Arizona Trail

THE OFFICIAL GUIDE

TEXT BY **TOM LORANG JONES**
WITH ASSISTANCE FROM THE
ARIZONA TRAIL ASSOCIATION

PHOTOGRAPHY BY **JERRY SIEVE**

WESTCLIFFE PUBLISHERS
westcliffepublishers.com

ISBN 10: 1-56579-279-3
ISBN 13: 978-1-56579-279-1

TEXT: Tom Lorang Jones, © 2005. All rights reserved.
PHOTOGRAPHY: Jerry Sieve, © 2005. All rights reserved. Other photos by Bob Rink, and the Arizona Trail Association (Larry Snead, Dori Peterson and Dave Hicks)
MAPS: Rebecca Finkel, © 2005. All rights reserved.

EDITOR: Dougald MacDonald
DESIGNER: Rebecca Finkel, F + P Graphic Design, Inc.; Fort Collins, CO
PRODUCTION MANAGER: Carol Pando

PUBLISHER: Westcliffe Publishers, Inc.
P.O. Box 1261
Englewood, Colorado 80150-1261
WESTCLIFFEPUBLISHERS.COM

Printed in China through World Print, Ltd.

LIBRARY OF CONGRESS CATALOGING-IN-PUBLICATION DATA:

Jones, Tom Lorang.
Arizona Trail: The Official Guide / text by Tom Lorang Jones ; photography by Jerry Sieve.
p. cm.
Includes bibliographical references (p.) and index.
ISBN: 1-56579-279-3
1. Hiking—Arizona—Arizona Trail—Guidebooks.
2. Arizona Trail (Ariz.)—Guidebooks. I. Title.
GV199.42.A72A755   2005
796.52'09791—dc21   2003049708

COVER PHOTOS:
From top to bottom, Arizona Trail Founder, Dale Shewalter, photo by Bob Rink; Trusty llamas carry the photographer's gear; A young biker explores the trail; Trail riders battle the midday sun

PLEASE NOTE:
Risk is always a factor in backcountry and high-mountain travel. Many of the activities described in this book can be dangerous, especially when weather is adverse or unpredictable, and when unforeseen events or conditions create a hazardous situation. The author has done his best to provide the reader with accurate information about backcountry travel, as well as to point out some of its potential hazards. It is the responsibility of the users of this guide to learn the necessary skills for safe backcountry travel, and to exercise caution in potentially hazardous areas. The author and publisher disclaim any liability for injury or other damage caused by backcountry traveling or performing any other activity described in this book.

Dedication

For Nancy, the reason why hiking the Arizona Trail
was only the second-best thing to happen to me during the last five years.

Acknowledgments

Many people provided invaluable help as I worked on this book. Larry Snead reviewed every word and asked others who knew the trail intimately to help. Thanks to Arizona Trail Association volunteers Chuck Horner, Jim Martin, Merle Parmer, Steve Saway, Dave Hicks, Dave Babcock, Bev Showalter, Dave Troutner, Denny Haywood, Carl Golnik, Richard Corbett, Glenn Jordan, Dick Walsh, Tom Coulson, Stephen Wood, and many others. Thanks also to AZT segment stewards for taking the time to review trail descriptions.

A variety of people provided shelter to me at different times. Thank you to Steve Anderson, Michael and Marilia Baker, Alec and Beth Rekow, and Carrie and Hap Robison for sharing their homes.

Many Forest Service and Bureau of Land Management employees took time to show me where the trail went, or was supposed to go, on maps. Thanks to Trish Callaghan, Kevin Cochary, Don Muise, Walt Thole, Brad Orr, Linda Holmes, Tom Folks, Catie Fenn, and John Nelson for your help. Also a special thanks to photographer Jerry Sieve for his help. I apologize to anyone whose name is missing.

The hospitality and assistance offered by several people deserve special mention. Cynthia Lovely, a great asset to the Arizona Trail, drove me around the Empire-Cienega area and discussed trail particulars during innumerable phone calls and visits. Jan Hancock and Phyllis Ralley helped in many ways—both are integral to the momentum behind the Arizona Trail. Dean Prichard offered his hospitality and waited for a visit that never came. (Sorry, Dean.) Hugh Dorathy rescued my dead truck from a remote road above Roosevelt Lake. Chuck and Adele Levy volunteered for a short shuttle drive that turned into a commitment of a couple of hours. Maryann Pratt gave me a lifesaving glass of cool lemonade on a hot day at her ranch, the LF Ranch, in the East Verde River Valley. Rich Mayfield and Peggy Hammes offered expert spiritual guidance. And thanks to Ted Olsen for giving me a large supply of his magic elixir, Bodhi Chai, which got me through some very cold nights in the White Canyon Wilderness.

I am grateful for the help of several equipment manufacturers. Sierra Designs' Clip Flashlight is one of the best superlight tents on the market. The hiking poles from Leki added years to the useful lives of my knees. Slumberjack rushed a warmer sleeping bag to me when the company learned I was ill-prepared for the desert winter. Trails Illustrated and DeLorme provided detailed maps. Mountainsmith gave me a handy little bike pack. Everything else I used came from Wilderness Sports in Silverthorne, Colorado.

I want to thank the people at Westcliffe Publishers—especially Linda Doyle and John Fielder—for sticking with me over a very long project. Thanks also to John Fayhee, who introduced me to Westcliffe.

Finally, I want to thank my dad, a great backpacking companion, and my mom, a great day-hiking companion, for their support through all of my outdoor pursuits.

Table of Contents

Arizona Trail Map

Bill Williams River

Gila River

Yuma

The Arizona Trail
Passages 1-43

—— Trail
– – – Proposed Trail
—— Road
—— River
○ City or Town
National Forest
National Park and
Wilderness Area

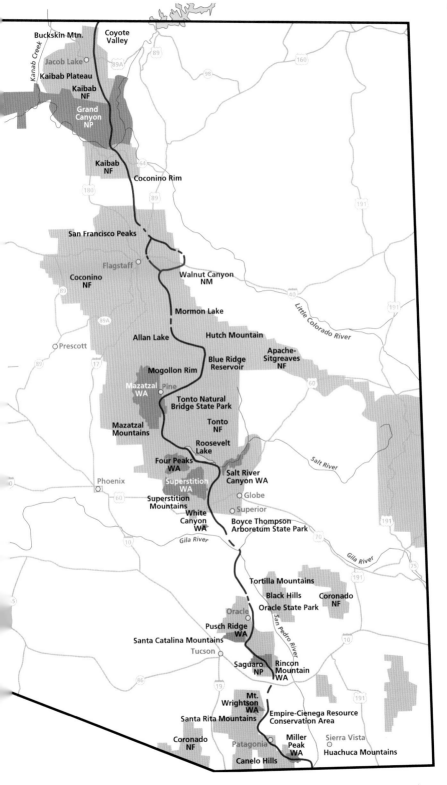

Segments Chart

PASSAGE	NAME	FROM	TO	MILEAGE
1	Huachuca Mountains	Mexico Border	Parker Canyon Lake	21.7
2	Canelo Hills East	Parker Canyon Lake	Canelo Pass	14.5
3	Canelo Hills West	Canelo Pass	Patagonia	17.4
4	Temporal Gulch	Patagonia	Gardner Canyon Rd.	19.4
5	Santa Rita Mountains	Gardner Canyon Rd.	AZ 83	17.2
6	Las Cienegas	AZ 83	I-10	Approx. 18.0
7	Rincon Valley	I-10	Hope Camp	Approx. 12.6
8	Happy Valley (Unused Passage)	NA	NA	0.0
9	Rincon Mountains	Hope Camp	Italian Trap	22.3
10	Redington Pass	Italian Trap	Prison Camp TH	15.7
11	Santa Catalina Moutains	Prison Camp TH	Mount Lemmon	15.5
12	Oracle Ridge	Mount Lemmon	American Flag TH	22.0
13	Oracle	American Flag TH	Tiger Mine TH	8.3
14	Black Hills	Tiger Mine TH	Freeman Rd.	28.2
15	Tortilla Mountains	Freeman Rd.	Kelvin-Riverside Bridge	Approx. 23.6
16	White Canyon	Kelvin-Riverside Bridge	White Canyon WA	Approx. 17.0
17	Alamo Canyon	White Canyon WA	Picketpost TH	11.5
18	Reavis Canyon	Picketpost TH	Rogers Trough TH	18.6
19	Superstition Wilderness	Rogers Trough TH	Roosevelt Lake	29.7
20	Four Peaks	Roosevelt Lake	Lone Pine Saddle	18.3
21	Pine Mountain/ Boulder Creek	Lone Pine Saddle	Sunflower	20.0
22	Saddle Mountain	Sunflower	Mount Peeley	16.0
23	Mazatzal Divide	Mount Peeley	The Park (Trails 23, 24)	22.0
24	Red Hills	The Park (Trails 23, 24)	East Verde River	14.3
25	Whiterock Mesa	East Verde River	Twin Buttes (FR 194)	11.4
26	Hardscrabble Mesa	Twin Buttes (FR 194)	Pine TH	12.0
27	Highline	Pine TH	FR 300	19.0
28	Blue Ridge	FR 300	AZ 87	15.8
29	Happy Jack	AZ 87	Allan Lake	31.5
30	Mormon Lake	Allan Lake	Marshall Lake	Approx. 28.0
31	Walnut Canyon	Marshall Lake	Cosnino (I-40)	18.2
32	Mount Elden	Cosnino (I-40)	Schultz Pass	14.8
33	Flagstaff (Resupply Route)	Fisher Point	Schultz Pass	13.8
34	San Francisco Peaks	Schultz Pass	Cedar Ranch	26.4
35	Babbitt Ranch	Cedar Ranch	Moqui Stage Station	28.7
36	Coconino Rim	Moqui Stage Station	Grandview Lookout Tower	19.0
37	Grand Canyon—S. Rim	Grandview Lookout Tower	Yaki Point/South Kaibab TH	23.3
38	Grand Canyon— Inner Gorge	Yaki Point/South Kaibab TH	North Kaibab TH	21.4
39	Grand Canyon—N. Rim	North Kaibab TH	NP–NF Boundary	11.8
40	Kaibab Plateau South	NP–NF Boundary	Telephone Hill	22.0
41	Kaibab Plateau Central	Telephone Hill	US 89A	17.0
42	Kaibab Plateau North	US 89A	Winter Rd.	17.0
43	Buckskin Mountain	Winter Rd.	Utah Border	10.8

DIFFICULTY	BIKE RATING	TRAILHEAD ACCESS	TOTAL ELEV. GAIN (FEET)	DESCENT	PAGE
Strenuous	Prohibited	Bumpy Road & Hiking	5,045	5,277	34
Moderate	Difficult	Bumpy Road	2,260	2,606	44
Moderate	Moderate	Smooth Road	959	2,239	50
Strenuous	Prohibited	Smooth Road	3,365	2,054	58
Moderate	Moderate	4WD Road	1,635	2,173	66
Strenuous	Easy	Smooth Road & Hiking	NA	NA	72
Moderate	Moderate	Smooth Road	NA	NA	78
NA	NA	NA	NA	NA	81
Strenuous	Prohibited	Hiking	5,887	5,041	82
Moderate	Difficult	4WD Road	2,577	1,701	90
Strenuous	Prohibited	Smooth Road	5,812	2,135	98
Strenuous	Not Ridable	Hiking	3,672	7,781	106
Easy	Moderate	Smooth Road	413	777	114
Moderate	Difficult	Bumpy Road	3,061	3,127	119
Strenuous	Not Ridable	Bumpy Road	NA	NA	127
Strenuous	Prohibited	Smooth Road	NA	NA	136
Moderate	Difficult	4WD Road & Hiking	NA	NA	142
Strenuous	Not Ridable	Bumpy Road	4,047	1,608	148
Strenuous	Prohibited	Bumpy & 4WD Road	5,185	7,776	156
Strenuous	Prohibited	Smooth Road	7,026	3,645	166
Moderate	Difficult	Bumpy Road	2,214	4,397	174
Strenuous	Prohibited	Bumpy Road	3,958	1,642	180
Strenuous	Prohibited	Bumpy Road & Hiking	3,729	3,595	188
Moderate	Prohibited	Bumpy, 4WD, & Hiking	2,265	4,863	194
Easy	Prohibited	Bumpy Road & Hiking	2,661	87	199
Moderate	Difficult	Bumpy Road	1,284	1,750	206
Strenuous	Difficult	Smooth Road	4,667	2,779	212
Moderate	Difficult	Bumpy Road	1,133	1,575	220
Easy	Difficult	Smooth Road	2,484	1,849	226
Easy	Moderate	Smooth Road	NA	NA	233
Easy	Moderate	Smooth Road	1,051	1,685	239
Easy	Moderate	Smooth Road	1,897	363	244
Moderate	Difficult	Smooth Road & Hiking	2,208	814	250
Strenuous	Moderate	Smooth Road	1,946	3,573	256
Easy	Easy	Bumpy Road	1,034	787	262
Easy	Easy	Bumpy Road & Hiking	1,790	905	268
Easy	Difficult	Bumpy Road	981	1,303	274
Strenuous	Prohibited	Smooth Road	5,760	4,723	280
Moderate	Moderate	Smooth Road	1,511	628	288
Easy	Moderate	Bumpy Road	1,808	2,078	294
Easy	Easy	Bumpy Road	571	1,897	300
Moderate	Easy	Smooth Road	188	1,177	306
Easy	Moderate	Bumpy Road	582	2,121	312

Setting out on a day of hiking
  Photo courtesy of The Arizona Trail Association

Preface

The bear was walking straight toward me. He looked big—about 250 pounds—so I assumed he was male. I had watched him descend the streambank across from my campsite and enjoy a long drink of water in the dim, early-morning light. The instant you see such a large wild animal you are seized with a flood of feelings: wonder, fear, defensiveness, awe, and joy. I watched apprehensively, grateful for the rare sight yet hoping the bear would just finish his drink and go back the way he had come.

But he didn't. The bear sniffed the ground a couple of times and then headed straight for my little perch above the stream. With a light breeze at his back, he still didn't know I was there. I knew that the closer he got before he noticed me, the more unpredictable and dangerous his reaction might be. I couldn't just wait for him. As my joy battled with fear, I wondered if I should race 25 yards to my right, where my camera was nestled in my backpack, or run the same distance to my left, where a can of pepper spray sat near my bedroll. Meanwhile, the bear kept moving toward me.

The stream he crossed flowed from snowfields I had traversed the day before on top of Mount Lemmon. I had followed a different creek down Cañada del Oro, a trickle that grew quickly into a crashing torrent. As I descended into an old pine forest, the vegetation grew denser and the sky seemed to shrink. Soon I was dazzled by old-growth ponderosa pines buttressed by mossy deadfall, too big for my outstretched arms to reach even one-third of the way around their girth. A deer bounded out of the grove and then disappeared again.

Any of these wonders—the bear, the deer, the giant trees nurtured by a crashing, icy stream—might be seen beside a long-distance trail in another mountain state, such as California, Colorado, or Wyoming. But the Arizona Trail (AZT) is different. The day before I reached this high-mountain paradise, I had walked along the trail through a beautiful garden of saguaro cactus, welcoming the occasional breeze in the 90-degree heat and taking a dip at dusk in an inviting watering hole called Hutch's Pool. This combination of extremes epitomizes Arizona, where it is possible to see a rattlesnake coiling amid desert cactus one day and watch a bear amble through a dark forest the next. Anyone who dismisses the Arizona Trail as a long walk in the desert does not know Arizona and is missing the majority of what this state has to offer.

In its own right, the Arizona desert is a wonderful place, with a plethora of mysteries waiting for the patient walker to discover. Add colorful walls of water-carved canyons, moist forests dressing snow-speckled peaks and "sky islands," high-desert hills where mischievous coyotes lurk among impossibly still juniper forests, and vast expanses of ponderosa pines where you can see hundreds of elk in a single day, and you have the unique and special blend of nature that can only be Arizona.

The Arizona Trail is perfectly placed to show off these wonders. Just when the thru-hiker gets used to his or her surroundings, a whole new world opens up. The flora is strange and stunning, from those giant pine trees to the stark ocotillo, and the fauna is remarkably diverse. Colorful birds were constant companions during my hike. I saw curious—and sometimes disconcertingly bold—javelinas in the Canelo Hills, the White Canyon Wilderness, and all along Hardscrabble Mesa near Pine. In the same area, wild turkeys scrambled across my path. I startled herds of elk on Anderson Mesa, lay on my back and watched two bald eagles soar for an hour over the Four Peaks Wilderness, and saw a turtle move 2 feet in the time it took me to eat lunch near the East Verde River.

During the first two months of my hike, from Mexico to the Mazatzals, I saw very few snakes. Then, as April brought its explosion of life and color to the desert, I was startled by snakes of all sizes and colors, including a 6-foot-long diamondback meandering across a dusty road above Sunflower. I found out how high I could jump when I stumbled across a harmless garter snake near Mormon Lake. And I gave a wide berth to a black rattler in the Mazatzals.

And then—the icing on the cake—I saw a bear in the wild for only the second time in my life. I had heard from the locals at Summerhaven, the small community atop Mount Lemmon, that they had been having trouble with bears recently. Someone recommended I carry pepper spray, and I bought some reluctantly, with the words of the sales clerk echoing in my mind for the next week: "This stuff is just seasoning to the bears." I thought about that as the bear ambled across the stream and came toward me. I raised my hands, clapped them loudly, and yelled, "Hey, hey, hey!" It was the moment of truth. The bear's head popped up. We may have made brief eye contact, and then, in a burst of strength and speed, he turned and ran as fast as I've ever seen an animal move. I stood with my mouth open for a few seconds, my heart pounding, and finally began to chuckle, with a glance toward the pack that still contained my unused camera. Then I sat back down to my breakfast, jotted a few notes, and began to study the map of the day's route, back to the nearby desert, deeper into the wilds of Arizona.

—TOM JONES
Evergreen, Colo.

A Short History of the Arizona Trail

The Arizona Trail began as the dream of one man, a fifth-grade teacher named Dale Shewalter. After attending college in Illinois, Shewalter was interested in hiking the Appalachian Trail, but he couldn't afford to do it right away. As a geophysicist, he felt Tucson would be a promising area to put some money in the bank before his East Coast hike. But after he moved to Arizona in 1974, his priorities soon changed. "I saw the Sonoran Desert and I was instantly converted," he said at his home in Flagstaff, as his horses whinnied nearby. "I started exploring the mountains around Tucson, and I thought you could connect the desert islands down there" with a single hiking trail.

That idea remained just a seed as Shewalter busied himself with work and volunteering at local schools. The latter appealed to him so much that he decided to get his teaching certificate, and he moved to Flagstaff in 1978 to teach full time. His yen for exploration was still strong, and in 1982 he walked the length of the Mogollon Rim, the fantastic escarpment that divides the lower-elevation deserts in southern Arizona from the higher-elevation, pine-clad plateaus of the north. After completing this east-west route, he started to look for a south-to-north hike to do. "I saw all the forests along the way, and I thought I could link them in one continuous hike," he recalled.

Thus, in 1985, Shewalter started with a light pack at Nogales, near the Mexican border, and made it to Flagstaff in a couple of weeks. (He was a long-distance runner at the time.) Shewalter continued on to Fredonia, a short distance from the Utah border, proving that a continuous trail linking the wildest parts of Arizona might be possible.

A few months later, Shewalter presented his idea to the Arizona Hiking and Equestrian Trails Committee, an advocacy group for nonmotorized trails. The members' instant enthusiasm evolved into strong public and governmental support for an official Arizona Trail. Then-Governor Bruce Babbitt created a coalition on recreation and public lands, and Kaibab National Forest, which surrounds Grand Canyon National Park, committed to building a section of the AZT across its jurisdiction. In 1988, the Forest Service dedicated this first segment of the trail, which ran 54 miles from Grand Canyon National Park's boundary north toward Utah. Shewalter's dream was well on its way to becoming reality.

The only thing missing was organized public involvement to complement the governmental agencies' work, and in 1994 a group of trail enthusiasts founded the Arizona Trail Association (to learn how you can get involved, see p. 322). Now, two decades after this visionary schoolteacher's first hike from Mexico to Utah, the AZT is almost complete, and hikers and other adventure seekers can follow a continuous path through some of the most stunning landscapes in the world.

Introduction to Arizona History

The earliest archaeological evidence of human life in Arizona, relics of hunting peoples who followed prehistoric big game across the continent, dates from approximately 10,000 B.C. By 8000 B.C., however, the mammoth and most of the other large species were extinct, and people turned to foraging edible vegetation and hunting small game for food. It was not until about 1000 B.C. that the people of Arizona, most notably the Cochise, began to grow corn and develop other agricultural methods.

By the first century A.D., three distinct native cultures had developed in Arizona: the Anasazi in the northeast, the Mogollon in the middle west, and the Hohokam in the southwest. Of these, the Anasazi are best known, thanks to their highly developed stone structures and artwork, and because of their mysterious and sudden disappearance.

Although the structures of the Arizona Anasazi appear not to have been as elaborate as those built by the Anasazi of New Mexico and southwestern Colorado, impressive examples of multiroom Anasazi dwellings survive as ruins near Navajo National Monument and other sites in Arizona. Scholars still don't know why the Anasazi abruptly abandoned their pueblos by the end of the thirteenth century, nor where they went. However, they recognize the Anasazi people's cultural and biological connections to many of the cultures that followed, including the Hopi, Zuni, Acoma, and Pueblo peoples.

Spanish Explorers

The first Europeans entered Arizona in 1540, when Francisco Vásquez de Coronado, a Spanish governor in western Mexico, led more than 300 Spaniards and 1,000 Native Americans in search of fabled cities of gold and silver. Although Spanish explorers and missionaries continued to travel into the region over the next two centuries, the Spanish did not establish permanent settlements in Arizona until the second half of the eighteenth century, spurred by the discovery of silver near present-day Nogales.

Numerous Native American tribes, including the Apache, Navajo, Hopi, and Pima, inhabited this area when Spanish explorers arrived. The Apaches and Navajos, both Athabascan-speaking tribes, likely had migrated as one group from Canada in approximately A.D. 1100, only diverging when they reached the Southwest around A.D. 1300. Both adopted matrilineal societies from the neighboring Pueblo tribes, and the Navajo, in particular, also learned horticulture and weaving from their neighbors.

When Spanish settlers arrived along the Rio Grande in the late 1500s, both the Navajo and Apache tribes attacked settlers' communities and stole cattle, horses, and sheep. Counterraids and bloody battles between native peoples and the newcomers continued for more than 300 years.

Mexico's ownership of the Southwest was challenged by Anglo rivals in 1846, at the onset of the Mexican-American War. After a year of bloody fighting, the war concluded in September 1847 with the Treaty of Guadalupe-Hidalgo. In return for $18.25 million, the United States gained ownership of Texas, California, and New Mexico, which at the time included Arizona north of the Gila River.

Opposite: Aspens, Saddle Mountain Wilderness

Mining Booms

In 1849, the great California gold rush brought tens of thousands of fortune-seekers across the nation and into Arizona via the harsh, dry Gila Trail. Few settled in Arizona, however, as they pursued their dreams onward to the West Coast.

But the face of Arizona began to change in 1857 when Jacob Snively discovered gold along the Gila River, near its junction with the Colorado. Mining camps quickly grew into mining towns across the state, as gold discoveries spread into central Arizona. Seven years after Snively's discovery, Henry Clifton discovered copper veins in the upper Gila River drainage. By the late 1870s, the mining town of Bisbee, in the Mule Mountains just north of the border with Mexico, had become one of the world's leading copper producers. Arizona still leads the nation in copper production, accounting for 65 percent of the total U.S. mine production.

Because only a few, rough roads connected Arizona's earliest centers of Anglo population, explorers such as Lieutenant Joseph Ives began investigating the potential for river travel. In 1858, Lieutenant Ives piloted an iron-hulled sternwheeler, the *Explorer,* up the Colorado River from Fort Yuma to beyond what is now the Hoover Dam. For his return journey, Ives left the sternwheeler and headed upriver, ultimately winding through the bottom of the Grand Canyon. The first white man to reach the Grand Canyon's floor apparently was unimpressed, remarking that, "After entering there is nothing to do but leave. Ours has been the first and will doubtless be the last party of whites to visit this profitless locality."

Native peoples in the area continued to fight against foreign encroachment. Although treaties were signed between the United States and the Navajo in 1852 and 1855, neither brought lasting peace. In 1862, U.S. military commanders ordered a hunter and Army scout named Christopher "Kit" Carson to round up the Navajo people and relocate them along the Pecos River in New Mexico. After brutally raiding Navajo settlements near Fort Canby and at Canyon de Chelly, Carson and his troops forced 8,000 Navajo survivors on the infamous 300-mile "Long Walk" to exile. There, the already weakened Navajo suffered from floods, drought, insects, and a devastating small-pox epidemic. In 1868, the United States finally allowed what remained of the tribe to return to land in northeastern Arizona, where their descendents still live.

Meanwhile, skilled Apache warriors continued to resist Anglo settlement. The Apache suffered their final defeat with Geronimo's surrender to General Nelson Miles near the mouth of Skeleton Canyon in 1886.

Railroad Expansion

Steamboats continued to travel up and down the Colorado during the years following Lieutenant Ives's historic journey, carrying freight, passengers, and soldiers. However, because most commerce in Arizona ran east and west, the arrival of the railroad in the late 1870s quickly overshadowed steamboats and the slow, often dangerous stagecoach service.

The first steam engine ceremoniously entered Arizona on the Southern Pacific Line from California in the spring of 1877. Low-paid Chinese and Mexican laborers continued to lay Southern Pacific tracks eastward, reaching Tucson by 1880. The Santa Fe Railroad also built lines through Arizona at a rapid pace, and the two companies competed fiercely for routes, knowing that control over Arizona's rail lines meant control over the lucrative lines along the Pacific coast.

As Thomas E. Sheridan explains in his excellent book, *Arizona: A History,* the railroad broadly exposed the United States, its industry, and its government to Arizona's ores and other natural riches for the first time, and also allowed large-scale export of those riches. Within just a few decades, Arizona had transformed from an isolated, struggling frontier society into a developed economy supplying metals, timber, crops, and cattle to a rapidly industrializing nation.

Modern Arizona
The railroad also allowed another Arizona industry to flourish: tourism. As the nation discovered the awesome beauty of the Grand Canyon, railroad companies battled over access routes to the canyon rim and interior, building hotels and restaurants nearby to add to the tourist draw. With the advent of the automobile and the establishment of the Arizona Highway Commission in the late 1920s, vacationers flocked to Arizona in ever-growing numbers to experience the state's warm climate and exotic desert scenery.

As popular interest in Native American culture grew, traders encouraged Arizona's native artisans to produce jewelry and decorative objects for sale to Anglo vacationers. Hopi and Navajo craftspeople revived ancient designs of pottery, weavings, and jewelry, and soon tourist "trading posts" lined the highways. Commercial crafts remain an important source of income for many Native American tribes, as well as a link to their cultural histories.

Heavy manufacturing started to develop in Arizona after World War II, and in the 1950s the electronics industry took root in the state. The populations of Phoenix and Tucson exploded. Agricultural towns in the White Mountains, Salt River Valley, and elsewhere evolved into summer retreats for city and suburban dwellers, and even into subdivided suburbs. Between 1960 and 1990, the state's population grew 181 percent, to 3.6 million people. The problems of supporting a large and growing population in a delicate desert environment remain among the state's most important challenges for the 21st century.

—NANCY N. POTTER
Evergreen, Colo.

North Kaibab Trail, Grand Canyon National Park

Planning Your Trip

Careful planning can eliminate many problems on the trail. For a long hike, you need to prepare an itinerary, plan for food drops, acquire and break in the gear you'll need, and get in shape. Make a detailed checklist and stick to it. No matter how much you prepare, however, you'll have to remain flexible once you hit the trail, because bad weather, illness, and other problems may cause delays.

When to Go

Avoid low desert areas in the summer months and higher alpine areas in late fall, winter, and early spring. South-to-north thru-hikers probably will start sometime in late winter or spring, while north-south thru-hikers will need to start in summer or fall.

Permits

The National Park Service (NPS) tightly regulates camping and travel in Saguaro National Park (Passage 9) and Grand Canyon National Park (Passages 36–39). Backpackers must reserve campsites well in advance, especially in the Grand Canyon. See the passage descriptions for more information.

The state of Arizona may require a permit for camping in parts of Passages 6, 14, 15, 16, and 35. See the descriptions of these passages.

Food

Your calorie requirements can more than double when you hike the AZT. According to *Backpacker* magazine, the average 200-pound man needs about 3,600 calories in day-to-day life. But he will require an additional 3,000 calories or more to carry a heavy pack for many miles a day. Carbohydrates should account for 60 percent to 70 percent of these calories, protein 10 percent to 15 percent, and fat 20 percent to 25 percent.

A balanced diet for one trail day might include oatmeal with dried fruit for breakfast; bagels with a thin layer of peanut butter for lunch, along with carrots, trail mix, granola, and more fruit; and pasta or rice for dinner, along with dehydrated vegetables, bread or rolls, and, of course, dessert. In addition, eat a snack every 60 to 90 minutes and occasionally add sport-drink mix to your water. For more advice, consult a nutritionist or a book on exercise and nutrition.

You can't carry all the food you need for a long-distance hike, so planning for resupplies is essential. When you prepare your food shopping list, estimate how much of each food item you will need per day on the trail, and then use your itinerary to multiply these amounts by the number of days between food drops. Factor in at least one extra day in each segment for emergency rations.

Prepare an individual box or other container for each food drop. Include a list of the perishable items you'll need, and ask the people doing food drops for you to purchase these perishables.

Be realistic about the amount of time it will take to hike between food drops and how much you can carry, and allow for unexpected delays. If you're meeting someone at a trailhead, you must stick to your itinerary!

You can mail boxes to yourself at most post offices. Just write "General Delivery" and your name above the post office address and include instructions to "Hold for

Arizona Trail Hiker." You'll find post office addresses and phone numbers under "Supplies, Services, and Accommodations" in the chapters describing passages near towns.

If you carry items that need to remain cool, such as cheese, wrap them in clothing for insulation. Remember, however, that in bear country it's best not to allow food smells to penetrate the clothes you'll be sleeping in.

Water

Because water does not occur naturally along much of the AZT, you must carry enough for yourself or stash it ahead of time along the trail. Consult the section on "Water" at the beginning of each chapter to determine which passages may require caches of water. "Alternate Access Points" listed for some passages may offer good places to drive to the trail with water.

Rancher-developed water on leased federal land or state trust land is the rancher's private property and cannot be used without first getting permission from the rancher, unless it is a life-or-death situation. Please respect the property rights of others. The Arizona Trail Association can help you identify ranchers' names and telephone numbers.

Conserve water by using a damp kitchen rag to clean pots and plates. Don't use soap, so you won't have to rinse as much. Pour unused hot water into your water containers. Use a disinfectant lotion, such as Purell, to wash your hands.

I found a GPS unit to be useful for making and finding water caches. Just remember that the GPS is only as good as its batteries and its digital electronics, and be confident that you can find your water stashes with a map and compass.

Before You Go

Test items such as your stove and water filter before you leave. Make sure your cook set will sit securely on the stove. Set up your tent, check your pack for frayed straps and loose pins, and test your rain gear in the shower.

A note about sleeping pads: My inflatable pads have about a 50 percent survival rate in the spine-rich environment of the desert. I believe a noninflatable pad is the way to go on the AZT.

Give yourself plenty of time before the hike to break in new boots. Don't take a chance on this—blisters can be painful and threaten your trip. In any event, carry light-weight shoes to wear around camp and give your feet a break.

Cutting weight in your pack is mostly common sense, but here are a few suggestions:

- Leave all but one pot at home. Use the lid as a plate.
- Avoid heavy food. Fresh fruit is nice, but it weighs much more than dried fruit. For dinners, freeze-dried food is very light, and its quality has improved in recent years.
- Eliminate packaging overkill. Don't take the granola bar box. Repackage liquids that come in glass in plastic bottles or bags.
- Avoid unnecessary luxuries, such as chair, shower, and CD player.
- Take plenty of clothes, but don't duplicate anything. Remember, no one else will have showered lately!
- Take only as much of each bulk item as you need. For example, you can squeeze a small amount of toothpaste into a lightweight container instead of carrying the entire tube.

- Use food drops to resupply with clothes, batteries, stove fuel, toothpaste, etc.
- Take only one good paperback. There's not nearly as much time for reading as you might think.
- Hiking any big stretch of the AZT, especially the entire trail, is a strenuous undertaking. Starting regular exercise well before your trip can make a big difference in your comfort and performance on the trail. Emphasize aerobic activity and leg-strengthening exercises.

On the Trail

Be realistic about how far you can hike in one day. You will enjoy the hike more if you don't kill yourself trying to set distance records. Naturally, it will be easier to hike farther per day after you've gotten your "trail legs."

Even for people in great shape, it doesn't take long to get run down when you carry 50 pounds on your back, climb thousands of feet per day, and breathe oxygen-poor air. A day of rest is amazingly rejuvenating after several days of hiking. One rest day every four to six days, particularly on stretches with a lot of climbing, is not unrealistic.

Safety Concerns

The AZT passes through land that is managed to provide a primitive experience to the backcountry traveler. In some places, help will be far away and preparation for hazards is essential. Anyone considering a hike along the AZT should carefully evaluate his or her ability to cope with potential dangers.

Flash Floods

Floods kill several people each year, and often with little warning—survivors have described flash floods as sudden, raging walls of water, not gradually increasing flows. To avoid these calamities, stay aware of the weather and the terrain.

Flash floods occur when thunderstorms quickly drop a large amount of rain and the ground cannot absorb all of the water. Obviously, dark skies and the sound of distant thunder are warning signs, but floods can develop many miles away, and the storm may not be evident downstream.

As for terrain, floods follow established waterways and seek the lowest ground. Thus it is important not to camp or linger in dry washes or near streams or rivers, especially during the rainy season or thunderstorms. Low-lying areas that are not obvious waterways can also be inundated. Err on the side of caution and always camp on high ground. Never enter an enclosed canyon when thunderstorms are present or likely.

Lightning

This serious danger can strike anywhere, but is most threatening at exposed high elevations, such as Arizona's sky islands or the high ridges of such wilderness areas as the Superstitions, the Mazatzals, and the Kachina Peaks. Lightning is most likely during Arizona's monsoon rainstorms of June, July, and August, and it usually occurs in the afternoon.

Lightning seeks the shortest path from earth to sky, so avoid high points of land or lone trees during a storm. Look for a low, treeless spot and squat there until the storm passes. It's also acceptable to take shelter in a low-elevation stand of trees of uniform height. Hiding in caves is dangerous, as they provide an ideal conduit for ground currents.

Contaminated Water

The greatest peril from drinking natural water is contamination, especially from *Giardia lamblia,* a small parasite that is transmitted via the fecal matter of animals and causes severe intestinal discomfort in humans. A hand-pumped water-purification system is the best defense against such impurities. Iodine tablets are also effective, but the health effects of long-term and frequent use are uncertain.

Dehydration

Arizona's low humidity, combined with the increased respiration rate during strenuous hiking, can result in potentially dangerous dehydration. Hikers may need up to a gallon of water per day, which must be carried or stashed along the route unless there are guaranteed natural sources. Each chapter's introduction provides information on water availability in a given passage.

Symptoms of dehydration include slurred speech, nausea, fatigue, dizziness, and loss of muscular control. If someone exhibits these symptoms, move the victim out of direct sunlight and give small sips of water immediately. Wipe the torso, head, and neck with cool, wet rags or clothing. Do not resume hiking until the day's heat has subsided.

Heat Exhaustion

The intense sun and heat along much of the AZT can pose a serious health threat. Heat exhaustion can overtake a person rapidly, and, because disorientation and confusion are common symptoms, a victim may never know what happened. Keep an eye on each other and be aware of these symptoms of heat exhaustion: chills, clammy skin, stumbling, and muscle weakness.

Treatment is similar to that for dehydration. Get the victim into the shade, give small sips of water, and cool the person with water or wet clothes. If there is a stream or pond available, immersion can help cool the victim, but you must be careful that the water is not too cold or that the cooling doesn't occur too rapidly.

If heat exhaustion advances, it may turn into heat stroke, which is even more serious. Skin will go from clammy to hot and dry, and unconsciousness may follow. A doctor should be consulted as soon as possible if these serious symptoms occur. Interim treatment is the same as for heat exhaustion, except that water immersion is not recommended.

Hypothermia

Arizona's weather can change at any time, and even in the low-elevation deserts snow and cold rain are possible. If you choose to hike during winter, carry warm clothing and avoid cotton, which does not insulate well when it gets wet. Wet clothing and wind can combine to cause hypothermia, a lowering of the body's core temperature to dangerous levels. Symptoms include loss of coordination, shivering, exhaustion, and confusion.

Hypothermia victims need to be warmed and protected from the elements immediately. They should be sheltered in a tent, stripped of wet clothing, and given many layers of dry

Opposite: One of the numerous creeks below the Mogollon Rim near Washington Park

clothes. Hot liquids (no alcohol!) are helpful, as is surrounding the victim with the warm bodies of fellow hikers. Victims will need plenty of water, high-energy food, and rest.

Acute Mountain Sickness

This common malady is caused by the lower air pressure at higher altitudes. It can strike anyone, but visitors from lower elevations are more susceptible. It's not uncommon, for example, for residents of Phoenix to suffer acute mountain sickness when they travel to the state's highest mountains from their low-level homes. (The high point on the AZT, in the mountains north of Flagstaff, is 10,400'.) At the altitudes in Arizona's mountains, a few days of acclimatization and a slow pace at the start of a hike usually eliminate any altitude sickness.

Symptoms of acute mountain sickness include headache, nausea, dizziness, shortness of breath, loss of appetite, and insomnia. The best treatment is to descend to a lower altitude, drink plenty of water, and rest.

Hikers should be aware of the rare but much more serious condition of high altitude pulmonary edema (HAPE), characterized by fluid buildup in the lungs. HAPE's symptoms include those of acute mountain sickness, as well as dry cough, difficulty with breathing, and gurgling sounds in the chest. This illness can be fatal, and the only treatments are rapid descent to a low altitude and/or immediate administration of oxygen to the victim.

Animals

Most animals you encounter in the backcountry will be more frightened of you than you are of them. However, a large animal occasionally may exhibit protective or aggressive behavior. Animals, and their prey, may be attracted by the smell of food. Maintain a clean camp and keep food in one place (such as a stuff sack) 100 yards from your tent to minimize the chance of confronting a hungry visitor. When there are trees near your campsite, try hanging food high off the ground from a slender branch.

Mountain lions and bears inhabit Arizona, but, for the most part, they are shy of humans. In the unlikely event that you have a threatening encounter, experts suggest standing up tall, waving your arms, making noise, and slowly backing up. Throwing rocks or a walking stick at a persistent mountain lion may also be effective. If you are attacked, fight back.

The best defense against snakes and scorpions is to avoid putting your hands and feet in places you can't see, such as deep grass, rock crevices, and holes. Almost all snakebites are the result of humans harassing snakes—not a very smart thing to do. If you see a rattlesnake, back away and leave the snake an escape route.

In spite of their reputation, rattlesnake and scorpion bites are rarely fatal, although victims describe them as being extremely painful. If you are bitten, the most important thing you can do is to remain calm. Keeping your heart rate down slows the spread of venom through your body. An article in the July 1996 edition of *The Distance Hiker's Gazette* gives succinct suggestions for treating a snakebite: "Calm the victim; gently wash the area with soap and water; apply a cold, wet cloth over the bite; and transport the victim to the nearest emergency facility. Do not apply a tourniquet, nor pack the area with ice or ice water, nor cut the wound, nor suck out venom by mouth."

The Gila monster is a rare creature, one of only two poisonous lizards in the world, with the ability to lock its jaw on a victim's appendage and pump venom into the wounds from ridges in its teeth. I've seen two Gila monsters in the wild, and they were among the shiest and slowest creatures I've ever encountered. They have a flat snout, a thick, stubby tail, and black and orange stripes. Watch from a distance, don't harass them, and you'll enjoy an exciting and rare sighting.

Africanized honeybees, also called killer bees, are hybrids of African bees and European honeybees, the most common bees in North America. Africanized bees are more aggressive and persistent, attack in larger numbers, and may pursue intruders farther from their hives than European bees. Their venom is the same as that of the European bee.

Because it is difficult to distinguish the two kinds of bees, it is best to treat all bees with respect. Wear light-colored clothing and avoid shiny jewelry. If you enter an area with a lot of bees, move away calmly. Never swat or kill a bee, because sudden movements and the odor of an injured bee stimulate the attack instinct in Africanized bees. If you are attacked, run away and keep running. Cover your head and face with clothing, because these are the first places bees will sting. Seek shelter. Unleash pets so they can escape too. If you are stung, scrape away the stinger but don't squeeze it, which will release more venom. And don't worry too much! Africanized bees have killed only 12 people in the United States, yet about 40 people die each year from European bee stings, mostly due to allergic reactions.

Children are more vulnerable to all wild creatures than adults are, so keep an eye on them. Avoid direct physical contact with any wild animal, regardless of its size, and never feed them.

Mine Shafts

Abandoned mine shafts dot the hillsides of Arizona. They are not maintained and are extremely dangerous. Not only are they subject to collapsing rock, they also may contain toxic fumes that can overcome a careless explorer. Give them a wide berth.

Snags

Snags are dead trees whose root structures may be decayed to the point that the tree is ready to topple over. They are particularly prevalent in burned areas. Although the danger of being hit by a falling tree is slight, they have killed a few people. Don't camp under snags, and remember that even live trees are susceptible to blowing over in a strong storm.

Leave No Trace

Most of the lands through which the AZT passes belong to every American. As the popularity of these areas grows, it's up to each individual who visits these last vestiges of American wilderness to preserve them in their natural state. Toward this end, the Forest Service and various partners developed the principles of Leave No Trace, which should govern the behavior of every visitor to the Arizona backcountry.

For more information on low-impact hiking and camping, call the Leave No Trace organization at (800) 332-4100, or visit the website at www.lnt.org. Here are some basic pointers for AZT travelers.

Plan Ahead

By equipping yourself with the right equipment, maps, and information, you can reduce your impact on the land. If you know your route, for example, you're less likely to get lost and tromp cross-country. If your footwear is appropriate, you won't have to walk around wet spots in the trail, which creates wider trails or new trails altogether. Advance knowledge of the terrain will help you pick appropriate campsites, avoid sensitive areas, and plan your use of water.

Respect other visitors' desire for a remote backcountry experience by keeping a low profile and picking campsites screened from the trail by trees or terrain features. When you meet other trail users, be courteous and give them room to pass. The standard rule is that mountain bikers and hikers yield to horses, and bikers yield to hikers—but the prudent hiker always makes room for a mountain biker. When passing a horse party, move off the trail on the lowest side until everyone has passed. Do not make any sudden movements or loud noises that might spook the horses.

Travel on Durable Surfaces

Most of the AZT follows established trails and roads. Hiking single file and staying on the trail avoids trampling fragile plants and soft ground, which can take years to recover from careless boot prints.

Be especially careful to avoid cryptobiotic soil, which is essential to the ecology of arid lands, according to the Leave No Trace publication *Desert & Canyon Country*. That pamphlet notes that "cryptobiotic soil crusts are self-sustaining biological communities that look like tiny, black, irregularly raised pedestals in the sand. By reducing erosion, fixing nutrients in the soil, and increasing water absorption, these soils create a hospitable environment in which other plants may establish themselves." Please avoid disturbing these very fragile soils.

In places where there is no trail, or where it is necessary to leave the trail, walk on the most durable surfaces, such as rocks, dry ground, or a carpet of pine needles. Groups should fan out to disperse their impact.

If you plan to use pack animals on the Arizona Trail, please learn to minimize the impact of large animals. Bring collapsible buckets to carry water to the animals so they don't damage streambanks. At camp, horses should be hitched to a highline. Avoid tethering them in a small area, which will concentrate their impact. Bring your own feed and make sure it is certified weed free to avoid introducing nonnative plant species.

Low-Impact Camping

In well-traveled areas, it is best to select an established campsite that has already seen a lot of use, in order to preserve the surrounding area. For a tent site, choose hard, dry ground with the least amount of vegetation. Make sure your camp is at least 200 feet from streams, lakes, and trails.

While moving about camp, be aware that each step is potentially harmful. If you are in a heavily used area, use existing trails instead of tromping down new ones. In less-visited areas, try not to use the same route each time you travel around camp so no single area becomes worn. Wear light shoes instead of hard-soled hiking boots once you arrive at camp.

Pack It In, Pack It Out

Nothing should be left in the forest or the desert that wasn't there before you arrived, with the exception of human waste. Everything else, including toilet paper, personal hygiene items, and uneaten food, should be packed out. Most trash, even paper, will not burn completely in a campfire. Leaving food for animals or giving it to them directly habituates them to humans, alters their diet, and makes them less self-sufficient. It also can result in more aggressive animals. In many cases, leaving food for animals is like a death sentence. Never feed a wild animal.

Waste Disposal

The best way to dispose of solid human waste is via the "cathole" method, which entails digging a hole 6 to 8 inches deep and filling it in with dirt after use. Catholes should be at least 200 feet from water or potential waterways, such as dry washes. Toilet paper should be packed out; a double plastic bag works well for this.

Use soap sparingly—even so-called biodegradable soap is an unnatural chemical in an outdoor environment. Never use soap near a water source. Use a small strainer to remove food particles when rinsing plates and pans, and pack out the solid residue. Spread the remaining wastewater over a large, dry area to lessen its concentration.

Leave What You Find

Leave the natural wonders along the trail for other visitors to enjoy. In most areas, it is illegal to remove cultural artifacts, such as potsherds and rock art. If you encounter ruins, consider viewing them from a distance. If you are compelled to enter, stay on established trails and avoid walking on artifacts, which are often contained in dark mounds of earth (middens). Don't break boughs off trees, hammer nails into trees, or pick flowers.

Use Fire Responsibly

Travelers in the natural world have long regarded campfires as a source of warmth and comfort, providing a sense of security in the vast darkness of the outdoors. But fires have an unnatural impact on the environment, leaving scars, gobbling nutrients, and sterilizing the soil. A small backpacking stove provides a quick, efficient way to cook, and I encourage the AZT hiker to experience the darkness of the forest or the desert on its own terms, without the glaring interruption of a fire. You'll see things you would have missed when blinded by flames, and you will hear sounds otherwise drowned out. Nocturnal animals may pass closer to camp than they would if driven back by a blazing fire.

If you must build a fire, make sure it's far from water sources or wetlands, in an area where there is an abundant supply of dead and downed wood. Never cut firewood from a standing tree, even if the tree is dead. Use an existing fire ring or build a "mound fire" —never build a new fire ring.

To build a mound fire, the method prescribed by the National Outdoor Leadership School in its Leave No Trace literature, find a source of mineral soil, such as a dry wash. Use a stuff sack to carry this soil to the fire site, lay down a ground cloth, and build a flat-topped mound of the mineral soil, 6 to 8 inches thick, on top of the cloth. Build the fire on this mound. When it's time to break camp, scatter the ashes, and then use the ground cloth to return the soil to its source.

Conserve Water

In the deserts and arid forests of Arizona, water is a precious resource. Please use it sparingly and avoid polluting it. On many stretches of the AZT, you will have to carry your own water or cache it along the way. When you do encounter water sources, please camp at least 200 yards away whenever possible. Use containers to carry water far from its source to bathe or cook. Don't let animals trample streambanks or defecate in water sources.

Arizona's rare riparian corridors—green strips of life cutting a line through the surrounding dry land—are inviting places for campers and hikers. But avoid the temptation to linger in these places. The vegetation is easily trampled, and the animals that rely on the water are frightened away by human presence.

American Flag Trailhead near Oracle

Tom Jones

How to Use This Guide

This book is written for the day hiker, overnight camper, thru-hiker, mountain biker, or equestrian seeking to experience the wonders of the Arizona Trail (AZT). Its trail descriptions are divided into 43 chapters that correspond to the 43 "passages" designated by the Arizona Trail Association. Each passage represents a distinct section of the trail, with starting and ending points at highways, dirt roads, or, in a few cases, hiking trails.

To help you plan a hike or ride, a chart on p. 8–9 lists each of the passages and their difficulty, trailhead accessibility, mountain bike access, and elevation gain and descent. A map of the entire trail is on p. 6–7.

The passages are arranged in geographical order from south to north, so a thru-hiker can follow the book from start to finish. Most thru-hikers travel from south to north because it is easier to avoid snow or excessive heat by hiking in this direction. The book also includes important information for southbound hikers, marked with this symbol:

Passage Information

The beginning of each chapter summarizes the important aspects of a passage, including its difficulty rating and length. A few paragraphs of text describe each passage's highlights and pitfalls, local history, and options for camping.

Difficulty ratings are easy, moderate, and strenuous. The background color of each passage's introductory page also corresponds to difficulty: green for easy, blue for moderate, and red for strenuous. Note that these ratings are highly subjective—a trail that is easy for the seasoned Arizona hiker may be quite strenuous for the novice. The chart on p. 8–9 shows all of the passages and their difficulty.

In each passage, four different mileage figures are given:

Passage Length: This is the total length of the passage in miles. Note that the mileages in this book may not match the figures posted on U.S. Forest Service signs, which are generally wrong. I am confident in the numbers I provide, as I used a pedometer and a GPS, and then cross-checked my figures using a map wheel. I also biked many sections of the trail with a very accurate odometer.

Quality Hiking Distance: This is a somewhat subjective figure designed to show how much of the passage follows off-road singletrack or little-used dirt roads. It eliminates paved roads or heavily traveled dirt roads, where some people may prefer to drive to reach the start of the best hiking.

From Mexico/To Utah: These figures list the total trail mileage from either border to the "Beginning Access Point" of each passage.

The introductory information also lists each passage's Land Managers (see Appendix A for contact information) and the Recommended Months for hiking that passage. Although it's certainly possible to hike most of the AZT's passages during any month, following the recommended times will give the most pleasurable experience.

Mountain Bike Notes

This section discusses each passage's accessibility to mountain bikes. The following symbols provide a quick visual reference:

 Most of the terrain is nontechnical, but there may be some elevation gain.

 You will find mostly intermediate riding, with a few sections of technical terrain.

 Mountain biking is technical or difficult, with steep and/or loose sections, and is not recommended for inexperienced riders. You may have to carry your bike in spots.

 Most of the terrain on the passage is not ridable due to rocks, steepness, lack of a trail, or other factors.

 The passage goes through a designated wilderness area, national park, or other area where bikes are prohibited.

The chart on p. 8–9 lists all of the passages and their mountain bike accessibility.

Water

This section lists the primary water sources, if any, along each passage. The source's GPS coordinates are usually given. Look for the following symbols within the passage descriptions:

 Stagnant or dirty water that requires purification before consumption. Availability may be intermittent.

 Fresh water whose presence is uncertain. As with all backcountry water, it still requires filtration and/or purification.

 Reliably available water. As with all backcountry water, it still requires filtration and/or purification.

Maps

Each chapter lists all of the maps that cover the passage, primarily the 7.5-minute quadrangles from the U.S. Geological Survey (USGS) and maps from the U.S. Forest Service. Where other useful maps are available, these also are listed.

The best maps for precise navigation are the USGS quadrangles. Their scale is 1:24,000, and their detail is excellent for navigation if you know how to use a map and compass and read contour lines. Eighty-five of these maps are required for the entire AZT, and they cost $6 apiece. Forest Service maps are particularly useful for identifying the many Forest Roads (FR) that the AZT follows or crosses.

See Appendix C for a list of map sources and Appendix D for a list of all of the maps that cover the trail.

Access Points

The AZT's passages have been divided so their beginning and ending points may be reached as easily as possible by car. However, the AZT traverses some of the most remote land in Arizona, and some passages must be reached by dirt or four-wheel-drive roads, or even by hiking. For a quick visual reference on trailhead accessibility, the following symbols precede each set of driving directions:

 The trailhead is accessible by a normal passenger car. The road is either paved or well-graded dirt.

 A normal passenger car may get to the trailhead, but the road is unpaved and may be quite rough. Adverse weather conditions may make these routes impassable.

 You will need a high-clearance, four-wheel-drive vehicle.

 A hike is required to reach the AZT.

The symbols may be used in combination, and the numbers after each indicate the distance required by each method. In the following example, you would drive 3.4 miles over rough roads and hike an additional 0.7 mile to reach the AZT.

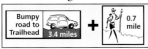 Note that the **Ending Access Point** for each passage refers the reader to the **Beginning Access Point** of the following passage. In some cases, southbound hikers may find it helpful to refer to both passages' trail descriptions to get started.

The chart on p. 8–9 lists each of the passages and its accessibility by vehicles.

Trail Markers

The markers illustrated below are often seen along the AZT, and the book refers to them frequently:

 AZT trail marker   rock cairn

Supplies, Services, and Accommodations

Trail users may find the information in these sections useful for planning an itinerary. All of the relevant services within a short walk or drive of the trail are described. If you plan to send boxes of supplies to post offices along the route before you depart, call first to check on business hours and to make sure they can accommodate general delivery.

Equestrian Notes

Information for riders appears in the introductory matter for a few passages.

Navigation

Much of the AZT is well marked and follows clear trails or roads. But other sections have not been completed or are poorly marked. Skill with a map and compass is essential for safe travel in these areas.

A few basics: The circular compass dial is divided into 360 equal units called "degrees," which are numbered starting with 0° at due north and increasing in a clockwise direction. Due east is at 90°, south is 180°, and west is 270°.

The needle always points toward magnetic north, but maps are based on "true north." The difference between the two, which varies across the continent, is listed in degrees at the bottom of the map. If magnetic north is 15° east of true north, then any direction you wish to find will lie 15° to the left, or counterclockwise, of the direction indicated by using the compass needle.

Phrases such as "slightly east of south" appear frequently in the text. In this example, you would take a bearing 5° or 10° toward the east from due south, or 170° to 175° on the compass dial. "Southeast," on the other hand, is a bearing precisely between due south and due east, or 135° on the compass dial. And "south-southeast" is a bearing precisely between southeast and due south, or 157.5°. Bearings provided in this book are based on true north and have a margin of error of ±10°.

In this book, particularly confusing or obscure areas along the trail are marked with this symbol:

GPS Coordinates

GPS coordinates, or waypoints, are provided throughout the trail descriptions. These coordinates are intended to help you to verify your position on the trail and to find trailheads or the trail itself should you stray from it. However, the waypoints do *not* constitute a route and will *not* guide you around obstacles and dangers such as cliffs, water, or buildings.

Coordinates are based on readings from a Garmin handheld unit, which lists a margin of error of ±15 meters (50 feet), and are given in degrees, minutes, and seconds. At the time I collected these coordinates, the U.S. Department of Defense added an intentional error of up to 100 meters into GPS transmissions. This has since been removed, so the readings on handheld consumer units should be more accurate than they were previously.

For more on this subject, see ATA Note (opposite).

New Trail Construction

Please note that the AZT is still under construction. The trail's route on entire passages may differ from the descriptions given here when the AZT is completed. In addition, completed sections of the trail occasionally may be rerouted. Contact the Arizona Trail Association (602-252-4794; www.aztrail.org) to learn about significant changes, particularly if you're planning a thru-hike across passages that were incomplete when this book was written.

Grand Canyon from Yavapai Point

ATA NOTE: GPS COORDINATES AND MILEAGES

Regarding the author's text on GPS coordinates (at left) and mileage information provided in the text of each passage, the Arizona Trail Association has since gathered new GPS coordinates with an accurate GPS unit for the completed sections of the AZT. We reviewed this guide and made substantial changes and additions to enhance its accuracy. In some cases, we omitted the author's original mileage information because no current figures were available. Because the AZT is a project in process, route changes designed to improve the trail experience still occur. *We recommend that users of this book treat its GPS data and mileage information as points of reference, not as guides for outings on the AZT.* In the future, we will make our GPS data available for ATA members to download to their mapping software or GPS units from our website. Please visit www.aztrail.org for more information.

—Arizona Trail Association

Passage I
Huachuca Mountains: Mexico Border to Parker Canyon Lake

North slopes of the Huachuca Mountains along the Arizona Trail

TOTAL DISTANCE	21.7 miles
QUALITY HIKING DISTANCE	21.7 miles
DIFFICULTY	Strenuous
TOTAL ELEVATION GAIN	5,045 feet
TOTAL DESCENT	5,277 feet
FROM MEXICO	0 miles
TO UTAH	771.9 miles
LAND MANAGERS	Coronado National Memorial, Coronado National Forest (Sierra Vista Ranger District)
RECOMMENDED MONTHS	March through November, depending on snowfall

INTRODUCTION From the trailhead at Montezuma Pass, this passage climbs onto the first of several landforms called "sky islands," which are unique to Arizona. These isolated mountain ranges rise several thousand feet above the surrounding desert, resulting in life zones that are wetter and greener than the lower elevations only a few miles away. In the cool, thin air, ponderosa pine and fir forests provide homes for a variety of mammals including bobcat, mule deer, and black bear; 265 species of birds; and 20 percent of North America's ant and bee species, according to Dr. Peter Warshall, an ecologist.

The experience of hiking across a sky island is unique. In the Miller Peak Wilderness, you will have the impression of tiptoeing across a narrow catwalk suspended high in the air. Yet, you may also feel a slight sense of claustrophobia, as your travel on either side of the trail will be limited by thick vegetation and steep hillsides. Be sure to avoid these lightning-prone sections during thunderstorms!

As the AZT follows the spine of the Huachuca Mountains, flat ground becomes a precious commodity and campsites are rare—plan your hike accordingly. There are flat places along the trail at mile 3.9 (not recommended for camping), mile 5.8 (no water), mile 8.5 (water usually found at mile 8.3), mile 9.7 (no water), mile 10.4 to 11.1 (no water), and from mile 13.8 to the end of the passage.

For thru-hikers, this passage may present other difficulties. Because of its high elevation, it holds snow later than nearby sections of the AZT. After a particularly wet winter, the snow may be waist deep, and snowshoes could be necessary. If you plan to hike here in late winter or spring, call the Sierra Vista Ranger District (see Appendix A) for a report on current conditions.

One more oddity of this passage: There is no way to access the beginning of the trail at the border with Mexico other than to walk southbound on the AZT itself, starting at mile 1.9 atop Montezuma Pass. (See "Beginning Access Point" on the next page.) You may want to walk this 3.8-mile round-trip the day before you start the more committing hike from Montezuma Pass into the Miller Peak Wilderness.

Note: There has been extensive illegal-immigrant and drug-smuggling traffic in the Huachuca Mountains passage along the Arizona Trail and other cross-country routes. Trail users should contact the appropriate land managers regarding current conditions, level of risk in the backcountry, and what to do if individuals or groups are encountered. Be aware that trash and discarded clothing commonly litter the Huachuca Mountains despite volunteer efforts to keep the trails clean.

MOUNTAIN BIKE NOTES

Bikes are not permitted on trails in Coronado National Memorial or Miller Peak Wilderness. Cyclists wishing to start at the international border will have to improvise by using existing roads outside the memorial boundary. (See the USGS Montezuma Pass map.) An easier alternative is to start at Montezuma Pass and ride west on FR 61 to FR 48 and the beginning of Passage 2, near Parker Canyon Lake. Passage 2 provides good to excellent mountain biking for advanced riders.

WATER

Mile 1.9, Montezuma Pass: Water is available during spring and summer months only. Call Coronado National Memorial to verify.

Mile 8.3, Tub Spring: This spring is reliable after a snowy winter (N31°24'20", W110°18'44").

Mile 9.7 (plus 0.5 mile off the trail), Bear Spring: This is a reliable spring with nice campsites, but it does require an extra mile round-trip.

Mile 13.8 to mile 16.6, Sunnyside Canyon: This 2.8-mile stretch of canyon usually contains flowing water during spring snowmelt.

Mile 20.5 (plus 1.6 miles off the trail), Parker Canyon Lake: You can reach Parker Canyon Lake by hiking 1.3 miles off the AZT from mile 1.0 in Passage 2. If you don't want to make the side trip to Parker Canyon Lake, there may be water elsewhere in Passage 2.

MAPS

USGS Quadrangles: Montezuma Pass, Miller Peak, Huachuca Peak
USFS: Coronado National Forest (Sierra Vista Ranger District)
Other: Hiker's Map of the Huachuca Mountains, Leonard Taylor; Arizona Public Lands Information Center, AZT Passage Topo Map 1—Huachuca

BEGINNING ACCESS POINT

Montezuma Pass: This passage is unique because the only way to get to the beginning is to start at mile 1.9 at Montezuma Pass and hike backward. From the town of Sonoita, follow AZ 83 south 30 miles to its intersection with FR 48. Turn left (south) onto FR 48 and continue 5.4 miles to FR 61. Continue east 8.8 miles to a large parking area at the summit of the pass (N31°21'22", W110°17'06").

Be sure to notify Coronado National Memorial headquarters if you plan to leave your car at the summit of Montezuma Pass overnight. The headquarters is about 4.5 miles east of Montezuma Pass (see Appendix A for phone and address).

To hike toward the border with Mexico, start at the kiosk in the southeast end of the parking lot, climb a short distance on a clear tread, and follow a sign for the Coronado Peak Trail. After 0.1 mile, turn left onto Joe's Canyon Trail, which follows the ridgeline to the southeast. Descend to a saddle and an intersection at mile 0.8, turn right (south) on the AZT, and follow switchbacks down Yaqui Ridge. At 1.9 miles from the parking lot, reach the fence that separates Mexico from the United States and another fence that runs up the ridge to the north. An obelisk here notes that the Treaty of 1853 established the international boundary. It also marks the beginning of the AZT. *Do not* cross the fence into Mexican territory!

To Reach Montezuma Pass from Sierra Vista, travel 14 miles south on AZ 92 and turn right (south) onto FR 61. Continue 8.3 miles, generally south and west, to the large parking area at the summit of the pass.

ALTERNATE ACCESS POINT

Sunnyside Canyon Trailhead (AZT trail mile 16.6): This is a good place to leave a vehicle for a shuttle hike. From the town of Sonoita, follow AZ 83 south 30 miles to its intersection with FR 48. Turn left (south) onto FR 48, continue 2.2 miles, and turn left (east) onto FR 228. Drive 0.9 mile to a fork and stay left. Continue 1.6 miles to a "T" intersection and turn right on FR 204. Drive 0.3 mile to a "Y" intersection and bear left on FR 204. Over the next 0.2 mile, ignore three left turns, following the road as it winds back to the right to intersect another road at a sharp angle. Turn left here and drive 0.5 mile to meet the AZT, which leaves the road on the left. Continue 0.1 mile to a small parking area at the wilderness boundary (N31°26'32", W110°23'36").

ENDING ACCESS POINT

Parker Canyon Lake: See "Beginning Access Point" for Passage 2.

TRAIL DESCRIPTION

The corner of two fences near an obelisk-shaped border marker indicates the beginning of the Arizona Trail (5,911'; N31°20'01", W110°16'55"). Follow the winding trail as it climbs north-northeast to a saddle and an intersection with Joe's Canyon Trail at mile 1.1 (6,520'). The mountain range to the southwest is Mexico's famed Sierra Madre. Turn left (west) and climb a short distance, then drop through several switchbacks to meet the Coronado Peak Trail at mile 1.8. Turn right and descend 0.1 mile to the parking lot at Montezuma Pass (6,570'). (A left turn at mile 1.8 would lead a short distance off the AZT to the top of Coronado Peak, where Flagstaff school-teacher Dale Shewalter sat with friends on a clear, cool evening and broached the question of whether it would be possible to link a series of trails across the entire state.)

Walk to the road (FR 61) at the north end of the parking lot, turn right (north-east), and continue 25 yards to the Crest Trail, a clear singletrack that takes off on the left (north). The trail climbs through many switchbacks along the east side of the ridge (not the west side, as indicated by the 1982 Montezuma Pass USGS map). You'll reach the ridge crest at mile 2.5 and earn stunning views to the south over the San Rafael Valley and Mexico.

The faint of heart won't like this section of trail, as it traverses a steep hillside that drops several hundred feet to the valley. At mile 3.9 the trail crests the main ridge, with great views to the east. The lone feature to the southeast is San Jose Peak. As the trail turns left (north-northwest) to climb along the ridge, notice a wide, flat spot right on the trail that makes a tempting campsite (N31°22'01", W110°16'57"). Avoid this temptation, because local authorities warn that drug smugglers and illegal immigrants use this site. In another 50 yards, the trail enters the Miller Peak Wilderness (7,750').

WILDERNESS ALERT

The **Miller Peak Wilderness** was designated in 1984 as "an area where the earth and its community of life are untrammeled by man, where man himself is a visitor who does not remain." It protects 20,190 acres of rugged pine and oak woodlands that conceal 14 species of hummingbirds and 60 kinds of reptiles, among other plants and animals.

Please follow these rules governing wilderness areas:
- Camp out of sight, at least 200 feet from lakes and streams, on dry, durable surfaces.
- Use a stove. If you must have a fire, use existing fire rings.
- Keep water sources clean by washing at least 200 feet away from them.
- Bury human waste 6 inches deep and 200 feet from lakes and streams. Pack out toilet paper.
- Hobble or picket livestock at least 200 feet from lakes and streams, and use only treated, weed-free grain and feed.
- Keep dogs on leashes at all times.
- Do not ride a mountain bike.
- Pack out all trash; don't attempt to burn it.

The effects of sunlight on vegetation become starkly clear as the AZT crosses to the shadier northeast side of the ridge. There is another flat place to camp at mile 5.8, where the trail bends to the right (northeast), but it is directly adjacent to the AZT (N31°23'00", W110°17'42").

Avoid side trails to Lutz Canyon and Bond Spring as you continue straight ahead to mile 6.5, where the trail crests the ridge at an intersection with the trail to the top of Miller Peak (9,050'; N31°23'29", W110°17'43"). To climb Miller Peak, turn right and continue 0.5 mile to the 9,466-foot summit. The AZT descends from this junction to the north (straight ahead).

The trail follows the ridge to the northwest for about a mile before dropping off to the right side and passing Tub Spring at mile 8.3 (8,550'; N31°24'20", W110°18'44"). This water source, which flows into an old bathtub, is reliable in springtime. Camping is not permitted within 200 feet of the spring — there are better sites at mile 8.5 anyway. Thirty yards past the spring, reach an intersection with the Miller Canyon Trail, which descends to the right. Make a sharp left turn (due north) and follow a sign for the Crest Trail.

Climb briefly to mile 8.5 where you should avoid the Carr Peak Trail by staying on the Crest Trail to the left (west). (The orientation of the Carr Peak Trail is marked incorrectly on the 1978 Miller Peak USGS map.) There are a few flat spots here for camping. *Note:* For the rest of this passage, the AZT does not appear on the USGS map.

Many switchbacks negotiate the steep descent to an intersection with the Oversite Canyon Trail at mile 9.2. Stay on the Crest Trail and walk due north, crossing a streambed in 0.1 mile.

Cross through Bear Saddle at mile 9.7 (8,060'), where there is one flat spot to pitch a tent about 2 feet off the trail. Be advised that illegal immigrants use this area and Bear Spring heavily.

If you turn left (south) at Bear Saddle onto the Bear Canyon Trail, you can descend 0.5 mile to reliable Bear Spring and some nice campsites. Note that this detour takes you off the Arizona Trail.

Now climb steeply to the west through ponderosa pines until the trail crosses the ridge into a beautiful, old fir forest at mile 10.2. There are a few flat spots next to the trail over the next mile. From a rocky outcrop at mile 10.8, look for stunning views to the west, including a view of Parker Canyon Lake far below. The views continue at mile 11.4 with Sierra Vista to the northeast and the impressive gray walls of Pat Scott Peak dominating the foreground to the north.

At mile 11.6, the AZT reaches the crest again and then becomes fainter as it descends to an intersection at mile 11.8. Leave the Crest Trail here by turning left (west-northwest) onto the Sunnyside Canyon Trail (#117) (8,500'; N31°25'27", W110°20'45"). The ensuing sharp descent through numerous switchbacks offers stunning views of the San Rafael Valley to the southwest. The highest point to the northwest is Mount Wrightson.

Stay on the Sunnyside Canyon Trail as it intersects the Eureka Canyon Trail at mile 12.8 and the Copper Glance Trail at mile 13.5. The descent finally abates near a nice place to camp at mile 13.8 (6,750'). As you continue to descend more easily along the canyon bottom, good campsites are frequent.

The bottom of Sunnyside Canyon often contains flowing water during snow-melt. Continue to the wilderness boundary at mile 16.6 (5,935'; N31°26'32", W110°23'36"). There is a small parking area here (see "Alternate Access Point" at the beginning of this passage). You'll find a good camping area outside the wilderness area, less than 0.1 mile down the road.

To continue on the AZT, follow the rough road through a turn to the left in 0.1 mile. Look for a somewhat obscure AZT sign on the right (north) side of the road. Turn onto the singletrack trail, cross a drainage, turn left to follow this drainage, and then veer right (west) in 0.1 mile to exit it.

At mile 17.2, cross a road at a right angle and enter a confusing series of roads. From the sign on the far side of the road, walk due west about 50 yards and look for more signs indicating the singletrack trail to the northwest. Cross a wash for the first of several times at mile 17.3.

At mile 18.0 the AZT passes through a fence near a dry well and windmill before bending right (west). Descend to a small canyon at mile 18.1, and cross this several times, with the help of some signs, over the next 0.7 mile.

At mile 18.9, join an old road and turn right to descend along a wash to the south-southwest. Don't pass through a gate at mile 19.5; turn left (southeast) and descend into the drainage (N31°25'35", W110°25'12"). Follow a singletrack through the drainage and then parallel it on the other side, heading south-southwest. At mile

20.3, climb a short hill and pass through a gate, turn right (west), and follow a rutted trail downhill.

Reach the main road (FR 48) at mile 20.5 (5,610'; N31°25'00", W110°25'43"), southeast of Parker Canyon Lake. To leave the trail and go to Parker Canyon Lake, turn right onto this road and follow it about 1.5 miles to AZ 83; then turn left and walk a short distance to the small shop by the lake.

To continue on the AZT, cross the main road due south (a little left) and pick up a singletrack marked by a sign. Descend an obscure trail 0.1 mile to a cottonwood grove and bend right (due west) to follow a fence through a wash (5,520'). Continue through a vehicle-accessible camping area that is marked by cairns and signs, and then pick up a clear singletrack that climbs a steep hill. There is a dramatic landscape change here as the AZT passes through a vast community of evenly spaced juniper trees.

Cross an old jeep road (at mile 21.2), a wash, a corral and gate, and another road. On the other side of this road are a parking area and a kiosk identifying the AZT. This marks the end of Passage 1 (5,680'; N31°25'11", W110°26'27").

Opposite: Yaqui Ridge looking into Mexico
Photo courtesy of The Arizona Trail Association

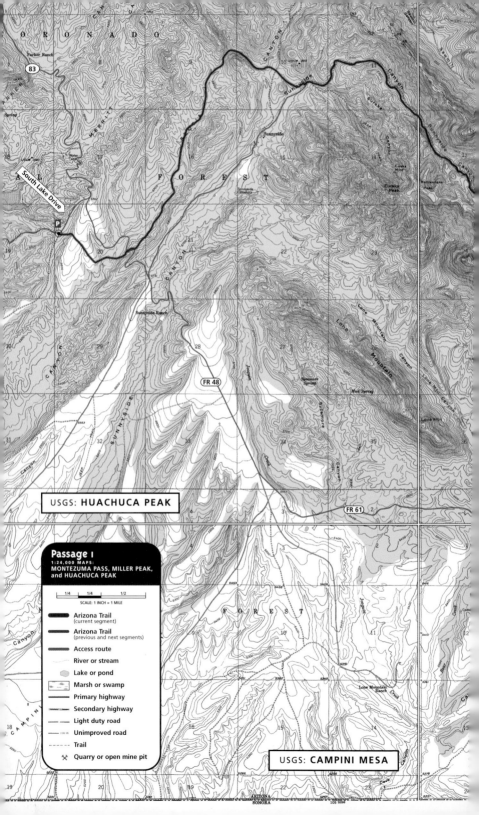

USGS: **HUACHUCA PEAK**

USGS: **CAMPINI MESA**

Passage 1
1:24,000 MAPS:
**MONTEZUMA PASS, MILLER PEAK,
and HUACHUCA PEAK**

1/4 1/4 1/2

SCALE: 1 INCH = 1 MILE

■■■ Arizona Trail
(current segment)

■■■ Arizona Trail
(previous and next segments)

━━ Access route

━━ River or stream

⬡ Lake or pond

Marsh or swamp

━━ Primary highway

━━ Secondary highway

─ ─ Light duty road

━ ═ Unimproved road

╌╌╌ Trail

✕ Quarry or open mine pit

USGS: MILLER PEAK

Bear Saddle

Tub Spring

FR 61

USGS: MONTEZUMA PASS

Passage 2
Canelo Hills East: Parker Canyon Lake to Canelo Pass

West of Parker Canyon Lake in the Canelo Hills

TOTAL DISTANCE	14.5 miles
QUALITY HIKING DISTANCE	14.1 miles
DIFFICULTY	Moderate
TOTAL ELEVATION GAIN	2,260 feet
TOTAL DESCENT	2,606 feet
FROM MEXICO	21.7 miles
TO UTAH	750.2 miles
LAND MANAGERS	Coronado National Forest (Sierra Vista Ranger District)
RECOMMENDED MONTHS	September through June. The winter months may be cold and wet, while the summer heat can be stifling.

INTRODUCTION After the AZT's skyscraping start in the Miller Peak Wilderness, this passage will get your feet back on the ground in the rolling Canelo Hills. But don't be deceived: The terrain here still offers its share of ups and downs. Although this is not a designated wilderness area, there is little evidence of humans along the trail.

Campsites are plentiful, but water is scarce. It is a good idea to stock up at the beginning of the passage and leave a cache at Canelo Pass. In springtime after a wet winter, water may trickle down the network of small canyons crossed by the trail, nurturing lush growth. Grasslands, oak savannahs, and groves of gnarled mesquite provide cover for healthy populations of javelina, deer, and smaller mammals.

The trail is easy to follow except in the frequent drainage crossings, where cairns mark the way. Camping is permitted unless signs indicate otherwise.

MOUNTAIN BIKE NOTES

Although this passage is not particularly technical, it has countless lung-busting climbs, loose rock, and sandy wash crossings. Pedaling with a full load will make it harder still. It is also a lot of fun—and a rare opportunity for a long bike ride into remote grassland and oak woodland ecosystems.

Southbound Cyclists: The long climbs of this passage are virtually impossible to ride. It is better to stick to the roads and avoid the actual AZT on this passage.

WATER

Parker Canyon: Clear water flows here throughout much of the year (N31°25'11", W110°28'24").

Unnamed Stock Tank: This offers murky water during periods of regular precipitation (N31°29'00", W110°30'43").

MAPS

USGS Quadrangles: Huachuca Peak, Canelo Pass, O'Donnell Canyon
USFS: Coronado National Forest (Sierra Vista Ranger District)
Other: Arizona Public Lands Information Center, AZT Passage Topo Map 2—
    Canelo East

BEGINNING ACCESS POINT

Bumpy road to Trailhead   0.5 mile

Parker Canyon Lake: From the town of Sonoita, follow AZ 83 south 30 miles to its intersection with FR 48. Turn left (south) onto FR 48, continue 0.5 mile, and turn right onto South Lake Drive. Proceed 0.5 mile to a parking area near an AZT kiosk (N31°25'11", W110°26'27").

ENDING ACCESS POINT

Smooth road to Trailhead

Canelo Pass: See "Beginning Access Point" for Passage 3.

TRAIL DESCRIPTION   From the kiosk at the trailhead (5,680'), follow an old, rocky road that descends to the west and reaches a sign that says "Closed to All Vehicles." The trail to Parker Canyon Lake leaves the AZT here (see "Supplies, Services, and Accommodations" below).

After a 0.1-mile climb to the top of a ridge, the trail fades. Cairns guide you through a bend to the right (north), and soon you'll have a view of Parker Canyon Lake, a popular fishing destination, on the right.

Pass through a gate and continue 0.1 mile to cross the drainage at the bottom of Parker Canyon (5,190'; N31°25'11", W110°28'24"). Clear water flows here throughout much of the year.

The AZT contours above the canyon, then crosses it several times over the next 0.5 mile. After passing through a gate, join a drainage heading north for about 100 yards. Head out of the drainage to the left (west) and make a substantial climb to the top of a small ridge (5,530'; N31°26'14", W110°28'52").

Ups and downs ensue, until a sustained climb begins and lasts until the AZT reaches a saddle (6,075'; N31°27'20", W110°29'49").

The trail descends along steep switchbacks, bottoms out, bends right (north), and starts to climb again. Pass through a gate and top out in a saddle, then bear left (north-northwest) to cross a ridge.

SUPPLIES, SERVICES, AND ACCOMMODATIONS

PARKER CANYON LAKE
Distance from Trail: 1.3 miles
Phone: (520) 455-5847
Services here are limited to a small store and tackle shop. You will find basic food, camping supplies, and water. The shop is closed in the off-season, so be sure to call ahead if you're counting on its services.

To reach Parker Canyon Lake's shop from the trail, follow the description for Passage 2 to mile 1.0, where you'll see a sign that says "Closed to All Vehicles" (N31°25'02", W110°27'18"). Look for an obscure dirt road descending to the right (north). Follow this 0.2 mile to a small wash and avoid a singletrack turning to the left (west). Continue straight (north) by going around a dirt barricade and climbing the opposite bank. Climb 100 yards, pass through a gate, and continue on a faint roadbed. At mile 0.4 from the AZT, you'll reach a road from which you can see Parker Canyon Lake. Turn left (west), walk 20 yards on the road, and turn right (north) onto another old roadbed by two signs that say "No Motor Vehicles." Continue 50 yards to a clear singletrack near the water and turn right (southeast). You can see the shop across the lake to the northeast. Walk along the east side of the lake until you reach the small buildings on the north side (N31°25'28", W110°26'57"). This is 1.3 miles from the AZT. This access is all bikable.

To drive to Parker Canyon Lake, follow AZ 83 south from the town of Sonoita for 30 miles to its intersection with FR 48. Do not turn onto FR 48, but continue straight (west) a short distance to a parking area near the lake and the shop.

Turn left (west) onto an old road (5,750') and climb 0.1 mile to a 4x4 post. From the 4x4 post, the road curves to the right (north) and descends gradually to reveal impressive views to the northeast. Signs on later 4x4 posts indicate a 180-degree turn through a gate to the left (south). Stay on this new road (FR 4633A) as it bends to the right (west) in about 25 yards.

Southbound Hikers: The 4x4 post here may be confusing if you're headed the other way. It appears to indicate you should leave the road and continue up the hill to the south. Instead, you should follow the road's turn to the left (east).

Near mile 8.9, you'll pass a stock tank that sometimes has murky water, and then bend to the right (northwest). Stands of sturdy ponderosa pines adorn the trail here. As you descend, a deep forest of pine, juniper, and oak trees envelops you. In the heart of these winsome woods, turn left (south) onto an intersecting jeep road (5,325'; N31°29'16", W110°30'59").

The AZT climbs over a ridge before descending to cross a wash (5,415'). From here, don't follow the road as it climbs a steep hill to the southwest. Instead, turn right (north-northwest) onto a singletrack trail that dances in and out of a small wash for the next 0.5 mile. The trail starts a committing climb (5,315'), bends right (north) near the top of a ridge, and continues a gentler climb along a fence to a high point (5,980'; N31°29'48", W110°32'39"). From this stretch, the sharp peak of Mount Wrightson, monarch of Passage 5, dominates the horizon to the west-northwest.

As Canelo Pass Road (FR 799) comes into view, pass through a gate in the fence and begin a switchbacking descent to the west. The trail comes within 20 feet of the road, then turns right (north) and climbs to cross the road at mile 14.5. Soon you'll reach the parking area and the end of Passage 2 (5,330'; N31°30'47", W110°33'28").

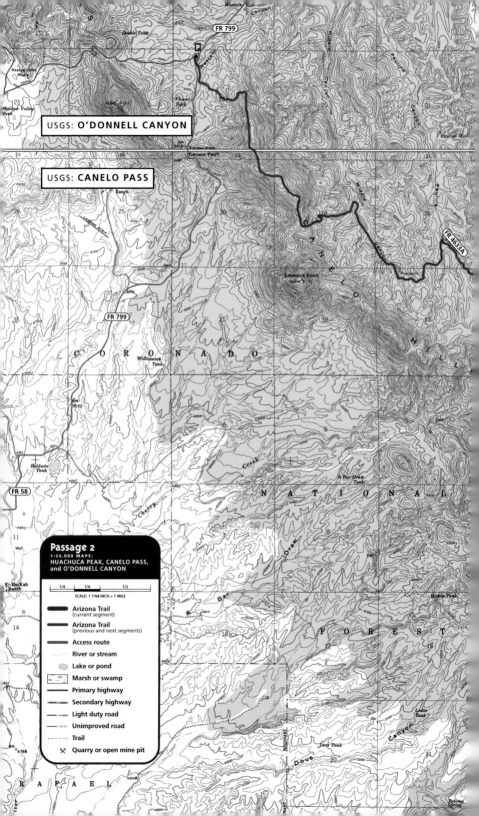

USGS: O'DONNELL CANYON

USGS: CANELO PASS

FR 799

Passage 2
1:24,000 MAPS:
HUACHUCA PEAK, CANELO PASS,
and O'DONNELL CANYON

| 1/4 | 1/4 | 1/2 |

SCALE: 1 7/64 INCH = 1 MILE

Arizona Trail
(current segment)

Arizona Trail
(previous and next segments)

Access route

River or stream

Lake or pond

Marsh or swamp

Primary highway

Secondary highway

Light duty road

Unimproved road

Trail

Quarry or open mine pit

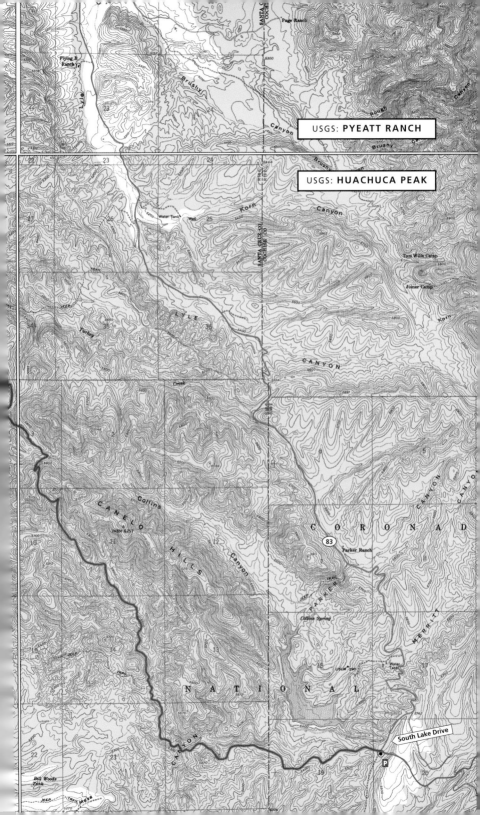

USGS: **PYEATT RANCH**

USGS: **HUACHUCA PEAK**

South Lake Drive

Passage 3
Canelo Hills West: Canelo Pass to Patagonia

Near Canelo Hills West

TOTAL DISTANCE	17.4 miles
QUALITY HIKING DISTANCE	14.1 miles
DIFFICULTY	Moderate
TOTAL ELEVATION GAIN	959 feet
TOTAL DESCENT	2,239 feet
FROM MEXICO	36.2 miles
TO UTAH	735.7 miles
LAND MANAGERS	Coronado National Forest (Sierra Vista Ranger District)
RECOMMENDED MONTHS	September through June, though the winter months may be cold and wet

INTRODUCTION Rolling, grassy hills mixed with patches of high desert define this passage. Hundreds of plant and animal species—some quite rare—thrive in the nearby Patagonia–Sonoita Creek Preserve, owned and managed by the Nature Conservancy. This preserve's 275 species of birds attract tens of thousands of bird enthusiasts each year. You might catch a glimpse of a rare violet-crowned hummingbird, northern beardless-tyrannulet, or gray hawk. For more information, see "Supplies, Services, and Accommodations" on p. 53.

This passage does not feel as isolated as the previous two did, but its rarely used, often charming ranch roads offer a moderate hike or a fun, nontechnical bike ride (albeit with a few difficult sections). Novice backpackers might enjoy a one- or two-night shuttle hike starting at Canelo Pass and ending at the trailhead on Harshaw Road (See "Alternate Access Point.") Plan hikes to avoid camping between mile 5.5 and about mile 6.3, where regulations prohibit overnight stays.

MOUNTAIN BIKE NOTES

 This passage of the AZT provides almost continuous riding, partially on excellent singletrack. It has short stretches of difficult terrain, with some rocky, steep sections, but most of the passage is accessible to intermediate cyclists.

WATER

 Down Under Tank: This stock pond may have murky water (N31°31'08", W110°35'48"). There might also be water in the streambed below, even when the tank is dry.

Red Bank Well: If there's no visible water, try lowering the float in the trough to activate the flow (N31°31'27", W110°38'30").

Gate Spring: The spring is off the trail about 150 meters to the south. Tread lightly because this is a sensitive area for threatened and endangered species (N31°31'55", W110°38'57").

MAPS

USGS Quadrangles: O'Donnell Canyon, Mount Hughes, Patagonia
USFS: Coronado National Forest (Sierra Vista Ranger District)
Other: Arizona Public Lands Information Center, AZT Passage Topo Map 3—Canelo West

BEGINNING ACCESS POINT

 Canelo Pass: From the town of Patagonia, follow Harshaw Road (FR 58) east 14.0 miles to an intersection where FR 58 makes a 90-degree turn to the right. Avoid this and continue straight ahead (east) on FR 799. In 5.0 miles, cross Canelo Pass and continue about a 0.5 mile down the other side to a large parking area on the left (west) side of the road. The trail toward Patagonia departs from the right side of a kiosk; the trail arriving from Passage 2 is on the left side of the kiosk (N31°30'47", W110°33'28").

  Canelo Pass: From the town of Sonoita, follow AZ 83 south for 18 miles to a turnoff on the right for FR 799. Continue 2.9 miles to a parking area on the right that is marked with Arizona Trail signs.

ALTERNATE ACCESS POINT

  Harshaw Road Trailhead: Park here to avoid the last 3.2 miles of this passage, which follow high-use roads. From Patagonia, take Harshaw Road (FR 58) east for 2.8 miles. You will see the trailhead on the left and a large parking area on the right (N31°31'39", W110°42'36").

ENDING ACCESS POINT

Patagonia: See "Beginning Access Point" for Passage 4.

TRAIL DESCRIPTION

Two singletracks lead away from the kiosk in the parking lot (5,330'). Follow the one on the right, to the west, climbing slightly. (The trail on the left is the end of the AZT's Passage 2.) Pass through a gate in a saddle at mile 1.1 (5,580') and descend fairly steeply through three switchbacks to the north edge of Meadow Valley at mile 2.1. Soon, a 4x4 post marks a turn left (southwest) onto an old jeep road.

At an intersection marked with a 4x4 Arizona Trail post at mile 2.4, turn right and follow the road over a small hill to the intersection with a more heavily traveled road (FR 765). A 4x4 Arizona Trail post directly across this road points the way to more than

The Arizona Trail in the Canelo Hills

a mile of recently constructed singletrack. This singletrack section slopes down gradually to the northwest, taking you into Redrock Canyon and terminating at the southeast end of the Down Under Tank dam. You rejoin the two-track ranch access road at the northwest end of the dam.

 If there is no water in Down Under Tank (N31º31'08", W110º35'48"), check in the streambed below the dam (first 100 to 200 meters).

Continue to descend through the pleasant, open oak savannah. At about mile 5.9, you'll reach a broken windmill where signs indicate camping is prohibited. The road veers

SUPPLIES, SERVICES, AND ACCOMMODATIONS

PATAGONIA

Distance from Trail: 0.0 mile

Area Code	520
Zip Code	85624
ATM	Patagonia Market (394-2962), on Naugle Ave., 1 block west and south of post office
Bank	Community First (877-226-5663), 3rd Avenue and McKeown Avenue; open M, F 10 a.m. to 3 p.m., T, W, Th 10 a.m. to 2 p.m.
Bicycle Shop	None
Bus	None
Camping	No commercial camping available
Dining	*The Home Plate* (394-2344), 277 W. McKeown Ave., kitty-corner from the post office, has good, inexpensive lunch food. *The Stage Stop* (394-2211), 303 W. McKeown Ave., 1 block south of the post office, offers good, reasonably priced Mexican and American food.
Gear	None
Groceries	Patagonia Market (394-2962), on Naugle Avenue, 1 block west and south of the post office
Information	Patagonia Tourist Information Center (394-0060), 305 McKeown Ave., the big, yellow building 1 block south of the post office; open M to Th, 8 a.m. to 1 p.m.
Laundry	Patagonia RV Park (394-2491), 566 Harshaw Rd., on the AZT at mile 16.2
Lodging	Stage Stop Inn (800-923-2211), 303 W. McKeown Ave., 1 block south of post office
Medical	Family Health Center (394-2262), 101 Taylor Ave.
Post Office	Located at the bend in Harshaw Avenue, 1 block east of AZ 82; general delivery held for 15 days; 394-2950
Showers	None

Other Attractions: If you have an open afternoon in Patagonia, visit the nearby Patagonia–Sonoita Creek Preserve, a fine example of Arizona's dwindling riparian areas. Nationally famous among birders, the preserve supports a wide variety of plants and animals and 275 species of birds. This Nature Conservancy–owned preserve is open Wednesday through Sunday, from 7:30 a.m. to 3:30 p.m. From town, go west on 4th Avenue and left on Pennsylvania Avenue. Cross Sonoita Creek and continue to the parking area at the main gate, about a mile and a half from the center of town. For more information, contact the Nature Conservancy of Arizona at (520) 622-3861.

right (north) to continue descending through Redrock Canyon and passes a north-facing no-camping sign near mile 6.3 (indicating you're leaving the no-camping zone).

Continue on this charming, old road to a fork at mile 7.5 (4,645'; N31°31'25", W110°38'29"). Bear right (north) to cross the drainage and pass the windmill at Red Bank Well (mile 7.6; N31°31'27", W110°38'30"). If there's no visible water, try lowering the float in the trough to activate the flow. Pass through a corral as the road ends and continue downcanyon to the north on a clear singletrack.

You'll pass near Gate Spring at mile 8.3 (N31°31'55", W110°38'57"). The spring is down the hillside about 150 meters to the south. Do not linger in this area, which is frequented by threatened and endangered species.

Turn right (north) at a fork at mile 9.3 (4,520'; N31°32'26", W110°39'28"), pass through a gate at mile 9.4, and, in 50 yards, follow a singletrack trail that leaves the drainage bottom to the left (northwest). A brief climb leads into an eerie forest of mesquite.

Continue straight across a road to the west at mile 10.6. At mile 11.0 (4,420'), pass through a wash and turn southwest to parallel the wash for 80 yards. Follow the trail left (south) out of the wash and climb through switchbacks to mile 11.9 (4,635') before descending to mile 12.7 (4,500'). You'll pass through a gate before reaching a saddle at mile 13.2 that offers a view of the Harshaw Creek Valley winding northwest to Patagonia.

Several switchbacks lead down to Harshaw Road (FR 58) at mile 14.2 (4,220'; N31°31'39", W110°42'36"). If you left a car here, cross the road and follow a singletrack a few yards to the parking lot.

Thru-hikers heading for Patagonia should turn right (northwest) and follow the road. Hitchhiking may be possible. Pass Patagonia RV Park at mile 16.3. At mile 16.9, the road winds to the left and enters the town. In another 0.1 mile, turn right at the post office and walk to Naugle Avenue (AZ 82), the main drag. Turn right and follow the road to 1st Avenue (4,067'; N31°32'38", W110°44'52"). This is the end of Passage 3; the next passage turns left onto 1st Avenue and continues to the northwest.

Opposite: The Arizona Trail near Meadow Tank

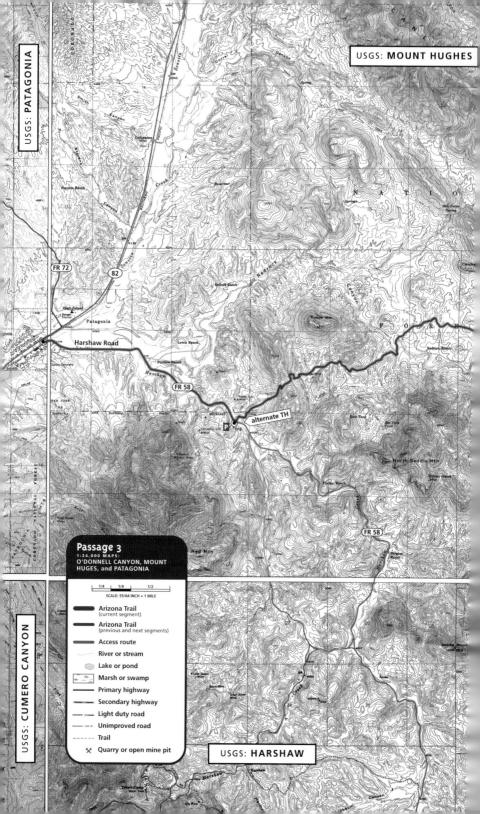

FR 72

82

Harshaw Road

FR 58

alternate TH

P

FR 58

N A T I O

F O R

Passage 3
1:24,000 MAPS:
O'DONNELL CANYON, MOUNT
HUGES, and PATAGONIA

1/4   1/4   1/2

SCALE: 55/64 INCH = 1 MILE

Arizona Trail
(current segment)

Arizona Trail
(previous and next segments)

Access route

River or stream

Lake or pond

Marsh or swamp

Primary highway

Secondary highway

Light duty road

Unimproved road

Trail

Quarry or open mine pit

Red Mtn

Kunde Mtn

North Saddle Mtn

83

FR 799

Passage 4
Temporal Gulch: Patagonia to Gardner Canyon Road

The town of Patagonia highlighted by the setting sun

TOTAL DISTANCE	19.4 miles
QUALITY HIKING DISTANCE	7.1 miles
DIFFICULTY	Strenuous
TOTAL ELEVATION GAIN	3,365 feet
TOTAL DESCENT	2,054 feet
FROM MEXICO	53.6 miles
TO UTAH	718.3 miles
LAND MANAGERS	Coronado National Forest (Nogales Ranger District)
RECOMMENDED MONTHS	March through November, depending on snow level

INTRODUCTION The first part of this passage follows a dirt road that is open to motorized vehicles, and most day hikers will prefer to drive 12.3 miles to the wilderness trailhead at Upper Walker Tank. But with views of the Mount Wrightson Wilderness and surrounding grasslands, this can be a pleasant walk for thru-hikers. It starts in a grassland ecosystem and climbs through oak savannah to reach the thick, cool oak and pine forest on the edge of the Mount Wrightson Wilderness.

This passage and Passage 5 offer an interesting contrast, as the route passes through remote, relatively untouched land, protected by the Mount Wrightson Wilderness, and then enters one of southern Arizona's most productive former mining regions. The Greaterville Mining District, which the AZT enters shortly after exiting the wilderness, drew hundreds of Mexican and American prospectors after gold was discovered in 1874. Interpretive signs describe the extensive water-diversion project that took water uphill from Gardner Canyon into Kentucky Gulch for high-pressure hydraulic mining.

The jewel of the Mount Wrightson Wilderness is its namesake 9,453-foot peak, a side trip off the AZT and possibly the most visible landmark in southern Arizona. The rugged wilderness that surrounds the peak is home to rare birds and some plants that occur nowhere else north of Mexico.

Early in spring, snow will blanket the higher reaches of the trail, making some hills difficult to traverse. Early-season travelers should wear sturdy boots, take their time on the snow, and travel with a friend.

MOUNTAIN BIKE NOTES

The road that constitutes the first 12.3 miles of this passage is easy to ride at first, but becomes steadily more difficult. It ends at a wilderness trailhead beyond which bikes are prohibited. The best way to bypass the wilderness is to skip this portion of the trail by following AZ 82 north to Sonoita. Turn left (north) onto AZ 83, ride about 1.3 miles, and turn left (west) onto FR 4104. Ride about 7 miles on an occasionally difficult road to FR 785, turn left, and continue west less than 2 miles to a sign on the right that marks the AZT.

The portion of the AZT from Tunnel Spring Trailhead through Passage 5 to AZ 83 provides excellent, moderate singletrack riding. You can ride point-to-point by leaving a vehicle at one of the access points, or do an out-and-back.

WATER

Temporal Gulch: The route of the AZT parallels this wash. It contains water during spring runoff (N31°36'11", W110°47'14").

Upper Walker Tank: This cement dam may retain fresh water after wet winters. Snow on the slopes of Mount Wrightson may indicate that you'll find water here (N31°40'19", W110°48'57").

Big Casa Blanca Canyon: This drainage should have water during a normal spring runoff.

 Bear Spring: Locals report finding water here even in autumn when the rest of the canyon is dry.

 Tunnel Spring Trailhead: Water in the stream next to the road is reliable under normal spring conditions (N31°42'08", W110°47'34").

MAPS

USGS Quadrangles: Patagonia, Mount Hughes, Mount Wrightson
USFS: Coronado National Forest (Nogales Ranger District)
Other: Arizona Public Lands Information Center, AZT Passage Topo Map 4—
Temporal Gulch

BEGINNING ACCESS POINT

 Patagonia: Take AZ 82 to the town of Patagonia. At the north end of town, on the south side of the high school, 1st Avenue heads northwest from the highway (N31°32'38", W110°44'52"). The AZT follows 1st Avenue (later FR 72) for the next 12.3 miles.

ALTERNATE ACCESS POINT

 **Walker Basin Trailhead:** Take AZ 82 to the town of Patagonia. At the north end of town, near the high school, turn northwest onto 1st Avenue. This road soon turns to dirt and becomes FR 72. At 6.5 miles from the highway there is a parking area and a trailhead for non-four-wheel-drive vehicles. Four-wheel-drives can continue 5.8 miles along the very rough FR 72 to a small parking area at the trailhead (N31°40'19", W110°48'57").

 Tunnel Spring Trailhead: From Sonoita, follow AZ 83 north 4 miles and turn left (west) onto Gardner Canyon Road (FR 92). Avoid side roads. You'll reach the Gardner Trailhead, this passage's end, 5.5 miles from the highway on the right side of the road. Continue another 0.8 mile and turn left (east) onto FR 785 at a sign for Gardner Canyon Trail. You'll cross the AZT twice as you continue 2.7 miles to a small parking area at the Tunnel Spring Trailhead (N31°42'08", W110°47'34"). The Utah-bound trail continues down the road you just drove up. The Mexico-bound stretch heads into the trees to the southwest on a singletrack trail.

ENDING ACCESS POINT

 Gardner Trailhead: See "Beginning Access Point" for Passage 5.

Opposite: Agave, mesquite, and Emory oak near Empire Ranch, with the Santa Rita Mountains and Mount Wrightson in the distance

TRAIL DESCRIPTION   From the intersection of 1st Avenue and AZ 82 (Naugle Avenue), walk northwest along 1st Avenue (4,067'). Please respect private residences. After crossing a cattle guard at mile 0.5, the road turns to dirt. Avoid side roads. At mile 0.8, the trail bends left, crosses a wash, and starts climbing.

At a fork at mile 2.0, avoid a left turn to the landfill—unless you're a thru-hiker who has accumulated an excess of trash! In 0.4 mile, a sign indicates FR 72. The rocky block of Mount Wrightson's summit dominates the horizon directly in front of you.

Stay on the main, graded dirt road. After you pass a sign indicating you are entering public lands, there are plenty of places to camp along the road. Pass a sign at mile 6.2 that says "Arizona Trail Trailhead ¼ mile" and avoid a fork to the left. In 0.2 mile, cross a cattle guard and follow a right fork to the trailhead (mile 6.5; 4,430'; N31°36'11", W110°47'14"). Motorists will require a four-wheel drive beyond this point.

Follow the road west through a small wash, and then bend to the right to parallel the wash to the north. You may find water here during spring runoff. Just after the trail crosses the wash again, you'll see several nice campsites. From here on, flat ground is difficult to find, but you might improvise a camping spot at the Walker Basin Trailhead.

WILDERNESS ALERT

The **Mount Wrightson Wilderness** was designated in 1984 to be "an area where the earth and its community of life are untrammeled by man, where man himself is a visitor who does not remain." It protects 25,260 acres of rugged canyons and steep slopes surrounding the impressive, 9,453-foot summit of Mount Wrightson.

Please remember these rules governing wilderness areas:

• Camp out of sight, at least 200 feet from lakes and streams, on dry, durable surfaces.
• Use a stove. If you must have a fire, use existing fire rings.
• Keep water sources clean by washing at least 200 feet from them.
• Bury human waste 6 inches deep and 200 feet from lakes and streams.
• Pack out toilet paper.
• Hobble or picket livestock at least 200 feet from lakes and streams, and use only treated, weed-free feed and grain.
• Keep all dogs on a leash.
• No mountain bikes.
• Pack out all trash; don't burn it.

Brown carsonite posts mark the rest of the passage. Avoid the occasional fork, such as FR 72A or the singletrack Temporal Trail. You'll reach a small parking area for the Walker Basin Trailhead (5,680'; N31°40'19", W110°48'57").

 A cement dam here contains water in springtime after a wet winter, but it may be empty during the summer or in dry years.

Walk the rocky road as it continues north into the Mount Wrightson Wilderness. Follow a singletrack trail as it continues a switchbacking climb along the lower reaches of Josephine Peak. The stunning views behind you reach far into Mexico.

The trail forks at a saddle (6,560'; N31°40'51", W110°49'20"), where you might find a place to camp but no water. A metal sign that says "Arizona Trail" marks this intersection, the high point of Passage 4. Turn 90 degrees to the right (east) and follow a side trail (not shown on the 1981 USGS map) as it descends through several switchbacks into Big Casa Blanca Canyon. The rocky throne of Mount Wrightson, to the west, presides over this canyon.

 The AZT crosses the canyon bottom (5,675'; N31°40'59", W110°48'18"), and you should find water during an average springtime. Locals report that nearby Bear Spring has provided water in autumn when the rest of the canyon was low on water.

For the next mile, the trail maintains its height as the canyon it is paralleling digs a deep path toward the flat grasslands to the southeast. The views here are grand, including the sometimes-snowcapped Huachuca Mountains to the southeast. The trail bends north to leave the canyon and exits the Mount Wrightson Wilderness.

You soon will pass the first of many interpretive signs describing the elaborate hydraulic mining system that existed here in the early 1900s. The trail meanders to the north and reaches the Tunnel Spring Trailhead and a dirt road (5,640'; N31°42'08", W110°47'34").

 Water in the stream next to the road is seasonal, so the stream might be dry.

Turn right (east) onto the road (FR 785), pass through a gate, continue 1.2 miles to a side road that breaks off sharply to the left (west), and turn onto it.

This turn is easy to miss—there is a sign here, but it faces the opposite direction along the road.

Cross the stream and pick up a clear singletrack turning back to the right (north). Follow this popular mountain-bike segment across FR 785. After crossing a cow pasture, two gates, and a wash, you'll reach the road again; turn right (northeast), walk about 100 yards, and pick up the trail branching off to the left. Continue 0.3 mile to the Gardner Trailhead and the end of Passage 4 (mile 19.4; 5,215'; N31°43'12", W110°45'11").

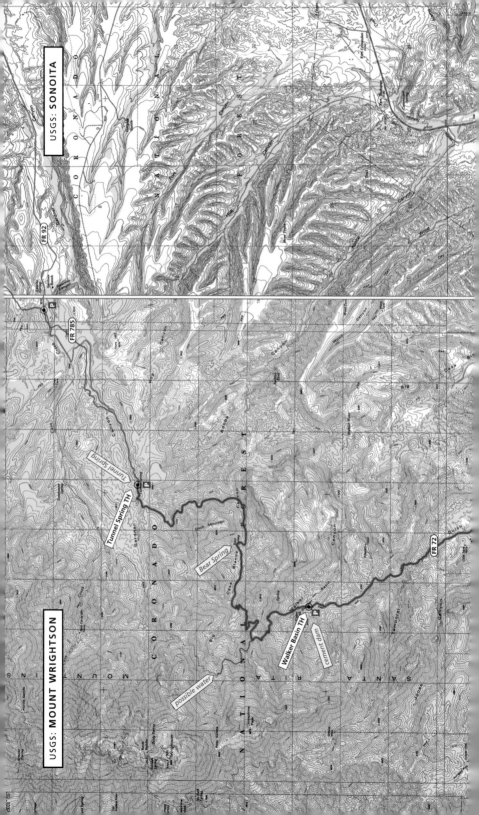

USGS: SONOITA

USGS: MOUNT WRIGHTSON

CORONADO NATIONAL FOREST

SANTA RITA MOUNTAINS

FR 92

FR 785

FR 72

Tunnel Spring

Tunnel Spring TH

Bear Spring

Walker Basin TH

cement dam

possible water

USGS: **MOUNT HUGHES**

USGS: **PATAGONIA**

Passage 4
1:24,000
PATAGONIA, MOUNT HUGES, and
MOUNT WRIGHTSON

SCALE: 27/32 INCH = 1 MILE

1/4   3/8   1/2

Arizona Trail
(current segment)

Arizona Trail
(previous and next segments)

Access route

River or stream

Lake or pond

Marsh or swamp

Primary highway

Secondary highway

Light duty road

Unimproved road

Trail

✕   Quarry or open mine pit

Passage 5
Santa Rita Mountains:
Gardner Canyon Road to AZ 83

Along the Arizona Trail in Coronado National Forest

TOTAL DISTANCE	17.2 miles
QUALITY HIKING DISTANCE	14.4 miles
DIFFICULTY	Moderate
TOTAL ELEVATION GAIN	1,635 feet
TOTAL DESCENT	2,173 feet
FROM MEXICO	73.0 miles
TO UTAH	698.9 miles
LAND MANAGERS	Coronado National Forest (Nogales Ranger District)
RECOMMENDED MONTHS	This passage is hikable year-round, though summer can be quite hot.

INTRODUCTION This passage is rich in mining history, much of which you can observe from the trail. After gold was discovered in 1874, the town of Greaterville sprang up and soon boasted saloons, dance halls, stores, a jail, and a public school. Many of the original buildings still stand, and some are inhabited by descendants of the early Mexican residents. The town, whose buildings are private and not open to visitors, is just a mile off the AZT.

The landscape around this passage might look significantly different if mining plans just after the turn of the century had come to fruition. After gold production around Greaterville fell off in the early 1880s, the boomtown quieted and most of its residents moved on to more promising venues. But there was a revival in 1904 when a well-financed Californian named James Stetson came to Greaterville with the idea of using hydraulic mining to reach previously inaccessible gold deposits in Kentucky Gulch. This system employed vast quantities of pressurized water to blast away the earth, revealing ore concealed beneath the surface. Since there was not enough reliable water in Kentucky Gulch, Stetson built a system of pipes to carry water over a ridge from nearby Gardner Canyon, which is fed by the snows on Mount Wrightson. There is plenty of evidence of this aqueduct along the AZT, and frequent interpretive signs describe aspects of the project, including the physics of moving water uphill without a pump.

Kentucky Gulch was spared the ravages of hydraulic mining because the life of Stetson's mining company was cut short—along with his own. During a trip to Tucson in 1905 to meet with investors, Stetson fell to his death from a third-story hotel room. The details of his untimely demise remain a mystery, but history suggests Stetson was neither suicidal nor drunk enough to stumble out of a window.

Much of Stetson's legacy remains in the form of Kentucky Camp, a collection of buildings constructed as a base for the mining operation. The AZT passes right through the camp, which is under renovation by the Forest Service and a dedicated group of volunteers called Friends of Kentucky Camp. (Membership in this group is $10 per person. More information is available at www.aztecfreenet.org/fkcamp/.)

MOUNTAIN BIKE NOTES

 This entire passage provides excellent, moderate singletrack riding. You can ride point-to-point by leaving a vehicle at one of the access points, or do an out-and-back.

WATER

 Kentucky Camp: There is an outdoor sink with fresh, running water here (N31°44'37", W110°44'27").

 FR 165: A not-too-reliable stock pond here has surprisingly clear water (N31°45'48", W110°46'34").

 Stock pond: Another unreliable pond is 0.3 mile before the end of the passage (N31°48'34", W110°42'54").

Mount Wrightson
Photo courtesy of The Arizona Trail Association

MAPS

USGS Quadrangles: Mount Wrightson, Sonoita, Empire Ranch, Helvetia
USFS: Coronado National Forest (Nogales Ranger District)
Other: Arizona Public Lands Information Center, AZT Passage Topo Map 5—
    Santa Rita Mountains

BEGINNING ACCESS POINT

Gardner Trailhead: From Sonoita, follow AZ 83 north 4 miles and turn left (west) onto Gardner Canyon Road (FR 92). Avoid side roads. You'll reach the Gardner Trailhead (not to be confused with Gardner Canyon Trail, which is farther west) 5.5 miles from the highway on the right side of the road. There is a large parking area here (N31°43'12", W110°45'11").

ALTERNATE ACCESS POINT

Kentucky Camp: Continue on Gardner Canyon Road, FR 92 (see "Beginning Access Point" above), and do not take any turnoffs or side roads until you reach the intersection with FR 4085 and FR 163 at approximately 3.4 miles. FR 4085 bears to the left, and FR 163 bears to the right. At about 1.1 miles, a gate and parking area will be on your left. Kentucky Camp is about 0.3 mile down the hill.

ENDING ACCESS POINT

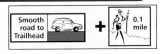

AZ 83: See "Beginning Access Point" for Passage 6.

TRAIL DESCRIPTION   The AZT skirts the north side of the parking area (5,215'), and then makes a steep climb to the northeast. Top out in 0.2 mile (5,415') after a few formidable switchbacks. Cross a minor high point and pass through a fence. The trail follows a water-diversion ditch to the northeast. Turn right (east) onto FR 4110 and follow it along a high finger of land (N31°43'55", W110°44'00"), where a single-track trail departs to the left. Descend this trail to the north and cross FR 4085 in less than a mile. Follow the trail uphill through a meadow as it swings back to the west to reach historic Kentucky Camp (5,125'; N31°44'37", W110°44'27"). Clear AZT signs will lead you through this area.

Running water, a modern outhouse, and a rental cabin are available here. For information on the cabin, contact the Nogales Ranger District at (520) 281-2296.

Climb away from Kentucky Camp on the dirt road heading north. Pass through a fence in 0.3 mile, continue 50 yards, and turn left (west) onto FR 163. Climb steadily to a fork in the road. Stay right (north) on FR 163. Bear left at the next fork, staying on FR 163 until you reach the intersection with FR 165 at the bottom of a very steep hill.

Turn left (southwest) onto FR 165 and follow it for 0.7 mile uphill to a small parking area and trailhead on the right (5,580'; N31°45'45", W110°46'27"). Pick up the singletrack trail that climbs to the north.

A stock pond just west of the trail here has surprisingly clear water. To reach it, walk 0.1 mile along the AZT beyond the trailhead to a flat spot and turn left (west) to bushwhack over a hill 0.1 mile to the pond.

The AZT soon joins an old roadbed and climbs gradually. Pick up a singletrack trail with a sharp turn to the right. The trail reaches a high point in 0.2 mile (5,845') and then begins descending to the north-northeast. Steep switchbacks lead to a drainage. The trail turns left (west-northwest) to join an old jeep road, and then it turns right (east) onto a second road. Watch for a 90-degree bend to the left (north).

The AZT crosses FR 62 (5,186'; N31°47'34", W110°44'48"). Look for a gate on the other side of the road and a singletrack trail continuing to the northeast.

In 0.1 mile, the trail turns left (north) onto an old road and climbs for the next 0.5 mile. Join another road and turn left (north). Make a sharp turn to the right (southeast) in 0.1 mile, then climb a ridge for 0.1 mile before taking off to the left (east) on a singletrack trail (5,400'; N31°48'15", W110°44'24").

After a short distance, join a road and turn left (north). Where the road appears to fork, avoid the clear road bending right (southeast) and turn left to follow a narrow track through a fence to the north. Continue to the top of a small knoll and take a right fork to the northeast. Pass through another gate.

Arizona Trail hiker
Photo courtesy of The Arizona Trail Association

Climb steeply for 100 yards and turn left (northeast) onto a singletrack. The trail rejoins the narrow track and continues east and northeast. Join FR 4072 and turn left (north). The road descends 50 yards before bending right (east) in front of a water tank.

You'll pass a stock pond. Sounds of the highway foretell the end of the passage, which you reach at a trailhead sign and former parking area at mile 17.2 (5,115'; N31°48'31", W110°42'37"). Note that vehicle access to this trailhead is now closed.

USGS: HELVETIA

USGS: EMPIRE RANCH

Passage 5
1:24,000 MAPS:
MOUNT WRIGHTSON, SONOITA,
EMPIRE RANCH, and HELVETIA

1/4   1/4   1/2
SCALE: 1 INCH = 1 MILE

• • • Arizona Trail
        (current proposed segment)

━━━ Arizona Trail
        (previous and next segments)

· · · · Arizona Trail
        (previous or next proposed segments)

━━━ Access route

       River or stream

       Lake or pond

       Marsh or swamp

       Primary highway

       Secondary highway

─ ─ ─ Light duty road

· · · · Unimproved road

- - - - Trail

   ✕   Quarry or open mine pit

FR 62

83

stock pond

Trail not exact

water hose

Kentucky Camp

FR 4085

FR 163

FR 92

USGS: MOUNT WRIGHTSON

USGS: SONOITA

CORONA

NATION

Passage 6
Las Cienegas: AZ 83 to I-10

Grasslands of the Empire/Cienega Resource Conservation Area north, of Sonoita, Arizona

TOTAL DISTANCE	Approximately 18.0 miles
QUALITY HIKING DISTANCE	NA
DIFFICULTY	Strenuous
TOTAL ELEVATION GAIN	NA
TOTAL DESCENT	NA
FROM MEXICO	90.2 miles
TO UTAH	681.7 miles
LAND MANAGERS	Coronado National Forest (Nogales Ranger District, Sierra Vista Ranger District), Arizona State Lands Department
RECOMMENDED MONTHS	September through April

INTRODUCTION An official route for this passage has not been established. The previously proposed route through the Empire-Cienega Resource Conservation Area, as reported in other publications, has been changed. The new route will proceed north from Oak Tree Canyon to Davidson Canyon at I-10. From there, the planned route goes through Colossal Cave Mountain Park and then into the Rincon Mountains from the south. As of this printing, full construction of the new trail is not expected for several years.

MOUNTAIN BIKE NOTES

Until a route is finalized, mountain bikers may want to follow AZ 83 north to I-10, then to the town of Vail, and on to Colossal Cave Mountain Park. Or, with a careful study of area maps, you could intermittently ride on some forest roads west of AZ 83 and north of Oak Tree Canyon, at least until reaching Sahuarita Road, which is approximately 15 miles north of Oak Tree Canyon.

WATER

Blacktail Tank: There's intermittent cattle-tank–grade water here (N31°53'36", W110°41'06").

Mile 11.0, Twin Tanks: There's available cattle-tank–grade water here (N31°54'38", W110°40'05").

MAPS

USGS Quadrangles: Empire Ranch, Mount Fagan
USFS: Coronado National Forest (Nogales and Sierra Vista Ranger Districts)

BEGINNING ACCESS POINT

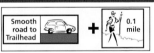

AZ 83: At the intersection of I-10 and AZ 83, drive south on AZ 83 to just near milepost 43. Turn right (west) on an unmarked road (FR 4072). The road has a gate preventing vehicles from proceeding very far. Park in this area and walk 0.1 mile south on the road to a large open area and the AZT trailhead sign (N31°48'31", W110°42'37"). This is Oak Tree Canyon. As of July 2004, this location is the end of the AZT's Passage 5.

ENDING ACCESS POINT

I-10: A walk-through culvert (N31°59'47", W110°39'11") passes under I-10, 0.25 mile west of the Davidson Canyon Bridge. It is not accessible by vehicle. Please do not exit your vehicle from I-10.

TRAIL DESCRIPTION As mentioned previously, there is not an official route through this passage. The following is only a suggested route. Based on very preliminary plans, the route is to proceed north out of Oak Tree Canyon and stay west of AZ 83 until reaching the junction of AZ 83 and Sahuarita Road. That's a distance of about 15 rugged miles. Until there is a constructed trail, hikers will have to walk roads and bushwhack their way. The rough terrain teems with whitethorn and other prickly vegetation. Some hikers may instead decide to hike along, or within earshot of, the paved AZ 83 until reaching Sahuarita Road.

Those wishing to stay off the paved road are in for some lovely views, although the going is slow and scratchy because of the shirt- and pant-grabbing desert plants. Off-road hikers should proceed north out of the west end of Oak Tree Canyon toward a place on the map, just over 2.0 miles away, called Rosemont Junction. Then follow FR 231 approximately 2.5 miles northeast to N31°50'55", W110°42'17". This spot is about 0.5 mile west of AZ 83. Bushwhack due north for approximately 1.5 miles, skirting the east side of private property (Hidden Ranch).

Then hike northeast and bushwhack a rugged 2.5 miles to Blacktail Tank (N31°53'36", W110°41'06"). You can possibly find cattle-tank–grade water there. From Blacktail Tank, continue northeast about 1.5 prickly-pear-filled miles to a spot called Twin Tanks (N31°54'38", W110°40'05"). This area is probably the best spot to camp since Oak Tree Canyon. And water is likely, too—in fact, it could be the last water you will find until reaching Colossal Cave Mountain Park. There are also houses and AZ 83 within 0.5 mile of Twin Tanks.

Leaving Twin Tanks, you must continue bushwhacking, but the terrain isn't too bad. Hike north-northeast for a couple of miles to avoid private property northwest of Twin Tanks. After about 2.0 miles, in order to stay west of the highway, turn northwest. The goal is to get to the junction of AZ 83 and Sahuarita Road (N31°57'47", W110°40'19"). Unfortunately, it's all fenced in at that junction, so find a place to crawl under the fences. Please don't climb over them!

The area east of the Sahuarita Road and AZ 83 junction looks more daunting than it is. Again, east of AZ 83 there is a fence. Climb under it and then proceed into a large wash and hike north for about 0.25 mile. Northeast of the wash is a faint old road. Follow it east as best you can for 0.5 mile until reaching a much better road. Cross the better road and crawl under some more fence, then bushwack northeast for another 0.5 mile until reaching a spot where you can see many utility lines and the interstate (N31°58'39", W110°39'19"). Hike north almost 2.0 miles, passing under the utility lines and into a large, vegetation-filled wash. Carefully pick your way through the wash until you reach the end of this passage at a large culvert (N31°59'47", W110°39'11"), which crosses under I-10 about 0.25 mile west of the Davidson Canyon Bridge.

Dave Hicks shows off the size of the barrel cactus.
Photo courtesy of The Arizona Trail Association

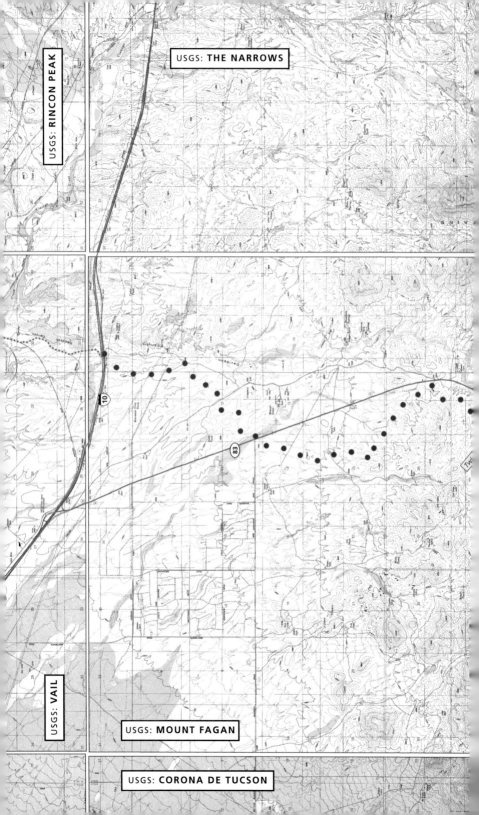

USGS: **RINCON PEAK**

USGS: **THE NARROWS**

USGS: **VAIL**

USGS: **MOUNT FAGAN**

USGS: **CORONA DE TUCSON**

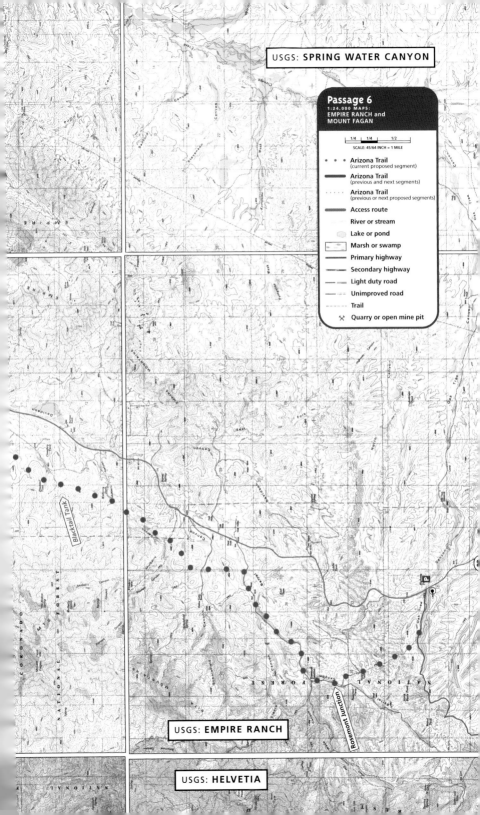

USGS: **SPRING WATER CANYON**

Passage 6
1:24,000 MAPS:
EMPIRE RANCH and
MOUNT FAGAN

| 1/4 | 1/4 | 1/2 |

SCALE: 45/64 INCH = 1 MILE

• • •   **Arizona Trail**
(current proposed segment)

━━━   **Arizona Trail**
(previous and next segments)

• • • •   **Arizona Trail**
(previous or next proposed segments)

━━━   **Access route**

      River or stream

◯   **Lake or pond**

      Marsh or swamp

━━━   **Primary highway**

━━━   **Secondary highway**

─ ─   **Light duty road**

─ ·· ─   **Unimproved road**

- - -   **Trail**

✕   **Quarry or open mine pit**

Blacktail Tank

CORONADO   NATIONAL   FOREST

Rosemont Junction

USGS: **EMPIRE RANCH**

USGS: **HELVETIA**

Passage 7
Rincon Valley: I-10 to Hope Camp

Rincon Valley new trail construction

TOTAL DISTANCE	Approximately 12.6 miles
QUALITY HIKING DISTANCE	Approximately 5 miles
DIFFICULTY	Moderate
TOTAL ELEVATION GAIN	NA
TOTAL DESCENT	NA
FROM MEXICO	108.2 miles
TO UTAH	663.7 miles
LAND MANAGERS	Saguaro National Park, Colossal Cave Mountain Park, Pima County, Arizona State Land Department, Empire-Cienega Resource Conservation Area
RECOMMENDED MONTHS	September through April

INTRODUCTION   As of this writing, much of the trail construction in this passage remains in progress, but there is new trail from the north boundary of Colossal Cave Mountain Park to Rincon Creek just south of Hope Camp. Much of the rest of the route is in Colossal Cave Mountain Park, either along roads or bushwhacking.

MOUNTAIN BIKE NOTES

The newly constructed trail north of Colossal Cave Mountain Park is accessible to bicycles. As of this printing, the Sonoran Desert Mountain Bicyclists were leading the trail construction of this passage. When completed, it will be very appropriate for mountain biking.

WATER

Colossal Cave Mountain Park: Fresh water is available year-round at both campsites and at La Posta Quemada Ranch.

Rincon Creek: Seasonal water is available here (N32º07'40", W110º38'38"). Also, Cienega Creek near the Pantano Road trailhead and bridge might have water, but it's a no-trespassing area.

MAPS

USGS Quadrangles: Mount Fagan, Vail, Rincon Peak, Tanque Verde Peak

BEGINNING ACCESS POINT

Smooth road to Trailhead

I-10: A walk-through culvert (N31º59'47", W110º39'11") passes under I-10, 0.25 mile west of the Davidson Canyon Bridge. It is not accessible by vehicle. Please do not exit your vehicle from I-10.

ENDING ACCESS POINT

3.0 miles

Hope Camp: From The Old Spanish Trail, approximately 7 miles southeast of the Saguaro National Park Visitor Center or 4 miles northwest of Colossal Cave Mountain Park, turn north on Camino Loma Alta Road. Go about 2.5 miles until it ends at a small trailhead/parking area. Hike 3.0 miles on Hope Camp Trail to Hope Camp (N32º07'59", W110º38'57"), the end of Passage 7.

TRAIL DESCRIPTION   From the north end of the walk-through culvert under I-10 (N31º59'47", W110º39'11"), walk east to a ridge and a two-track road. Follow this road north about 1.5 miles to a Las Cienegas National Conservation Area trailhead (N32º00'50", W110º38'51") next to Pantano Road. Walk northeast across the car bridge. Immediately turn left (west) after crossing the bridge and cross a fence. New trail construction is scheduled to be completed to this point in 2005. The new trail leads to La Posta Quemada Ranch (N32º02'58", W110º38'09), part of Colossal Cave Mountain Park. Exit the park north of La Selvilla Picnic Area, which is 2.5 miles from the ranch. Follow constructed trail northwest about 5.5 miles, crossing two well-traveled dirt roads (Pistol Hill, then X-9 Ranch) before crossing Rincon Creek and reaching the run-down and deserted Hope Camp (N32º07'59", W110º38'57").

Passage 7
1:24,000 MAPS:
MOUNT FAGAN, VAIL, RINCON
PEAK, and TANQUE VERDE PEAK

1/4   1/4   1/2

SCALE: 45/64 INCH = 1 MILE

· · · **Arizona Trail**
(current proposed segment)

— **Arizona Trail**
(previous and next segments)

· · · · **Arizona Trail**
(previous or next proposed segments)

— **Access route**

—— **River or stream**

◯ **Lake or pond**

▦ **Marsh or swamp**

—— **Primary highway**

—— **Secondary highway**

—·— **Light duty road**

— = = **Unimproved road**

- - - - **Trail**

✕ **Quarry or open mine pit**

Passage 8
Happy Valley: Unused Passage

View at sunrise of the Galiuro Mountains from the Rincon Mountains

INTRODUCTION   This passage number is not currently being used. It might be used in the future as an alternate route for this area.

Passage 9
Rincon Mountains: Hope Camp to Italian Trap

The Rincon Mountains rise in the distance

TOTAL DISTANCE	22.3 miles
QUALITY HIKING DISTANCE	22.3 miles
DIFFICULTY	Strenuous
TOTAL ELEVATION GAIN	5,887 feet
TOTAL DESCENT	5,041 feet
FROM MEXICO	120.8 miles
TO UTAH	651.1 miles
LAND MANAGERS	Coronado National Forest (Santa Catalina Ranger District), Saguaro National Park
RECOMMENDED MONTHS	March through November. In winter, snow blankets the higher reaches of the Rincon Mountains, while summer temperatures approach 100° in the last couple of miles of this passage.

INTRODUCTION   Saguaro National Park, which hosts this passage of the AZT, evokes images of the stately, silent, statuesque cacti that gave the park its name. But there is another side to this park, where deep snows might cover the mountaintops four months of the year and chilly breezes strum the boughs of magnificent Douglas fir and ponderosa pine trees year-round. In fact, the AZT hiker will see few saguaros in Saguaro National Park.

Because the pine-fir forest community atop the Rincon Mountains is similar to forests of southern Canada, the 14.5-mile traverse of the park, including a 4,407-foot climb to the high point of Passage 9, at 8,602 feet, is akin to a 5,000-mile walk to Canada and back. AZT hikers will pass through six distinct biotic communities, each occupying a certain elevation range: desert scrub, desert grassland, oak woodland, pine-oak woodland, pine forest, and mixed conifer forest. This variety of biomes supports 986 different species of plants.

NOTE: Saguaro National Park prohibits backcountry camping and requires permits and reservations for overnight stays. Permits can be acquired by writing to or visiting Saguaro National Park's East Visitor Center, 3693 South Old Spanish Trail, Tucson, AZ 85730. For information, phone (520) 733-5153. Same-day walk-in permits are issued before noon, depending on availability. The campgrounds rarely fill during the week. To guarantee a spot, you may request a permit up to two months in advance.

MOUNTAIN BIKE NOTES

Bikes are prohibited in the Rincon Mountain Wilderness.

Cyclists continuing through from the previous passage can choose from a variety of routes here. Use the Coronado National Forest (Santa Catalina Ranger District) map to plan a route north to bypass the wilderness area and take Redington Road west to the Bellota Trailhead for a difficult ride to the Santa Catalina Highway. Ride this paved road to the top of Mount Lemmon to avoid the Pusch Ridge Wilderness. Then take Mount Lemmon Road to Oracle, or use primitive roads or trails to reach the AZT at Oracle Ridge.

You can also avoid all of the pavement by linking roads and trails east of the Santa Catalina Mountains, and then ride to Summerhaven, Dan Saddle, or down Mount Lemmon Road to the American Flag Trailhead. Before planning any bike trip here, you should consult the Forest Service to verify your route.

WATER

Mile 8.8, Grass Shack Campground: There may be water here in Chimenea Creek (N32°11'01", W110°35'34").

Mile 13.4, Manning Camp: The National Park Service recommends treating water obtained here (N32°12'22", W110°33'15").

Mile 15.9, Italian Spring: This is generally reliable into the summer months (N32°13'44", W110°32'07").

Mile 19.6, Italian Spring Trailhead: There may be a large pool of water here (N32°15'30", W110°32'50").

MAPS

USGS Quadrangles: Tanque Verde Peak, Mica Mountain, Piety Hill
USFS: Coronado National Forest (Santa Catalina Ranger District)
Other: Trails Illustrated #237 (Saguaro National Park); Arizona Public Lands Information Center, AZT Passage Topo Map 9—Rincon Mountains

BEGINNING ACCESS POINT

 Hope Camp: The beginning of this passage is not accessible by vehicle. You must hike there following the directions in Passage 7, or hike along the old road from the Loma Alta Trailhead, about 3.0 miles west of Hope Camp.

ALTERNATE ACCESS POINT

 Loma Alta Trailhead: Take I-10 east from Tucson to exit 279. Turn left (north) on Vail Road and follow it for 2.8 miles. Turn left onto Camino Loma Alta Road and proceed for approximately 5.5 miles until it ends at the Loma Alta Trailhead.

ENDING ACCESS POINT

 Italian Trap: See "Beginning Access Point" for Passage 10.

TRAIL DESCRIPTION

The stretch from the North Hope Trailhead (3,130'; N32°07'59", W110°38'57") at Hope Camp to the old Madrona Ranger Station site (3,390'; N32°09'04", W110°36'33") involves cross-country hiking and the use of old two-track roads. Contact the Arizona Trail Association for the current status of this section of Passage 9 (602-242-4794 or ata@aztrail.org).

From Madrona, the Manning Camp Trail climbs steadily north up into the foothills of the Rincon Mountains. The trail parallels the Chimenea Creek drainage and eventually reaches a trail junction at about the 4.2-mile mark (N32°11'12", W110°35'58") from Madrona.

 Taking the right fork and proceeding another 0.7 mile brings you to the Grass Shack Campground (5,290'; N32°11'01", W110°35'34"), where you must have a permit to camp. Here you'll find three campsites, an outhouse, and seasonal water in Chimenea Creek.

From the campground, the trail again heads uphill. It follows a ridgeline between Chimenea and Madrona Canyons. There is a trail junction about 3.5 miles from the campground (N32°11'52", W110°33'11"). Stay left here and continue across Chimenea Creek and up to Manning Camp, about 9.5 miles from Madrona.

> ### WILDERNESS ALERT
>
> The trail enters the **Rincon Mountain Wilderness,** which overlaps and helps to protect Saguaro National Park. Established by federal law in 1976 to be "an area where the earth and its community of life are untrammeled by man, where man himself is a visitor who does not remain," this wilderness area protects 38,590 acres of dry saguaro forests, cool stands of pine, and about 980 other plant species in between.
>
> Please remember and follow these rules when traveling in this backcountry paradise:
> - Off-trail travel below 4,500 feet in elevation is prohibited.
> - Open campfires are prohibited at Douglas Spring and Grass Shack Campgrounds.
> - The Park Service strongly recommends gas stoves at all other campgrounds. If you must build a fire, use the steel fire grate, make sure your fire is completely extinguished and cool before you leave, and burn only dead and downed wood.
> - Motorized and mechanized vehicles, including bicycles, are prohibited.
> - Dogs and other pets are prohibited, with or without a leash.
> - Do not shortcut switchbacks.
> - Bury human waste at least 150 yards from any trail, water source, dry streambed, or meadow. The hole should be 4 to 6 inches deep.
> - Pack out all trash, including toilet paper.
> - Only biodegradable soaps are allowed.
> - Firearms, traps, and other weapons are prohibited.
> - Unauthorized entry or use of government facilities is prohibited.
> - Digging trenches around tents is prohibited.
> - Hikers must yield the right-of-way to stock animals. Stand quietly off the trail on the downhill side.

Manning Camp (N32°12'22", W110°33'15") has six tent sites (reservations required). There is a faucet with running water on the east side of the main ranger building; the Park Service recommends you treat the water before using it. The campground also has an outhouse.

To continue on the AZT, turn right (east) from the junction at mile 13.4 and follow the Mica Mountain Trail. Numerous trails loop through this area. Go straight at an intersection at mile 13.9; turn right at a fork 40 yards beyond that; and turn right (east) at a "T" intersection at mile 14.8 (8,602'). Avoid the Bonita Trail branching to the right in 0.1 mile, and continue straight to the east. At mile 15.2 (8,475'; N32°13'20", W110°32'11"), turn 90 degrees to the left (north) onto the North Slope Trail, which descends steeply through switchbacks to mile 15.6, where it levels somewhat and fades among the remnants of a forest fire.

Follow metal markers on trees past a flat point that offers sweeping views to the east. The trail then bends back to the left (northwest) and continues descending via switchbacks.

You'll reach reliable Italian Spring and the trail named for it at mile 15.9 (7,980'; N32°13'44", W110°32'07"). Turn right onto this trail and descend through serious fire damage to the east.

The trail soon bends back to the west, where it crosses several small streams, including one at mile 17.2 (6,990'; N32°14'06", W110°31'57"). The rugged Santa Catalina Mountains rise in the distance to the northwest—the next obstacle on the AZT.

Vegetation has overgrown the trail where you exit the national park at mile 17.5 (6,720'; N32°14'14", W110°32'12"), but circular metal tabs tacked to trees show the way. Follow cairns when the trees become sparse as you descend into the high desert. Pass through a fence and reach Italian Spring Trailhead at a metal sign at mile 19.7 (5,095'; N32°15'30", W110°32'50").

Pass through a fence and reach Italian Spring Trailhead at a metal sign at mile 19.7 (5,095'; N32°15'30", W110°32'50").There is a large pool of water here.

Turn right and walk due north along an old roadbed, parallel to a fence. At mile 20.7, follow the road's bend to the left (west).

Southbound Hikers: At this point (mile 20.7; 4,685'; N32°16'18", W110°32'53"), Mexico-bound hikers will be on a dirt road heading east. Don't miss the right (south) turn here, marked by a sign that says "Trail."

Welcome back to the still heat of the desert grassland ecosystem. The trail joins a road in a wash at mile 22.0 (N32°17'00", W110°34'04"). This is the first vehicle-accessible point since the beginning of the passage. The road immediately exits the wash and continues to the west.

After you pass through a fence at mile 22.1, continue to the west and, in 0.2 mile, reach the end of Passage 9. This area is called Italian Trap, but no sign identifies it; a group of corrals and fences and a large, metal AZT sign are your landmarks (mile 22.3; 3,962'; N32°17'00", W110°34'09").

Opposite: Saguaro cacti grow along the AZT
Photo courtesy of The Arizona Trail Association

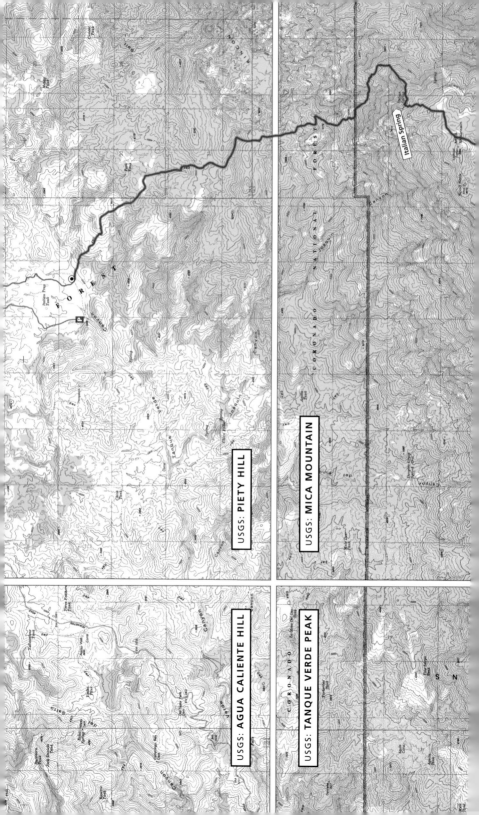

USGS: PIETY HILL

USGS: MICA MOUNTAIN

USGS: AGUA CALIENTE HILL

USGS: TANQUE VERDE PEAK

Italian Spring

Passage 9
1:24,000 MAPS:
TANQUE VERDE PEAK, MICA
MOUNTAIN, and PIETY HILL

SCALE: 37/64 INCH = 1 MILE

Arizona Trail
(current segment)

Arizona Trail
(previous and next segments)

Access route

River or stream

Lake or pond

Marsh or swamp

Primary highway

Secondary highway

Light duty road

Unimproved road

Trail

X Quarry or open mine pit

Madrona Ranger Station

Passage 10
Redington Pass: Italian Trap to Prison Camp Trailhead

The Santa Catalina Mountains as seen from near Agua Caliente Canyon

TOTAL DISTANCE	15.7 miles
QUALITY HIKING DISTANCE	12.5 miles
DIFFICULTY	Moderate
TOTAL ELEVATION GAIN	2,577 feet
TOTAL DESCENT	1,701 feet
FROM MEXICO	143.1 miles
TO UTAH	628.8 miles
LAND MANAGERS	Coronado National Forest (Santa Catalina Ranger District)
RECOMMENDED MONTHS	September through June

INTRODUCTION This passage provides a link between Saguaro National Park and the Pusch Ridge Wilderness. You may encounter mountain bikes, as this section presents a fun, challenging ride.

Massive fires in 2003 changed a few miles within this area. The final 2.7 miles of Passage 10, from Molino Basin Campground, were burned. Consult the Santa Catalina Ranger District at (520) 749-8700 for current information.

Molino Basin Campground, near the end of Passage 10, closes for the summer at the end of April, and the water is shut off at that time.

MOUNTAIN BIKE NOTES

 This entire passage is ridable, but it presents a challenging 1.5-mile climb beginning at West Spring Tank. The ride from Bellota Trailhead past Molino Basin Campground and on to Prison Camp Trailhead is classic, with everything from easy, flat spinning to lung-wrenching climbs and a crazy downhill. Advanced riders only!

Passage 11 enters the Pusch Ridge Wilderness, so thru-riders must take the paved Santa Catalina Highway to the top of Mount Lemmon. From there, follow Mount Lemmon Road to Oracle, or use primitive roads or trails to reach the AZT at Oracle Ridge.

WATER

 Stock Pond: This appears on maps as "The Lake" (N32°19'18", W110°37'15").

 Stream: A seasonal flow of water, along with large cottonwood trees, offers a cool rest stop (N32°19'17", W110°38'51").

 West Spring Tank: This tank collects water in a cement cistern and is generally reliable (N32°19'47", W110°40'27").

 Molino Basin Campground: The water is shut off when the campground is closed, from May to September (N32°20'15", W110°41'27").

MAPS
USGS Quadrangles: Piety Hill, Agua Caliente Hill
USFS: Coronado National Forest (Santa Catalina Ranger District)
Other: Arizona Public Lands Information Center, AZT Passage Topo Map 10—
    Redington Pass

BEGINNING ACCESS POINT

 Italian Trap: From Tucson, go east on Tanque Verde Road, which becomes Redington Pass Road after you leave the city. The road turns to dirt near mile marker 3. From that point, continue to just past mile marker 12 on Redington Pass Road. At the top of a small ridge, passenger vehicles should park on the right, as the remainder of the route is very rocky and bumpy. The AZT crosses

Redington Road here. There are AZT signs off both sides of the road. Those who wish to reach Italian Trap by high-clearance four-wheel-drive may descend the other side of the ridge to the south and continue 2.0 miles. Park at a large, metal AZT sign near some corrals and fences (N32°16'56", W110°34'32"). The last stretch of Passage 9 on the AZT arrives on the road from the east.

ALTERNATE ACCESS POINT

Bellota Trailhead: From Tucson, go east on Tanque Verde Road, which becomes Redington Road after you leave the city. The road turns to dirt near mile marker 3. Drive 0.3 mile past mile marker 10, and then turn left onto FR 36 at a sign for Bellota Ranch. Follow this bumpy road 2.1 miles to a confluence of roads and washes near a metal AZT sign (N32°19'18", W110°37'15").

ENDING ACCESS POINT

Prison Camp Trailhead: See "Beginning Access Point" for Passage 11.

TRAIL DESCRIPTION   From the metal AZT sign (3,962') at Italian Trap, follow the road's curve to the north. After 2 miles, crest a hill and avoid a side road on the right. Continue 0.1 mile past trail mileage signs to a well-maintained dirt road (Redington Road). Cross Redington Road and head northeast past a large, bullet-riddled AZT sign. This easy-to-follow trail soon turns west and in 4 miles arrives at the Bellota Ranch Road. When approaching the road, jog left (you'll pass a trail mileage sign) about 100 yards before crossing Bellota Ranch Road. Continue west across the road for 125 yards, where another large, bullet-scarred AZT marker greets you (3,980'; N32°19'18", W110°37'15").

"The Lake" is northeast of the AZT marker about 100 yards off the trail (N32°19'18", W110°37'15"). Look closely as there are two water basins. Tenacious plants thrive in this area's dry heat, including wiry manzanita, stout barrel cactus, spindly ocotillo, and small-leafed trees and shrubs such as juniper and mesquite.

The rest of this passage is a fun mountain-bike ride with a little bit of everything. Bear left from the metal sign, follow a wash for about 100 yards, and then pick up the singletrack Bellota Trail (#15), which takes off to the left (southwest).

After about 7.5 miles, pass through a fence. (Please leave all gates along the AZT as you find them, which usually means closed.) The trail rolls through rocky hills and soft and pleasant vegetation, descending to cross an upper finger of the Agua Caliente drainage on the right (north) at 3,870'.

 A seasonal flow of water and the shade of large cottonwood trees here offer a cool place to rest (N32°19'17", W110°38'51").

Opposite: Heading to Redington Pass
Photo courtesy of The Arizona Trail Association

The trail turns left (west) onto a dirt road. Just past here, stay on the trail to the right. (Don't take another cairn-marked trail, the Milagrosa Ridge Trail, which is on the left.) In 1.5 miles, pass through an old gate and climb out of a wash.

The road ends 0.4 mile later at a cement cistern that collects water from nearby West Spring (4,080'; N32°19'47", W110°40'27"). Hop on a singletrack trail that departs to the west and then climbs steeply to the northwest. After plenty of switchbacks, the trail tops out in a saddle (4,860'; N32°20'17", W110°40'56"). Mount Lemmon's sheer cliffs to the north-northwest are evidence of the rocky terrain in Passage 11.

SUPPLIES, SERVICES, AND ACCOMMODATIONS

TUCSON

Tucson is a large city with every service you could hope for. Most of the services listed below are near the intersection of Catalina Highway and Tanque Verde Road, which is about 10.5 miles from the AZT. These businesses are the ones with addresses between 8900 and 9100 on East Tanque Verde Road. The distances from this intersection to businesses farther from the trail are noted in parentheses.

Distance from Trail: 10.5 miles

Area Code	520
Zip Code	85749 (East Tanque Verde Road)
ATM	See "Bank"
Bank	Bank of America, 9015 E. Tanque Verde Rd., 760-2121
Bicycle Shop	Sabino Cycles, 7131 E. Tanque Verde Rd., 85715, 885-3666 (2.7 miles west)
Bus	None from trail to town
Camping	Best closer to trail
Dining	*Kickstart Grill*, 8987 E. Tanque Verde Rd., 760-3013; *Casa Vallarta*, 8963 E. Tanque Verde Rd., 749-1339
Gear	*Ace Hardware,* 9135 E. Tanque Verde Rd., 749-0288 (limited selection, including white gas); *Summit Hut,* 5045 E. Speedway Blvd., 85712, 325-1554 or (800) 499-8696 (6 miles south and west; complete selection of outdoor gear)
Groceries	Safeway, 9125 E. Tanque Verde Rd., 760-6087
Information	Tucson Metropolitan Chamber of Commerce, 465 W. St. Mary's Rd., 85701, 792-1212
Laundry	Pantano Wash & Dry Cleaning, 7621 E. Speedway Blvd., 85710, 296-8615 (3.2 miles southwest)
Lodging	Many motels and hotels of all price ranges can be found.
Medical	El Dorado Hospital, 1400 N. Wilmot, 85712, 886-6361 (4.1 miles west)
Post Office	According to the U.S. Postal Service, the only post office with general delivery is one block south of the intersection of South Cherry Avenue and 22nd Street. This is about 12 miles west and south of the intersection of Catalina Highway and Tanque Verde Road. The zip code there is 85713. Use the general post office telephone number of (800) 275-8777. There is a Mail Boxes Etc. at 9121 E. Tanque Verde Rd., 85749, 749-0277, but it does not accept general delivery.

The trail makes a steep descent to the west through many switchbacks, which can be hair-raising for cyclists. Reach the bottom of the drainage and a "T" intersection and turn left (west). Cross the Catalina Highway in 0.1 mile and enter Molino Basin Campground (4,355'; N32°20'15", W110°41'27"). To reach Tucson, turn left when you reach the Catalina Highway and descend for 10.5 miles.

Note: From this point on, the AZT enters the area burned by the 2003 Aspen Fire, which damaged portions of this and the next passage extensively. Contact the Santa Catalina Ranger District at (520) 749-8700 or the Arizona Trail Association (602-252-4794 or ata@aztrail.org) for an update on the trail route and conditions.

To continue from Molino Basin Campground, bear right, go around the bathroom facilities to the northwest corner of the parking lot, and find a trail marker for the singletrack Molino Basin Trail (#11). Walk west on this trail about 50 yards to a "T" intersection, turn right, and then make a quick left to avoid going through campsite #1. Descend through a wash, cross the road to the southwest, and continue on a trail that curves to the right (west).

The next 3.9 miles are popular with mountain bikers. While still in the campground, the trail crosses a road and begins a gradual climb to the northwest. Soon a sign indicates Upper Molino Basin Campground 0.1 mile to the right (north). Stay on the main trail. The AZT crests a small rise and begins to descend into an adjoining canyon. At a fork in 30 yards, take a left (southwest). As you finish this passage, a spur trail leads right to the Prison Camp parking lot and the end of Passage 10 (4,820'; N32°20'15", W110°43'09"). To stay on the AZT, continue straight (west) and pick up the description for Passage 11.

Mt. Lemmon Highway

Upper Molino Basin Campground

Molino Basin Campground

2003 Aspen Fire

West Spring

West Spring Tank

Catalina Highway

Mt. Lemmon Highway

C O R O N A D O   N A T I O N A L   F O R E S T

seasonal water

Passage 10

1:24,000 MAPS:
PIETY HILL and AGUA
CALIENTE HILL

1/4   1/4   1/2

SCALE: 1 3/32 INCH = 1 MILE

▬▬▬	**Arizona Trail** (current segment)
▬▬▬	**Arizona Trail** (previous and next segments)
▬▬▬	Access route
~~	River or stream
◯	Lake or pond
	Marsh or swamp
▬▬▬	Primary highway
▬ ▬ ▬	Secondary highway
- - -	Light duty road
·-·-·-	Unimproved road
------	Trail
✕	Quarry or open mine pit

USGS: AGUA CALIENTE HILL

FR 36

Redington Road

Redington Road

FR 37

Stock Pond

USGS: PIETY HILL

Passage 11
Santa Catalina Mountains: Prison Camp Trailhead to Mount Lemmon

Snowmelt flows past yuccas in the West Fork of Sabino Creek Canyon.

INTRODUCTION The following description of Passage 11 is from my hike before the devastating fires of 2003. The trail may no longer be hikable. Consult the Santa Catalina Ranger District for current information at (520) 749-8700, or contact the Arizona Trail Association at (602) 252-4794 or ata@aztrail.org.

As with the other AZT passages that traverse sky islands—isolated mountain ranges that rise from the Sonoran Desert—this passage presents difficulties because of its extreme elevation range, from 3,640 to 8,560 feet. By the time snow melts in the

TOTAL DISTANCE	15.5 miles
QUALITY HIKING DISTANCE	15.5 miles
DIFFICULTY	Strenuous
TOTAL ELEVATION GAIN	5,812 feet
TOTAL DESCENT	2,135 feet
FROM MEXICO	158.8 miles
TO UTAH	613.1 miles
LAND MANAGERS	Coronado National Forest (Santa Catalina Ranger District)
RECOMMENDED MONTHS	Spring and fall are best.

higher reaches, temperatures in the lower sections may be 90° to 100°. (Tucsonans wishing to escape the desert heat used to drive to a small ski resort atop Mount Lemmon and make a few runs.) So, as you pack shorts and T-shirts for the first part of this hike, be sure to throw in some warmer clothes for the high forests.

Hikers should also be prepared for strenuous walking. After leaving Hutch's Pool, the AZT climbs almost a vertical mile to reach the end of the passage. This undertaking is even more demanding if you're carrying supplies for the next passage, instead of stopping on Mount Lemmon. The total hiking distance from the beginning of this passage to the end of Passage 12, near Oracle, is about 40 miles.

Halfway through this passage, you'll enjoy the refreshing waters of Hutch's Pool. This large, deep swimming hole is a unique reward for the weary AZT hiker after a gritty hike through rocky high desert. Be sure to take a swimsuit, because this spot is well-known among Tucsonans, and it can attract a crowd on a hot spring or summer weekend. Try to plan your trip so you arrive on a weekday, especially if you want to camp at this ideal location. Please practice "Leave No Trace" camping to help Hutch's Pool retain its natural beauty.

In the mid-1990s, the residents of Summerhaven, the small resort community near the summit of Mount Lemmon, had some trouble with curious bears. In 1998, I was fortunate enough to see a bear near Catalina Camp in Passage 12. These incidents should not cause undue concern—as soon as I warned the bear of my presence with a hand clap, he turned and hightailed it into the forest. Nevertheless, you should keep your campsite clean and put all of your food in a bag or other container that can be hung high above the ground. For more information on safe travel in bear country, see "Safety Concerns" on p. 21 or consult the Forest Service.

If you're planning to end your hike atop Mount Lemmon, add 1.7 miles of walking distance to the length of this passage, bringing it to 17.2 miles, because the nearest parking area is 1.7 miles off the AZT. Equestrians should not attempt this passage because of a very steep and rocky section near Romero Pass.

Distant Rincon Peak as seen from Romero Pass

MOUNTAIN BIKE NOTES

Bikes are not allowed in the Pusch Ridge Wilderness, which encompasses this entire passage. Cyclists can follow the paved Catalina Highway to the top of Mount Lemmon. See "Mountain Bike Notes" for Passage 10.

WATER

Water is scarce after Hutch's Pool (N32°22'30", W110°47'31"), just when the difficult work of climbing Mount Lemmon begins. Hikers should carry as much as a gallon of water per person, depending on the heat, as they leave Hutch's Pool.

Sycamore Reservoir: This small reservoir is 100 yards off the trail and is usually reliable (N32°20'58", W110°44'46").

Hutch's Pool: This permanent water source is big enough for swimming and is a popular summer destination for Tucsonans. It is the last reliable water on this passage (N32°22'30", W110°47'31").

MAPS

USGS Quadrangles: Agua Caliente Hill, Sabino Canyon, Mount Lemmon
USFS: Coronado National Forest (Santa Catalina Ranger District)
Other: Arizona Public Lands Information Center, AZT Passage Topo Map 11—
Santa Catalina Mountains

BEGINNING ACCESS POINT

  Prison Camp Trailhead: Be prepared for a fee station partway up the Catalina Highway. Follow Tanque Verde Road east from Tucson and turn left (north) on the Catalina Highway. Drive about 9 miles and pass Molino Basin Campground. Continue 1.7 miles after the campground and take the left turn to Prison Camp. Drive 0.3 mile to a parking area. Follow a trail out of the south end of the parking lot for 40 yards to reach a "T" intersection with the AZT. Turn right to follow the trail description for this passage (N32°20'15", W110°43'09").

ENDING ACCESS POINT

Mount Lemmon: See "Beginning Access Point" for Passage 12.

WILDERNESS ALERT

The **Pusch Ridge Wilderness,** designated in 1978, protects 56,933 acres of rugged cliffs and cool pine forests that entice crowds of visitors from nearby Tucson. It is showing signs of wear, making these rules governing wilderness areas all the more important:

- Camp out of sight, at least 200 feet from lakes and streams, on dry, durable surfaces.
- Use a stove. If you must have a fire, use existing fire rings.
- Keep water sources clean by washing at least 200 feet from them.
- Bury human waste 6 inches deep and 200 feet from lakes and streams. Pack out toilet paper.
- Hobble or picket livestock at least 200 feet from lakes and streams, and use only treated, weed-free feed and grain.
- All dogs must be on a leash.
- No mountain bikes.
- Pack out all trash; don't attempt to burn it.

TRAIL DESCRIPTION   Head right (west) from the intersection with the short access trail from Prison Camp Trailhead (4,820'). Soon, you'll follow an old dirt road downhill to a confluence of roads. Walk straight to the west-northwest, following a sign for Sycamore Reservoir Trail. The road immediately passes through a wash and then bends right (northwest). You'll find many nice places to camp in this shady, oak-lined valley.

In less than a half mile, the road turns into a wash. Continue along a gentle, winding climb. The trail leaves the wash to the south (left) and climbs to a metal AZT sign and the wilderness boundary in a low saddle (5,010'; N32°20'32", W110°44'01"). Descend into the wilderness on the singletrack Sycamore Reservoir Trail (#39).

 As the trail reaches a road (N32°20'51", W110°44'38"), watch for an obscure singletrack branching to the left (northwest). Follow this trail into a steep, rocky descent that lasts for 0.1 mile and ends in a lush valley of oak, willow, and riparian flora. At the bottom, you'll pass between a large boulder and the remains of an old wall.

 From here, you can make a side trip to Sycamore Reservoir by continuing straight ahead to the northwest for 100 yards. This small reservoir is usually reliable in the spring (N32°20'58", W110°44'46").

To continue on the AZT from the old wall, make a big U-turn to the right (southeast) and follow a singletrack trail 35 yards to a large cairn. The trail forks here. Turn left (northeast) and follow the trail as it bends further to the left (north).

 In another 0.2 mile, the trail disappears into a sandy wash. Follow cairns and traces of singletrack north, staying close to the slopes on the left. Keep your eyes open for a clear singletrack trail that exits this valley to the left (west-northwest). Avoid the temptation to stay in the valley as it ambles to the northeast.

Follow an old roadbed over a low ridge in 0.1 mile. On the other side, switchbacks lead into another lush valley of juniper, sycamore, and willow. At the bottom, turn sharply right (north) at a "T" intersection and follow a clear singletrack. The trail parallels a seasonal streambed and then joins it. Bear left where the stream forks, following an intermittent trail. In 0.3 mile, avoid an obscure trail marked by cairns that breaks off to the left (west). Instead, continue straight (north). After passing through a thick forest of manzanita, the trail descends to the left to cross the rocky main drainage and then climbs to a saddle (4,590'; N32°21'34", W110°45'22"). Take the right (north) fork here and descend through countless switchbacks into Sabino Canyon East Fork.

At an intersection with the Palisades Trail (#99), turn left (west) and continue to descend toward Sabino Canyon. Avoid Box Camp Trail at another intersection and continue straight ahead (west) on the East Fork Trail. The AZT reaches a junction in a sycamore grove at the bottom of a side canyon of Sabino. Saguaro cacti on the hillsides seem out of place near this oasis. You may find a small amount of water here; if not, there is reliable water 1.7 miles ahead at Hutch's Pool. Turn right (north-northeast) toward the West Fork Trail (#24). Watch for poison ivy in the canyon over the next 8 miles.

Cairns mark an immediate bend left to cross the Sabino Canyon East Fork drainage. Climb out along a rocky, dry streambed and continue on a very clear singletrack into a veritable desert botanic garden, with saguaro, yucca, agave, mesquite, ocotillo, prickly pear, and dozens more desert species. You'll soon have a fleeting view down narrow Sabino Canyon with the Tucson plain in the background. Cross to the left (southwest) side of the drainage on large boulders.

At a junction, the AZT heads left (northwest), while the right fork descends north 100 yards then climbs a short distance to Hutch's Pool (3,880'; N32°22'30", W110°47'31"). You'll know if you miss this cutoff to the pool because the main trail immediately switchbacks to the left (south) and climbs high above the canyon bottom. Beautiful Hutch's Pool is a popular swimming hole for Tucsonans and tired AZT hikers. It is also the last source of water near the trail until the intermittent sources in the next passage about 12 and 20 miles away. Hikers who are stopping at the parking area on Mount Lemmon have 12 miles of hiking and more than 5,000 feet of elevation gain remaining.

At a trail intersection, avoid the Cathedral Rock Trail (#26) and turn sharply right (east) to continue on the West Fork Trail (#24). The scenery just keeps getting better as you reach Romero Pass and an intersection (6,080') with the Romero Canyon Trail and Mount Lemmon Trail (#5). Follow the Mount Lemmon Trail right (north) to a steep, rocky, difficult climb along the ridge. This is the stretch that prevents pack animals on this passage—you almost have to use your hands in some spots. Soon, the climb peaks and then descends toward a saddle in a refreshing stand of ponderosa pine. Avoid the Wilderness of Rock Trail and continue straight ahead on the Mount Lemmon Trail. You'll reach the end of Passage 11 at an intersection (8,560'; N32°25'46", W110°48'19") with the Sutherland Trail (#6).

To continue on to Passage 12 of the AZT, turn left (north) onto the Sutherland Trail. To exit Passage 11 and reach the parking lot atop Mount Lemmon, turn right (east-northeast) and follow the road 1.6 miles to an obscure turn right (east) onto a singletrack that leads 0.1 mile to the parking lot. Don't worry if you miss this final turn—when you hit a paved road in 40 yards, turn right, continue 100 yards, and turn right into the parking lot.

USGS: **MOUNT LEMMON**

Mt. Lemmon Highway

Sutherland Trail

N A T I O N A L   F O R E S T

Wilderness of Rock Trail

Romero Canyon Trail

P U S C H   R I D G E   W I L D E R N E S S

Cathedral Rock Trail

Hutch's Pool

water

Passage II

1:24,000 MAPS:
AGUA CALIENTE HILL, SABINO
CANYON, and MOUNT LEMMON

| 1/4 | 1/4 | 1/2 |

SCALE: 1 3/32 INCH = 1 MILE

━━━ **Arizona Trail**
(current segment)

━━━ **Arizona Trail**
(previous and next segments)

━━━ **Access route**

╌╌╌ **River or stream**

◯ **Lake or pond**

Marsh or swamp

━━━ **Primary highway**

━━━ **Secondary highway**

╍╍╍ **Light duty road**

╍╍╍ **Unimproved road**

╌╌╌ **Trail**

✕ **Quarry or open mine pit**

P U S C H   R I D G E   W I L D E R N E S S

N A T I O

USGS: **SABINO CANYON**

USGS: **MOUNT BIGELOW**

USGS: **AGUA CALIENTE HILL**

Passage 12
Oracle Ridge: Mount Lemmon to American Flag Trailhead

Rocky Ridge, north of Mount Lemmon

TOTAL DISTANCE	22.0 miles
QUALITY HIKING DISTANCE	22.0 miles
DIFFICULTY	Strenuous
TOTAL ELEVATION GAIN	3,672 feet
TOTAL DESCENT	7,781 feet
FROM MEXICO	174.3 miles
TO UTAH	597.6 miles
LAND MANAGERS	Coronado National Forest (Santa Catalina Ranger District)
RECOMMENDED MONTHS	March through November. The lower elevations at the end of the passage can be quite hot in summer.

INTRODUCTION   The following description of Passage 12 is from my hike before the devastating fires of 2003. The trail through this passage was closed following the fires but has since reopened. The trees and brush have been removed by the fire. Consult the Santa Catalina Ranger District at (520) 749-8700 for current information.

Steep-sided forest canyons, cascading spring runoff, and prickly plants of the high desert defined this passage, which starts near the summit of Mount Lemmon and ends 4,150 feet lower near the town of Oracle. The deep, lush Cañada del Oro was beautiful and pristine before the fires, and you could see majestic, old ponderosa pine trees in a community that had been undisturbed for thousands of years. Many of these trees were more than 12 feet around, dwarfing human visitors.

This is a demanding, remote passage of the AZT with limited water availability. When I hiked it in April, after a particularly wet winter, water roared down Cañada del Oro, smaller springs flowed, and there was a reliable stream at the Red Ridge Trail. There is also reliable water at Rice Spring most of the year, at High Jinks Ranch, and at the ranch house at the American Flag Trailhead.

Most backpackers should plan at least two nights to complete this passage. You must hike 1.7 miles from the parking area atop Mount Lemmon just to reach the AZT, and then it is 22 miles to the American Flag Trailhead near Oracle. A faint trail in Cañada del Oro may slow you down, but it would be difficult to become completely lost because the trail follows the bottom of the canyon. Forest Service personnel told me that, during extreme runoff periods, the canyon can become impassable. Areas of overgrown brambles and downright malicious plants such as catclaw might make you appreciate a pair of long pants, particularly after the AZT leaves Cañada del Oro.

MOUNTAIN BIKE NOTES

Mountain bikes cannot negotiate the steep trail through Cañada del Oro. However, most of the trail along Oracle Ridge, north of Dan Saddle, is ridable (although some sections will require walking). You can reach Dan Saddle by descending the difficult Oracle Ridge Trail (#1) from the top of Mount Lemmon, or by riding in from the east on forest roads. Before you plan any mountain bike route, check with the Forest Service.

WATER

There is seasonal water near the trail until mile 9. The final 13 miles are dry.

Shovel Spring: This is a light flow just below the USGS map's depiction of Shovel Spring (N32°26'30", W110°48'57").

Red Ridge Trail: A stream here is often reliable. It is the last natural water along this passage (N32°28'46", W110°45'47") until Rice Spring.

Rice Spring: Rice Spring is just north of Rice Peak. You might have to shovel dirt out of the spring's concrete bowl, but the water flow is often reliable.

High Jinks Ranch: You can fill up on water at the privately owned ranch house.

 American Flag Trailhead: Water is available at the ranch house here, but it is not reliable because the faucet is sometimes turned off (N32°34'51", W110°43'13").

MAPS

USGS Quadrangles: Mount Lemmon, Mount Bigelow, Oracle, Campo Bonito
USFS: Coronado National Forest (Santa Catalina Ranger District)
Other: Arizona Public Lands Information Center, AZT Passage Topo Map 12—
Oracle Ridge

BEGINNING ACCESS POINT

 Mount Lemmon: Follow Tanque Verde Road east from Tucson and turn left (north) on the Catalina Highway. After about 28 miles, turn right toward Ski Valley. In 1.5 miles, drive straight past Ski Valley and continue 1.7 miles to a power substation on the left. Turn into a parking lot in front of the substation.

Find a trailhead in the southwest corner of the parking lot, next to a fence that surrounds the substation, and follow this trail 0.1 mile west to a road. Turn left (south) on the road, which forks in about 10 yards. Take the right fork, pass through a gate, and follow the road as it descends to the southwest. Avoid forks by staying on the best road. After 0.5 mile, continue straight (southwest) on the Mount Lemmon Trail (#5) and avoid a road on the left. After 1.7 miles of walking, you'll reach the end of the road at the AZT (N32°25'46", W110°48'19"). Make a 90-degree turn to the right onto the Sutherland Trail (#6) to follow Passage 12 toward the American Flag Trailhead near Oracle, or walk straight ahead (west) to follow Passage 11 south toward Prison Camp Trailhead.

ENDING ACCESS POINT

 American Flag Trailhead: See "Beginning Access Point" for the next passage.

TRAIL DESCRIPTION   From the intersection (8,560') of the Mount Lemmon Trail (#5) and the Sutherland Trail (#6), turn right (north) onto the Sutherland Trail and descend via numerous switchbacks through a large burn area. In 0.3 mile, the trail reaches a saddle and climbs slightly up the opposite side. At an intersection with the Samaniego Ridge Trail (#7), turn right (northwest) and continue through another saddle in 0.1 mile. At the Cañada del Oro Trail (#4) junction (7,740'; N32°26'15", W110°49'03"), turn right.

At mile 1.5, you'll notice on your left a flat area that has seen some camping and, just above it, a green tank that once held water. A small spring originates in the streambed that descends from the camping area and parallels the trail.

 I found a small flow of water a couple of tenths of a mile below the location of Shovel Spring on the 1981 USGS Mount Lemmon map (7,400'; N32°26'30", W110°48'57").

The trail seems to end in a mess of downed timber and overgrown vegetation. Work your way through this short section and continue descending to the northeast. In 0.1 mile, bear right (northeast) at a trail junction with the Cañada del Oro Shortcut Trail (#4A). The AZT immediately bends more to the right (south-southeast) and descends quite steeply into Cañada del Oro. The trail is overgrown and annoying at times, but the gorgeous stands of ponderosa pines make up for it.

The trail reaches the drainage bottom, crosses to the east side, and then parallels it, heading downhill to the north. Keep heading downstream where deadfall obscures the trail. Cairns mark the way in particularly confusing sections.

Soon you would have reveled in the deep, dark beauty of an old-growth forest, but regretfully, fire destroyed it here. Some of the ponderosa pines were so big, you couldn't reach even one-third of the way around them. As you continue to lose elevation, sycamore and alligator juniper trees replace the pines, and soon you're solidly into an oak-woodland community.

At an intersection (4,875'; N32°29'48", W110° 46'51"), the AZT leaves Cañada del Oro by turning right (east). As the trail climbs, it sometimes resembles a dry streambed, but cairns offer guidance. With talons of catclaw beginning to thrash your legs, it's worth considering long pants. The AZT continues straight (east) as the Red Ridge Trail (#2) branches to the right (5,670'; N32°28'46", W110°45'47").

There's a nice place to camp near the trail here. If you walk 100 yards down the Red Ridge Trail, you may find water in a stream well into the summer.

You'll pass the first of the cabins at historic Catalina Camp. Near the second cabin, the trail turns into an old roadbed that continues to switch-back up the hill.

Trusty llamas carry the photographer's gear.

The trail reaches an intersection at Dan Saddle (6,910'; N32°28'52", W110°44'54"). Turn left (northeast) onto a singletrack that climbs away from the saddle. A right turn would have led 3.4 miles to Summerhaven, but this community was destroyed in the 2003 fire.

Southbound Hikers: Those headed toward Mount Lemmon will reach a sign painted on a rock shortly after they turn right at Dan Saddle. Although the sign says, "Keep off, Private Road," ignore this and continue descending on the road.

Don't be fooled into thinking the climbing ends at Dan Saddle. Soon, your extra effort on a steep trail will earn nice views southwest of the scraggly Reef of Rock and, just behind that, the lush rift of Cañada del Oro. Farther north, in the lowlands just

SUPPLIES, SERVICES, AND ACCOMMODATIONS

ORACLE

There are several ways for thru-hikers to reach Oracle from the AZT. You can leave the trail at mile 19.5 and continue about 3 miles north and northwest, following Trail #1 and then maintained roads. Or, if you complete Passage 12 at American Flag Trailhead, follow Mount Lemmon Road 4 miles into town. (This is 4.5 miles farther than walking to town directly from mile 19.5 on Passage 12.) Another option for thru-hikers is to walk the first 8.6 miles of Passage 13, leave the AZT there, and continue 1.2 miles to the trailhead near Oracle. Then it is 1.3 miles southwest along American Avenue to town.

All of the services listed here are on the south side of American Avenue, except for Hildreth's Market on the north side. Distances are measured from the trailhead on American Avenue reached by leaving the AZT at mile 8.6 of Passage 13 (not from the American Flag Trailhead on Mount Lemmon Road).

Distance from Trail: 2.5 miles to 4 miles, depending on trailhead

Area Code	520
Zip Code	85623
ATM	Gordon's Market, 896-2491 (1.5 miles)
Bank	None
Bicycle Shop	None
Bus	None
Camping	Proposed future camping at American Flag Trailhead
Dining	*Casa Rivera's Taco Express*, 896-3747, small but good (3.0 miles); *Nonna Maria's Pizza*, 896-3522 (1.6 miles); *Oracle Inn*, 896-2211 (1.4 miles)
Gear	None. You can find white gas at Gordon's Market.
Groceries	*Gordon's Market*, 896-2491, best selection (1.5 miles); *Hildreth's Market*, 896-2471 (1.1 miles)
Information	None
Laundry	Next to Oak Tree Video (3.1 miles)
Lodging	Chalet Village Motel, 896-9171 (2.6 miles)
Medical	None
Post Office	General delivery is available with a 15-day limit, 896-2641 (1.0 mile)
Showers	None

to the right of Samaniego Ridge, behind Cañada del Oro, you can see the white, odd-shaped buildings of Biosphere II.

The AZT continues to climb and then descends steeply to a saddle before climbing again. At N32°30'22", W110°44'39", descend to cross through a gate, and then turn left (north) onto a road. This road is open to motorized vehicles, but they are rarely seen. The road is flat or descends slightly until it forks. Take the left (westernmost) fork.

The steady descent continues to where FR 4475 leaves the AZT sharply to the right (southeast) to descend to Rice Spring, where water is often available. Walk down this two-track approximately 100 feet and descend into the gully to the left. There is a small, dugout concrete bowl at the spring. You might have to shovel dirt out of it, but the water flow is often reliable.

Back on the AZT, continue straight (north) to mile 15.9, where the road makes a sharp bend to the right. Just before that bend, leave the road by turning left (north) to pass through a fence and follow the singletrack Oracle Ridge Trail (#1).

The AZT rolls along the ridge for about 1.5 miles before passing through two gated fences to traverse along the steep west side of Apache Peak. The town of Oracle soon comes into view to the north. Looming beyond it in the distance are the peaks and ridges of Pinal County, including the Black Hills and Tortilla Mountains, which are crossed in Passages 14 and 15 of the AZT. After Apache Peak there is a long, steady descent through many switchbacks, which ends at a crossing of Trail #639. The trail then climbs, joins an old roadbed that is now a singletrack, and levels somewhat.

You'll pass a gate on the left that has an AZT marker on it. Continue straight (north-northeast) up the steep hill in front of you and top out. Ignore the occasional trail branching to the right until you reach an intersection with the Cody Trail (#9) at N32°34'27", W110°45'01". Take the right fork, as an AZT marker indicates, and begin a long, switchbacking descent to the east. (To reach the town of Oracle directly from here, continue north on Trail #1 for about 2.0 miles, and then northwest on maintained roads for about 1.0 mile.)

In 1.1 miles, the switchbacks abate somewhat. The trail heads south-southeast another 0.4 mile to reach a fork with the trail to High Jinks Ranch, which is on the National Register of Historic Places. From the AZT, you can elect to take the fork to the right and climb up slightly to the ranch entrance. You can rest here and fill up on water at the privately owned ranch house.

Continuing on the AZT, take the left fork into a switchback to the left (north-northeast), and avoid a couple of side trails. Descend through more switchbacks and cross a road (N32°34'30", W110°43'42").

All of this descending is interrupted by a 0.25-mile, 130-foot climb at mile 21.5. A few more switchbacks then drop to the American Flag Trailhead and the end of Passage 12 at mile 22.0 (4,410'; N32°34'51", W110°43'13"), where you might find water at the ranch house.

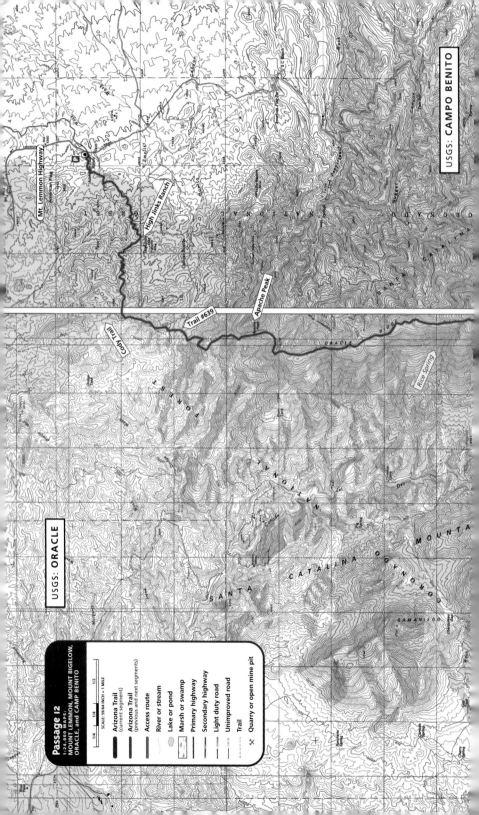

USGS: CAMPO BENITO

USGS: ORACLE

Mt. Lemmon Highway

High Jinks Ranch

Apache Peak

Trail #639

Cody Trail

Rice Spring

SANTA CATALINA MOUNTA...

COCHISE

SAMANIEGO

Passage 12
1:24,000 MAPS:
MOUNT LEMMON, MOUNT BIGELOW,
ORACLE, and CAMP BENITO

SCALE: 59/64 INCH = 1 MILE

1/4   1/4   1/2

- Arizona Trail (current segment)
- Arizona Trail (previous and next segments)
- Access route
- River or stream
- Lake or pond
- Marsh or swamp
- Primary highway
- Secondary highway
- Light duty road
- Unimproved road
- Trail
- ✕ Quarry or open mine pit

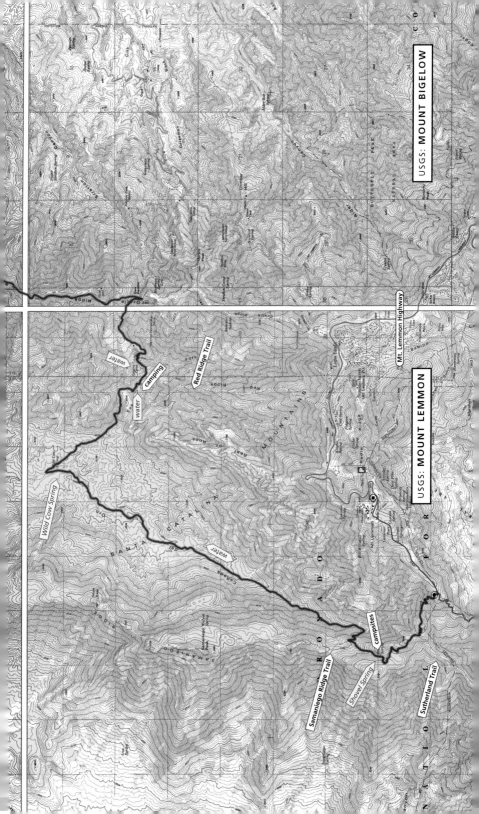

USGS: MOUNT BIGELOW

USGS: MOUNT LEMMON

Mt. Lemmon Highway

water

camping

Red Ridge Trail

Wild Cow Spring

water

Samaniego Ridge Trail

Shovel Spring

campsites

Sutherland Trail

Passage 13
Oracle: American Flag Trailhead to Tiger Mine Trailhead

The Arizona Trail near Oracle

TOTAL DISTANCE	8.3 miles
QUALITY HIKING DISTANCE	6.9 miles
DIFFICULTY	Easy
TOTAL ELEVATION GAIN	413 feet
TOTAL DESCENT	777 feet
FROM MEXICO	196.3 miles
TO UTAH	575.6 miles
LAND MANAGERS	Pinal County Department of Public Works
RECOMMENDED MONTHS	September through June

INTRODUCTION This short passage ambles through washes and across low ridges speckled with the plants of the high desert, including yucca, prickly pear, cholla, the occasional juniper tree, and a variety of shrubs and grasses. The trail is clear except where it enters washes, and then it is well marked with rock cairns. Local mountain bikers enjoy incorporating this stretch of the AZT into improvised loop rides.

This passage is ideal for a point-to-point day hike. To avoid walking on a road, use a side trail that leaves the AZT at mile 6.3 to reach a convenient parking lot just outside the town of Oracle on American Avenue. (See "Alternate Access Point" below.) The AZT itself continues onto Tiger Mine Road and into the Black Hills of Passage 14.

MOUNTAIN BIKE NOTES

 This passage provides a fun ride frequented by local cyclists. Where the AZT wanders into the deep sand of washes, bypasses provide ridable alternatives. Some of these are steep and rocky, but those sections are short. Most of the bypass intersections are marked with 4x4 posts. Cyclists out for a day ride should take a detour at bike-mile 6.3 to reach the alternate trailhead near Oracle. Thru-riders can continue on the AZT to Tiger Mine Road and into the next passage.

WATER

There is no reliable source of water on this passage. You can find water in the town of Oracle.

 Mile 0.0, American Flag Trailhead: Sometimes the water faucet at American Flag Ranch is turned off (N32°34'51", W110°43'13").

 Mile 4.4, Kannally Wash: Sometimes there is water in a tank at a windmill in Oracle State Park (N32°37'28", W110°43'06").

MAPS

USGS Quadrangles: Campo Benito, Mammoth
USFS: Coronado National Forest (Santa Catalina Ranger District)
Other: Arizona Public Lands Information Center, AZT Passage Topo Map 13—Oracle

BEGINNING ACCESS POINT

 American Flag Trailhead: From Oracle, turn south at the eastern intersection of AZ 77 and American Avenue, drive 1.5 miles on American Avenue, and then turn left onto Mount Lemmon Road. Continue 4.0 miles to trailheads on both sides of the road, including parking areas and log gateways that say "Arizona Trail." The trail on the left (east) side of the road is the start of Passage 13; the previous passage arrives from the west (N32°34'51", W110°43'13").

ALTERNATE ACCESS POINT

 **American Avenue Trailhead:** From the east intersection of AZ 77 and American Avenue, turn south onto American Avenue toward the Oracle business district.

Drive 0.25 mile, turn left (east), and continue 0.25 mile to a parking lot. A 4x4 post marks the trailhead on the south side of the parking lot. Follow this trail for 0.8 mile to meet the AZT at mile 6.3 of Passage 13. To continue toward American Flag Trailhead, turn right and follow the trail description backward from mile 6.3. To walk along Tiger Mine Road toward the next passage, follow the description forward from mile 6.3.

ENDING ACCESS POINT

Tiger Mine Trailhead: See "Beginning Access Point" for Passage 14.

TRAIL DESCRIPTION   A clear singletrack leaves the parking area (4,410') and immediately turns to the left (north) to descend. At mile 1.6, the trail reaches a road and fence. Turn right (north-northeast) to parallel the road for 0.2 mile before going through a gate. Turn right on the road, go 35 yards, and take off on another singletrack on the left (north) (N32°35'50", W110°42'50").

Follow the trail mostly downhill and in and out of washes. At mile 4.5, the AZT turns left (northwest) onto an old road and descends sharply into a gully. In another 50 yards, the road meets a major wash (3,980'; N32°37'28", W110°43'05"), Kannally Wash, where the tank at the windmill sometimes has water. Go straight across the wash to the north-northwest on an old roadbed.

Follow the old roadbed into a sustained climb, followed by alternating climbs and descents. Pass through a junction at mile 5.6 (N32°37'39", W110°43'48"), and when the trail splits again in about 100 yards, stay left and climb another old roadbed.

At mile 6.3, you come to the junction with the trail that leads to the American Avenue Trailhead. Continue on the main route until you reach a major wash next to the highway at mile 6.9 (N32°37'54", W110°44'22").

You will notice a culvert that crosses under AZ 77, 30 yards to the northwest across the wash. To reach it, you must go through a gate in a barbed-wire fence. On the other side of the highway, near the culvert, scramble up a steep bank to a dirt road. This is Tiger Mine Road, which is not signed (mile 7.0; 4,070'; N32°37'56", W110°44'23").

To get to the beginning of the next passage, turn left and follow this well-traveled dirt road. After 1.2 miles, you'll be traversing a steep hill that drops into a valley on your left side. In 0.1 mile, the ridge on your right drops to the level of the road, and 0.1 mile beyond that you'll see a brown fiberglass post with the AZT symbol on the left (north) side of the road. This is the end of Passage 13 and the beginning of the next one (mile 8.3; 4,060'; N32°39'02", W110°43'53").

The American Flag Trailhead—Photo by Tom Jones

Tiger Mine Road

BM
4081

USGS: MAMMOTH

Wash

Apod

WC

4049

VABM
4296   20

Cherry   Valley   21

Wash

4053

Cottonwood

22

4098

4338

4189

4000

4012

4054

4094

Kannally

Wash

30   29   28   27

American Ave

alternate access

4342

4200

29   28   27

4134

4163

4738

Wash

Kannally

4383

4200

4738

VABM
4144

Wash

Cottonwood

Wash

4400

Kannally Ranch
32

4432

33

4200

34

4400

Cherry
Valley
Ranch

Passage 13
1:24,000 MAPS:
CAMPO BENITO and
MAMMOTH

1/4   1/4
SCALE: 61/64 INCH = 1/2 MILE

▬▬▬ **Arizona Trail** (current segment)
▬▬▬ **Arizona Trail** (previous and next segments)
▬▬▬ **Access route**
〰〰 River or stream
Lake or pond
Marsh or swamp
Primary highway
Secondary highway
Light duty road
Unimproved road
Trail
✕ Quarry or open mine pit

4853

5000

Ray

4328   Windmill

4132

4200

4

Ray Spring
Hill
BM
4534

Mt. Lemmon Road
BM
4360

American Flag

4221

American Flag
Hill

5246
5200

4773

Wash

4400

American Flag
Ranch
4428

USGS: CAMPO BENITO

8   9   10

Passage 14
Black Hills: Tiger Mine Trailhead to Freeman Road

The Arizona Trail winds through a remarkable variety of well-adapted plants in the heart of the sublime Sonoran Desert.

TOTAL DISTANCE	28.2 miles
QUALITY HIKING DISTANCE	26.4 miles
DIFFICULTY	Moderate
TOTAL ELEVATION GAIN	3,061 feet
TOTAL DESCENT	3,127 feet
FROM MEXICO	204.6 miles
TO UTAH	567.3 miles
LAND MANAGERS	Pinal County Department of Public Works, Arizona State Land Department
RECOMMENDED MONTHS	March, April, October, and November offer the most comfortable weather. Winter can be nice, but be prepared for cold temperatures and rain. Avoid the furnacelike heat of summer!

INTRODUCTION   As this book was being written, volunteers were still building the trail for this passage. The trail has subsequently been completed and signed all the way to Freeman Road. Because I was able to hike the planned route for most of the trail, this description should be mostly accurate. Check with the Arizona Trail Association at (602) 252-4794 or ata@aztrail.org to verify the status.

Navigating here became significantly easier in 2001, when volunteer Chuck Horner put up over 2,500 aluminum reflector strips to mark the route of this passage and the next. Most of these markers were removed as the trail was built, but be sure to think of Chuck when you see those than remain!

Passage 14 is the AZT's gateway to the low-elevation ecosystem of the Sonoran Desert. Characterized by ubiquitous cactus, sandy soil, and hot, dry weather, the desert is shunned by many as an inhospitable wasteland. But visitors will find a rich, complex community of plants and animals in delicate coexistence. The opportunities for solitude are as limitless as the Arizona sky, and the clear, diamond-studded heavens come alive at night.

Of course, hikers should be aware of the desert's serious challenges. It's wise to keep long pants accessible because of the abundant scratchy plants. Temperatures routinely top 100° from June through September. In winter, temperatures plunge and torrents of water can fill the otherwise dry washes in minutes. The mesmerizing uniformity of the terrain can make navigation difficult. Precise planning is imperative to ensure a safe and successful trip, especially where water caches are concerned.

Water may present the single greatest planning challenge to the AZT hiker on desert passages. It's necessary to drink up to a gallon of water per day, and there are few reliable natural sources. All available water along this passage is owned by ranchers, whose permission you must secure before using it. This leaves two alternatives: Either you must stash water along your route prior to your hike, or you must arrange for people to meet you.

This passage crosses Arizona state lands, and a permit is required if you are not on or near the AZT. If you stay near completed construction of the trail, you do not need a permit. To acquire a permit, write or visit Arizona State Land Department—Public Records, 1616 West Adams, Phoenix, AZ 85007. Phone: (602) 542-4631.

MOUNTAIN BIKE NOTES

Although much of this passage follows roads that are easy to ride, other portions are on singletrack that will present difficulties for novice riders.

WATER

Note: All water sources along this passage require ranch-owner permission to use.

Mile 15.3 (plus 0.6 mile off the trail), Yellowjacket Well: This well seems reliable (N32°47'56", 110°51'02").

Mile 19.6, Beehive Well: This well may contain murky water (N32°49'23", W110°48'24").

MAPS

USGS Quadrangles: Mammoth, North of Oracle, Putnam Wash, Black Mountain
Other: Arizona Public Lands Information Center, AZT Passage Topo Maps 14A and
14B—Black Hills

BEGINNING ACCESS POINT

Tiger Mine Trailhead: From the east entrance to the town of Oracle, drive 0.8 mile east on AZ 77 to mile marker 105 and turn left (north) onto an unsigned dirt road. After 1.2 miles on this road, you'll be traversing a steep hill that drops into a valley on your left side. In 0.1 mile, the ridge on your right drops to the level of the road, and 0.1 mile beyond that a brown fiberglass post with the AZT symbol marks the trailhead on the left (north) side of the road (N32°39'02", W110°43'53"). Parking is available to the right of the road.

ENDING ACCESS POINT

Freeman Road: See "Beginning Access Point" for Passage 15.

TRAIL DESCRIPTION

Follow a clear singletrack north-northeast from the trailhead (4,060'). The trail generally descends, following numerous switchbacks, to reach a wash at mile 1.7 (3,680'; N32°40'01", W110°43'59"). Cross the wash, looking for cairns, then climb via switchbacks and top out at mile 2.1. After crossing another wash, the trail tops out on another ridge at mile 2.9 (3,840'). A few switchbacks descend to mile 3.2 (N32°40'24", W110°44'42").

Continue descending to a small wash, and then climb to a low ridge at mile 3.5. The ensuing descent gets gradually steeper until you reach a prominent wash at mile 3.7 (3,670'). Follow cairns as you cross this wash a bit west of north.

A short climb leads to the top of a low ridge at mile 4.0. In 0.3 mile, reach the bottom of Tucson Wash, which four-wheel-drive vehicles use as a road (3,640'; N32°40'59", W110°45'04"). Cross just west of north, following cairns.

After climbing out of Tucson Wash, the trail continues north-northwest to a ridge at mile 5.1 (3,800'; N32°41'15", W110°45'23"). From here the trail drops down to another wash at mile 5.5 and then proceeds due north to an old utility road at mile 6.0 (3,715'; N32°41'55", W110°45'23").

The dictionary's definition of a straight line should be illustrated with this road. It rolls up and down, into and over washes and low hills, but consistently cuts a straight shot into the heart of the Sonoran Desert. The trail follows this utility road as it heads northwest across the desert. After a short, steep climb that tops out at mile 6.9, the road makes a quick detour to the right. As you resume the straight course, the horizon is mostly featureless with the exception of a single, volcano-like mountain straight ahead. This is Antelope Peak, and it will be the central feature of the next 20 miles of the AZT.

Over the next 8.0 miles, avoid side roads as you pass through the occasional gated fence. A fairly long descent leads to Camp Grant Wash and a tangle of roads at mile 11.3 (3,115'; N32°45'30", W110°48'25"). Stay on what appears to be the main road and cross the wash to the northwest. About 100 yards past the wash, cross a dirt road at a right angle and continue up a hill to the north-northwest on the fainter gas-line road.

After another significant wash at mile 12.4, the road passes through numerous washes before curving through some small hills and finally switchbacking to a high point at mile 14.6 (3,550'; N32°47'38", W110°50'16").

 Descend a steep hill, cross a wash at mile 15.0, and continue north-northwest to a road in Bloodsucker Wash at mile 15.2 (3,407'; N32°48'02", W110°50'34"). A tank on the right is usually empty, but you may find water at Yellowjacket Well. To reach it, follow the road to the left (west) for 0.6 mile (N32°47'56", W110°51'02"). Some "No Trespassing" signs block further passage on the pipeline road at Bloodsucker Wash.

To continue on the AZT from mile 15.2, turn right (east) into this very sandy wash and follow the road in it downstream. The hillsides above the wash are mostly barren until mile 16.8, where you'll notice two short, pinkish brown, sandstone cliff bands on the left (north) about 0.1 mile away. At mile 17.4, there is a small, rocky hill on the left, followed by a significant wide spot in the wash. Continue 0.1 mile and look on the left for a cairn and markers that indicate the departure of the singletrack AZT to the left (north) (3,025'; N32°48'17", W110°48'22".)

The trail trends north along the right (east) side of this wide area in the wash. Several switchbacks soon lead to the top of a bank, which you'll reach 0.25 mile after leaving the road. The AZT bends right, follows a gradually descending ridge another 0.25 mile, and then turns left (northeast) onto a dirt road at mile 18.2 (3,070'; N32°48'33", W110°48'03").

Southbound Hikers: Keep your eyes peeled here for the unmarked right turn onto a singletrack trail.

 At mile 19.1, bear right at a fork. Cross a wash at mile 19.3 (3,060') and climb 0.1 mile to a view down to charming Beehive Well. After a short descent to the well, turn right (north) to walk between the windmill and the tank, which usually contains murky water (mile 19.6; 3,026'; N32°49'23", W110°48'24"). *Note:* AZT officials may build a singletrack here that continues west and northwest to mile 19.8 on the road instead of turning right to go between the windmill and the tank. Just past the windmill, curve to the left (west) into Putnam Wash and continue up the road.

In 0.2 mile, a cliff band on the left side of the valley curves close to the road. Just 0.1 mile beyond that, at mile 19.9, a ridge juts into the wash from the right side. Turn right (northeast) just before that ridge onto a singletrack trail. The AZT climbs briefly and then bears left (west) atop another ridge that parallels the wash you just left. Where the tread is faint, cairns mark the way.

The trail works its way up to a ridge at mile 21.7 overlooking Antelope Tank, and then down to a road crossing at mile 22.3 (3,560'; N32°50'09", W110°50'11"). After crossing the road, the trail continues west to a gate and road crossing at mile

22.9 and then up to another road crossing at mile 23.3. From here, the trail heads north and then west until it works its way up to a low saddle at the base of the rocky northern slopes of Antelope Peak at mile 26.2. Continue straight about 40 yards to an old road and turn right (northwest) on it (N32°51'20", W110°51'53").

Southbound Hikers: You should see the left turn onto the singletrack AZT just before the road you're on starts climbing very steeply up the lower slopes of Antelope Peak.

Descend on the road 0.4 mile to a "T" intersection with another road. Turn right (northwest). Continue 1.3 miles on this rough four-wheel-drive road to a "T" intersection with the wide and well-maintained Freeman Road at mile 27.9 (3,960'). Turn left, cross a cattle guard in 0.1 mile, and continue another 0.2 mile to a two-track dirt road on the right. This marks the end of Passage 14 (mile 28.2; 4,015'; N32°52'16", W110°52'56"). To continue on the next passage, turn right onto the dirt road, walk about 10 yards, and then turn left (northwest) onto a clear singletrack trail.

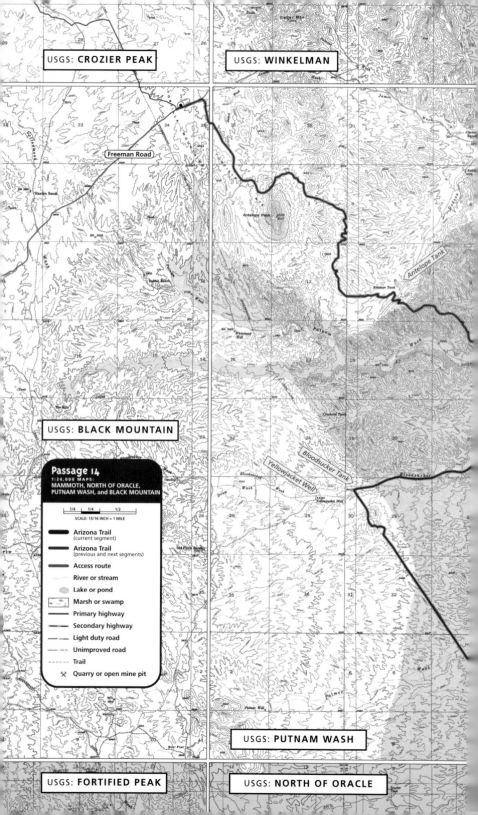

USGS: **CROZIER PEAK**

USGS: **WINKELMAN**

Freeman Road

Antelope Peak

Antelope Tank

Antelope Tank

USGS: **BLACK MOUNTAIN**

Whitehead Well

Putnam

Cottonwood Tank

Bloodsucker Tank

Bloodsucker

Yellowjacket Well

Yellowjacket Well

Passage 14
1:24,000 MAPS:
MAMMOTH, NORTH OF ORACLE,
PUTNAM WASH, and BLACK MOUNTAIN

| 1/4 | 1/4 | 1/2 |

SCALE: 13/16 INCH = 1 MILE

━━━ **Arizona Trail**
(current segment)

━━━ **Arizona Trail**
(previous and next segments)

━━━ **Access route**

River or stream

Lake or pond

Marsh or swamp

Primary highway

Secondary highway

Light duty road

Unimproved road

Trail

✕ **Quarry or open mine pit**

USGS: **PUTNAM WASH**

USGS: **FORTIFIED PEAK**

USGS: **NORTH OF ORACLE**

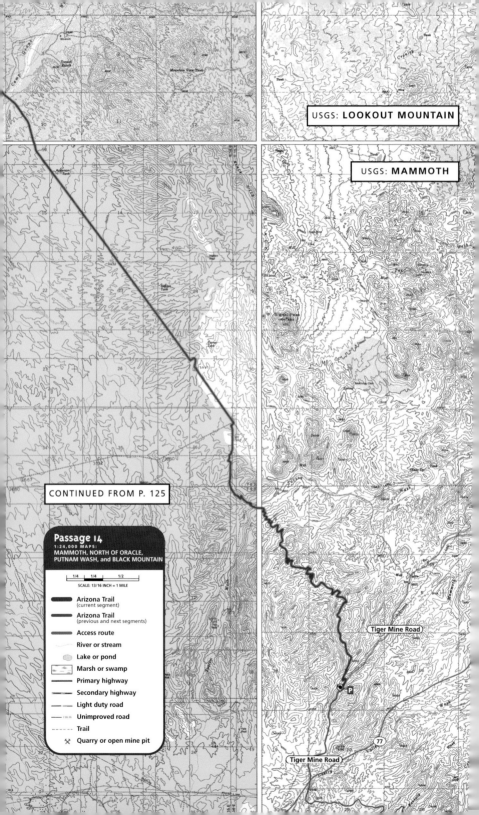

USGS: **LOOKOUT MOUNTAIN**

USGS: **MAMMOTH**

CONTINUED FROM P. 125

Passage 14
1:24,000 MAPS:
MAMMOTH, NORTH OF ORACLE,
PUTNAM WASH, and BLACK MOUNTAIN

SCALE: 13/16 INCH = 1 MILE

1/4	1/4	1/2	

Arizona Trail
(current segment)

Arizona Trail
(previous and next segments)

Access route

River or stream

Lake or pond

Marsh or swamp

Primary highway

Secondary highway

Light duty road

Unimproved road

Trail

✕ Quarry or open mine pit

Tiger Mine Road

Tiger Mine Road

77

CONTINUED ON P. 126

USGS: **DUDLEYVILLE**

USGS: **LOOKOUT MOUNTAIN**

USGS: **MAMMOTH**

Passage 15
Tortilla Mountains: Freeman Road to Kelvin-Riverside Bridge

Rolling terrain in the Tortilla Mountains

TOTAL DISTANCE	Approximately 23.6 miles
QUALITY HIKING DISTANCE	Approximately 23.6 miles
DIFFICULTY	Strenuous
TOTAL ELEVATION GAIN	NA
TOTAL DESCENT	NA
FROM MEXICO	232.8 miles
TO UTAH	539.1 miles
LAND MANAGERS	Pinal County Public Works Department, Arizona State Land Department
RECOMMENDED MONTHS	March, April, October, and November offer the most comfortable weather. The winter months can be nice, but be prepared for cold temperatures and chilly rains. Avoid the furnacelike temperatures of summer!

INTRODUCTION   Because volunteers had not begun trail construction when I hiked here in 1998 and 2000, portions of my hike required serious bushwhacking with a map and compass. Since that time, much of the trail along this passage has been completed, but not all. If you plan to hike this stretch, check with the Arizona Trail Association at (602) 252-4794 or ata@aztrail.org to verify the status of the trail. If you find that the portion you wish to hike has not yet been completed when you are planning your hike, you may use my description, but you should be well acquainted with orienteering. For me, significant portions of this passage required cross-country navigation. Attempting to follow these directions without the necessary skills may result in injury or death. Navigating with a GPS unit that you know how to operate would be helpful.

This passage crosses Arizona state lands, and a permit is required if you are not on or near the AZT. If you stay near completed construction of the trail, you do not need a permit. Again, check the trail's status with the Arizona Trail Association. To acquire a permit, write to Arizona State Land Department—Public Records, 1616 West Adams, Phoenix, AZ 85007. Phone: (602) 542-4631.

Due to the often thick and prickly vegetation on this passage, it is a good idea to carry long-sleeved shirts and pants.

MOUNTAIN BIKE NOTES

Although much of this passage follows roads that are easy to ride, other portions are on singletrack that will present difficulties for novice riders. Additionally, if trail construction is not complete, the incomplete sections will not be ridable. Check this passage's status with the Arizona Trail Association.

WATER

Water is virtually nonexistent on this passage. All available water is rancher-owned, so you must have the rancher's permission to use it. The only way to guarantee water along the route is to cache it in advance. See "Alternate Access Point" for a suggested place to cache water at trail mile 16.1.

   Mile 19.0 (plus 0.5 mile off the trail), Ripsey Wash: A spring and small tank may offer water here (N33°01'27", W110°58'55").

MAPS

USGS Quadrangles: Black Mountain, Crozier Peak, Kearny, Grayback

BEGINNING ACCESS POINT

Bumpy road to Trailhead 19.5 miles   **Freeman Road:** Because of a lack of landmarks, this description will take you 0.3 mile past the trailhead and instruct you to turn around. From the town of Florence, drive 21 miles south on AZ 79 and turn left (east) onto Freeman Road. (From the south, drive north from Oracle Junction on AZ 79 and turn right onto Freeman Road.) The following mileages indicate the distance from AZ 79: At about 14 miles, continue past Barkerville Road. At 15.5 miles, bear left at a fork. At 19.5

miles, cross over a cattle guard on a fence line. Just 0.1 mile farther, you'll see a primitive road on the right. This is the AZT arriving from the south. Turn around here and backtrack over the cattle guard. Continue 0.2 mile to a primitive two-track road on the right (north). Ten yards down this road on the left, the AZT departs as a single-track to the northwest (N32°52'15", W110°52'58").

ALTERNATE ACCESS POINT

Mile 16.1: This remote access point, a little over halfway through the passage, offers a logical place to cache water. A lone paloverde tree makes a good landmark. From Florence, drive 1.5 miles south on AZ 79 and turn left (east) on the Florence-Kelvin Highway, a dirt road. Continue on this road for 22 miles, then turn onto a primitive, unmarked road on the right (south) by a sign that says "State Trust Land—No Trespassing." If you are accessing the AZT, you may proceed. At a fork in 50 yards, go left (southeast). Continue 0.7 mile, and then take a right fork (southwest). In another 0.3 mile, there is a gate and another fork. Take the right (south-east) fork and continue another 0.7 mile to yet another fork. Bear left and continue 0.9 mile to a fence. Continue 0.4 mile beyond the fence and you'll see the paloverde tree on a rise on the left (N33°00'31", W111°00'15").

To reach the same point from the town of Kelvin (15.5 miles south of Superior), drive west on the Florence-Kelvin Highway for 9.0 miles to the primitive road mentioned in the preceding paragraph, turn left (south), and follow the directions above.

ENDING ACCESS POINT

Kelvin-Riverside Bridge: See "Beginning Access Point" for Passage 16.

TRAIL DESCRIPTION   *Note:* Much of the following information is changing as tread is being built. Please check with the Arizona Trail Association (602-252-4794 or ata@aztrail.org) for the current trail status before hiking this passage.

Walk about 10 yards from Freeman Road along the dirt road and turn left (north-west) onto a clear singletrack (4,015'). The trail fades after crossing a small, steep-sided ditch at mile 0.1, but if you look closely, it's still there. Continue 0.2 mile just north of west to a gas-line road (mile 0.6; N32°52'25", W110°53'25"). Turn right (north), walk 50 yards, and stay left at an intersection. Follow this road 1.0 mile and look for a very large rock cairn on the left. This marks a singletrack trail heading west (3,975'; N32°53'12", W110°53'53"). Follow this trail and cross a road in 0.3 mile. Continue 0.2 mile to Haydon Ranch Road at mile 2.2. When I hiked here in spring 2000, flagging marked the path of the trail to the west and northwest, but the tread had not been constructed. I took the road to the right, heading northwest.

After 1.7 miles on this road, you'll reach a gate with a sign that says "Arizona State Trust Lands—No Trespassing Without Permission from the State Land Commissioner." Continue through the gate, provided you have a state lands permit. In another 0.3 mile, turn left (northwest) at a four-way intersection. Continue 1.5 miles to the gate for Tecalote Ranch (3,712'; N32°55'07", W110°56'51").

At this point, the road enters private property owned by Tecalote Ranch. Until the trail is constructed here, you must bushwhack around the property. The terrain does not offer many distinct landmarks, but with a map and compass you should not get lost.

The west-central portion of the 1949 Crozier Peak USGS map shows the ranch, at N32°55'34", W110°57'27". The private property comprises all of Section 12 on this map. The best way I found around the property involves walking west along the south line of Section 12 to the corner of Sections 11, 12, 13, and 14 (N32°55'04", W110°57'53"), then walking north along the west line of Section 12 to the corner of Sections 1, 2, 11, and 12 (N32°55'56", W110°57'54"). From corner to corner, each section line is one mile. Metal stakes mark the corners, but they are difficult to see. If you have a GPS, use the coordinates in this paragraph to walk around the property and rejoin the description at the wire gate (N32°55'59", W110°57'53").

If you don't have a GPS unit, the following description, combined with a map and compass, should help. When you reach the gate for Tecalote Ranch, you are facing west. Walk through the gate. Turn left (due south) onto a primitive dirt road to parallel the fence you just came through. In 0.1 mile, pass through a small, overgrown wash. Turn right (west) in a second wash (N32°54'52", W110°56'51"), wider than the last one and a bit less overgrown. You are now 1.0 mile (in straight-line distance) from the first section corner. Use your compass to walk as close to due west as possible. This wash offers a relatively clear path in that direction. You'll see a power line and some pinkish hills off to your right, and you might see some of the buildings of Tecalote Ranch in that area.

You'll intersect at a right angle a road that goes north-south (N32°55'03", W110°57'28"). Continue across it to the west. You'll reach the hard-to-see marker at the southwest corner of the section (3,560'; N32°55'04", W110°57'53"). Make a 90-degree right-hand turn and head due north. In about 1.3 miles, you'll hit a fence. If

Cactus in bloom—Photo by Tom Jones

you're west of the north-south section line, you'll hit the fence and see the road beyond it. Turn right, walk east along the fence, and follow its 90-degree turn to the left (north). Continue to the road and turn left (west). If you're east of the north-south section line, you'll hit the road first. Turn left. Either way, the road will lead you through a wire gate to exit the Tecalote Ranch property (N32°55'59", W110°57'53").

The road soon bends to the right (north), and it joins a large wash and dances in and out of it over the next 1.2 miles. At times this road is not much more than a singletrack. Some saguaro cactus pop up near the road 0.25 mile before you reach the ruins of Ripsey Ranch, which include a windmill, a stock tank, and a corral. There is also a magnificent, huge cottonwood tree surrounded by lush grass.

A clear road exits the wash to the right. The road climbs north-northwest to a low ridge speckled with saguaro cactus as the wash curves off to the west.

The road goes through a little saddle and descends to a small wash. Climb and descend through numerous ridges and small washes. From a ridge, you can see the power line to your right disappearing behind a ridge directly in front of you. Continue to where the road starts to veer left (west); leave the road here and bushwhack due north to a prominent, multiarmed saguaro cactus on the horizon of the near ridge. Reach that ridge after 0.2 mile and continue due north, toward the second-nearest power-line tower. Reach the remnants of an old road and follow it 0.1 mile to the tower. Now strike out due north toward the left side of a low, flat spot on the horizon and what appears to be a wall of saguaro cactus standing guard.

Descend gradually, cross a wash, and pass by a line of giant saguaros. Aim for a fence with a gate about 0.4 mile ahead. If you reach the fence and there is a road in front of it, turn left. If there is no road along the fence, turn right (east). When you reach the gate (N32°59'18", W110°59'17"), pass through it to the north and follow the road through nice stands of saguaro. Within a mile, the road veers left (northwest) to curve around the upper reaches of deep Ripsey Wash. After 1.5 miles, continue straight where another road comes in at a sharp angle from the left. Cross through a small wash. Continue 0.1 mile and turn left (northwest) as the road forks.

You'll see a lone paloverde tree on a small rise on the right side of the road (3,300'; N33°00'31", W111°00'15"). This tree is a good spot for a water cache, as described in "Alternate Access Point" at the beginning of this passage.

Leave the road here and begin bushwhacking past the paloverde tree (just east of north). Walk a short distance to a fence and cross it without benefit of a gate. In 50 yards, crest a ridge above a deep valley and cross the valley in the same direction (just east of north). Climb the ridge on the other side and reach the top in about 0.5 mile. Loose rock and many little gullies will impede your progress here.

After crossing several more ridges, you'll top out on one with a view of a road to the north. Descend to the road by staying west of a prominent, rocky hill. After you reach a network of roads, follow the one that descends to the northwest into a deep wash. Stay in the wash as the road exits it to the east under a power line (N33°01'08", W110°59'20"). Follow the wash 1.0 mile to reach large, wide Ripsey Wash, (2,725'; N33°01'47", W110°59'08"). Turn right (southeast) and walk up this wash 0.1 mile, watching for a prominent wash (which may contain tire tracks) entering on the left-hand side (east-northeast). Turn to go up this wash (N33°01'48", W110°59'01").

If you continue up Ripsey Wash for 0.5 mile, you'll come to a spring and a tank on the left (N33°01'27", W110°58'55").

Back on the route of the AZT, continue up the tributary wash for about 0.4 mile to a fence (N33°01'57", W110°58'49"). Pass through a gate and follow the trail, heading for a high, cone-shaped peak. After about 1.0 mile from the gate, you will be on the southwest side of the peak, where you will begin a series of switchbacks. The trail skirts the west side of the peak and continues to the beginning of a ridge (3,510'; N32°02'37", W110°58'21").

Follow this ridgeline to the northwest. After about 0.8 mile, the route turns to the right (east), and then after another 0.4 mile, it turns left (north). In about another 0.6 mile, the trail crosses a saddle and turns left (west) again. After another 0.6-mile stretch, the trail crosses another highpoint and begins a northern descent. There are numerous switchbacks in this section and the trail eventually reaches the bottom of a deep wash (2,750'; N33°03'59", W110°59'05").

The trail climbs out of this wash and after another 0.3 mile passes through a gate in a fence. From here, the trail works its way to another wash in about 0.5 mile (2,450'; N33°04'30", W110°59'16"). After you climb out of this wash, it is only about 0.25 mile to a road (N33°04'31", W110°59'09"). Turn left (south) on this road.

Follow the road into a significant wash and descend until you reach the Florence-Kelvin Highway (2,045'). Turn right (northeast), descend along this dirt road for 1.1 miles, and cross the bridge over the Gila River. The railroad tracks on the far side mark the end of Passage 15 (1,775'; N33°06'14", W110°58'26").

Sunrise on the Arizona Trail
Photo courtesy of The Arizona Trail Association

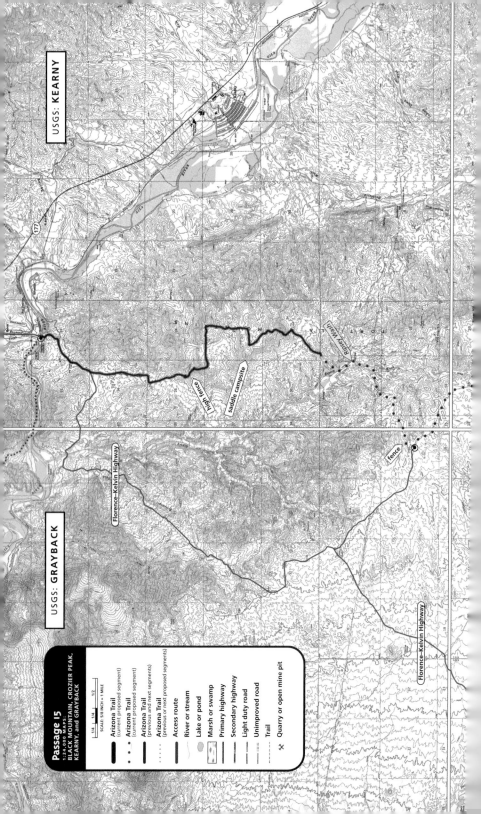

USGS: KEARNY

USGS: GRAYBACK

Florence-Kelvin Highway

Florence-Kelvin Highway

Ripsey Wash

high fence

saddle campsite

fence

Passage 15
1:24,000 MAPS:
BLAK MOUNTAIN, CROZIER PEAK,
KEARNY, and GRAYBACK

SCALE: 5/8 INCH = 1 MILE

1/4   1/4   1/2

Arizona Trail
(current proposed segment)

Arizona Trail
(current proposed segment)

Arizona Trail
(previous and next segments)

Arizona Trail
(previous or next proposed segments)

Access route

River or stream

Lake or pond

Marsh or swamp

Primary highway

Secondary highway

Light duty road

Unimproved road

Trail

✕ Quarry or open mine pit

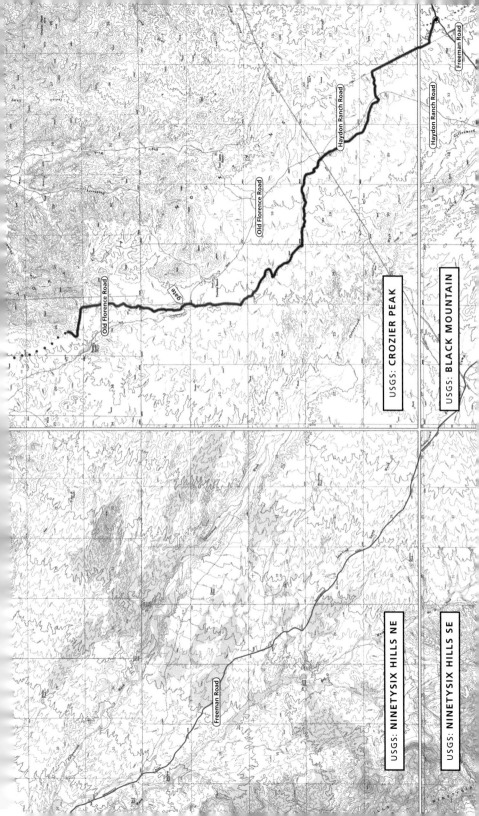

USGS: CROZIER PEAK

USGS: BLACK MOUNTAIN

USGS: NINETYSIX HILLS NE

USGS: NINETYSIX HILLS SE

Old Florence Road

Old Florence Road

Haydon Ranch Road

Haydon Ranch Road

Freeman Road

Freeman Road

gate

Passage 16
White Canyon: Kelvin-Riverside Bridge to White Canyon Wilderness

In the "Narrows" of White Canyon, White Canyon Wilderness

INTRODUCTION At the time I wrote this in 2002, this passage of the AZT was not complete. I describe one cross-country route that, based on discussions with trail stewards and volunteers, is the general route that thru-hikers frequently use. Please note that it is not an official route endorsed by the Arizona Trail Association.

I used a railroad grade, old roads, and significant bushwhacking to complete the passage. The cross-country hiking is quite rugged and difficult—even more difficult than in Passage 15. Steep, trailless hillsides, dense brush, and abundant cactus con-

TOTAL DISTANCE	Approximately 17.0 miles
QUALITY HIKING DISTANCE	Approximately 17.0 miles
DIFFICULTY	Strenuous
TOTAL ELEVATION GAIN	NA
TOTAL DESCENT	NA
FROM MEXICO	256.4 miles
TO UTAH	515.5 miles
LAND MANAGERS	BLM Tucson Field Office, Arizona State Land Department
RECOMMENDED MONTHS	March, April, October, and November offer the most comfortable weather. The winter months can be nice, but be prepared for chilly rains. Avoid summer!

spire to impede your progress. After you leave the river at mile 2.1, you can't count on water until an artesian spring at mile 13.0. Thus, great caution is required. Inexperienced hikers should not attempt this passage before it is completed.

For those willing to brave this hike before the trail is built, or who are able to hike it once volunteers complete the trail, Passage 16 offers a scenic sample of the varied landscape of Arizona. A desert canyon carved by the perennial Gila River is flanked by thick desert flora. The stunning Spine, a massive ridge of steep rock, dominates the route as you climb out of the Gila River canyon and into labyrinthine White Canyon. This incredible natural area features narrow side canyons and breathtaking cliffs on Battleaxe Butte.

The mining company ASARCO owns the land around Copper Butte, another impressive natural feature near mile 11.0. This company plans to mine copper in the area, and the trail most likely will be routed south and west of Copper Butte, into Walnut Canyon. Contact the Arizona Trail Association for more information.

This passage crosses state land, and a permit is required for travel and camping. Apply in writing or in person at the Arizona State Land Department—Public Records, 1616 West Adams, Phoenix, AZ 85007. Phone: (602) 542-4631. The permit is valid for one year and is also required to cross state lands in or surrounding Passages 14, 15, and 35.

Because of the thick and prickly vegetation on this passage, long-sleeved shirts and pants are a must.

MOUNTAIN BIKE NOTES

This area is not ridable. Once the trail is completed, it may be possible to bike most of the passage, but it will likely be very difficult riding. And keep in mind that this passage enters a wilderness area, where bikes are prohibited. At this time, the best way to bypass this passage and the next is to ride north from Kelvin on AZ 177 for 16.7 miles to the town of Superior.

WATER

Mile 13.0, Artesian Spring: This permanent source is 50 yards off the trail and pours from a small pipe sticking 18 inches out of the ground (N33°09'24", W111°04'47").

MAPS

USGS Quadrangles: Kearny, Grayback, Teapot Mountain

BEGINNING ACCESS POINT

Kelvin-Riverside Bridge: From the town of Superior, take AZ 177 south 15.5 miles and then turn right (south) toward the town of Kelvin. Continue 1.2 miles to the bridge. The trail description starts from the north side of the bridge and heads west (N33°06'14", W110°58'26").

From Florence, drive 1.5 miles south on AZ 79 and turn left (east) on the dirt Florence-Kelvin Highway. Continue 31 miles to the town of Kelvin and the bridge over the Gila River.

ENDING ACCESS POINT

White Canyon Wilderness: See "Beginning Access Point" for Passage 17.

TRAIL DESCRIPTION   Where the road and the railroad tracks intersect (1,775'), take a dirt road west. After 50 yards this road curves to the right (north), and at mile 0.1 it curves back to the left to cross a streambed on a bridge. Continue another 50 yards, turn left off the road, and head south toward the railroad line. At mile 0.2, as you approach the rail line, you'll run into a thicket of willows; climb an embankment on the right (southwest) through some saguaro cacti. Descend to the train tracks at mile 0.3 and turn right (west) to follow them. These are active tracks and extreme care is required! Keep an escape route in mind in case a train comes along. For the most part, it's better to stay on the river side of the tracks.

Continue along the tracks to mile 1.8, where a trestle comes into view. At mile 2.1, walk right up to this bridge, but don't cross on it. Instead, walk down a bank on the right side of the trestle and then branch off to the right and work your way to the northwest through thick brush. A game trail here makes for easier going. Once you're well past the trestle, a steep, rocky cliff descends all the way to the river (mile 2.4). At this point you should be on a very clear trail that climbs well above the river (N33°06'24", W111°00'12").

You can see the A-Diamond Ranch down the river to the southwest. At mile 2.6, the trail fades; continue climbing across the rocky, saguaro-studded desert to the northwest. You'll reach a rocky ridge at mile 2.8 (1,900'; N33°06'27", W111°00'17"). Look to the northwest at 305° on the compass, and you'll see the tops of two power-line towers. Head for a saddle in a ridge in that direction. (This is the saddle due north of the point marked 2,065' on the USGS Grayback map.) Maintain a fairly even contour around the large, wide valley by staying to the right (north). You'll reach the saddle in 0.7 mile. Continue northwest again (at about 305°) to another, less distinct saddle in the next ridge, again skirting the intervening valley on the north side. You'll reach that ridge at mile 4.5 (1,940'; N33º06'57", W111º01'00").

From here, walk due west a couple hundred yards to a road and turn right (north) to climb along a deep wash. The road soon curves to the left to trend west and north. At mile 5.1, reach the road's peak (2,180'; N33º07'10", W111º01'20") and begin a rapid, winding descent. The large wash below and to the left (west) is your goal. The road reaches a tributary of this wash at mile 5.5. Turn left (west) into this tributary and follow it 0.5 mile to the main wash. (Until volunteers build the trail here, you may decide to follow any of a number of drainages that serve as shortcuts.)

Turn right (northwest) into the main wash (mile 6.0; 1,940'; N33º07'20", W111º01'39"). At a fork at mile 6.6, take the right (north) option. At mile 6.8 (2,160'; N33º07'45", W111º01'46"), follow an obscure road that climbs abruptly out of the wash to the left and heads north.

 If you reach a power line crossing the wash, you've gone too far by 0.2 mile.

The road soon veers left (west). After some dipsy-doodles, it arrives in a wash at mile 7.1. Turn right (north) and walk upstream to mile 7.7, where a jeep road branches left (northwest) in a side wash (N33º08'12", W111º02'03"). Follow this side wash for 60 yards, and then turn onto a clear road taking off to the left (west). The road makes a gradual but steady climb until it tops out at mile 8.3 (2,450'), with impressive views of the rugged land to the northwest. The road then descends gradually to a wash at mile 8.9 (2,355'; N33º08'29", W111º02'48").

At mile 9.5, turn left (west) into a wash, follow it 0.1 mile to another wash, and then turn right (north). Turn left (west) at a corral onto Battleaxe Road at mile 11.0 (2,520'; N33º09'34", W111º03'10") and descend directly toward Copper Butte. In 0.2 mile, turn right onto another road and descend to the northwest.

Stay on the main jeep road and avoid the numerous washes until mile 12.0, where you join a wash and turn left (west). At mile 13.0 (2,040'), the wash seems to split in two.

The AZT continues up the right fork in the wash, but the artesian spring is 50 yards down the left fork. Look for a pipe sticking about 18 inches out of the ground with water coming out of it (N33º09'24", W111º04'47").

Continuing up the right fork, the trail climbs sharply to mile 13.7 before descending to mile 13.8. Avoid a road forking right (north) and continue straight west 0.2 mile, where the road veers left to cross a small drainage. Avoid this left turn and look for a primitive dirt road that continues to the west behind a brown carsonite post (mile 14.0; 2,240'; N33º09'37", W111º05'31"). This is the White Canyon Wilderness boundary (p. 145).

Walk west past the carsonite post and follow the primitive road (2,240') as it winds steeply to the west and northwest. The road disappears and a few rock cairns lead you northwest. After about 2.5 miles into the wilderness area, you will face a rock formation aptly named Hole in the Rock (N33º10'41", W111º07'07"). The difficult-to-see trail is left (south) of Hole in the Rock. In a few hundred yards, a wooden AZT post and rock cairns materialize. You have just exited the White Canyon Wilderness and reached the end of Passage 16.

USGS: **TEAPOT MOUNTAIN**

Battleaxe Road

White

artesian spring

Battleaxe Butte

Copper Butte

Copper Butte Mine

Walnut

Spring

The Spine

Passage 16
1:24,000 MAPS:
KEARNY, GRAYBACK, and
TEAPOT MOUNTAIN

1/4   1/4
SCALE: 11/16 INCH = 1/2 MILE

— Arizona Trail
(current segment)

— Arizona Trail
(previous and next segments)

— Access route

— River or stream

◉ Lake or pond

— Marsh or swamp

— Primary highway

— Secondary highway

— Light duty road

--- Unimproved road

---- Trail

✕ Quarry or open mine pit

USGS: **GRAYBACK**

USGS: **HOT TAMALE PEAK**

ower line too far

USGS: **KEARNY**

Florence–Kelvin Highway

Passage 17
Alamo Canyon: White Canyon Wilderness to Picketpost Trailhead

Cliffs high above the White Canyon Wilderness

TOTAL DISTANCE	11.5 miles
QUALITY HIKING DISTANCE	11.5 miles
DIFFICULTY	Moderate
TOTAL ELEVATION GAIN	NA
TOTAL DESCENT	NA
FROM MEXICO	273.4 miles
TO UTAH	498.5 miles
LAND MANAGERS	Tonto National Forest (Globe Ranger District)
RECOMMENDED MONTHS	October through April. Be prepared for cold temperatures, chilly rains, and snow in winter. Avoid the high temperatures of summer.

INTRODUCTION Hikers will enjoy the isolation of the first part of this passage. The desert hiking experience continues until Picketpost Trailhead. Much of this route is on old two-tracks that often follow washes; don't camp overnight in these washes. Progress is under way for a singletrack trail south of Picketpost Trailhead that will take the trail off the current old road and out of the washes. But until a new trail is complete, the existing trail is marked and will continue as official Arizona Trail.

MOUNTAIN BIKE NOTES

 The passage south from the Picketpost Trailhead to the beginning access point is ridable. There are some stiff uphill climbs and several stretches in washes; the washes are quite challenging. Please be aware that biking east of this passage is not allowed in the White Canyon Wilderness.

WATER

It's advisable to carry all the water you'll need on this stretch.

 Windmill: Locals report that this windmill and the pond it feeds are reliable sources (N33°14'00", W111°10'10").

 Windmill: A less reliable windmill is 0.5 mile northwest of the Picketpost Trailhead, just off the AZT.

 Boyce Thompson Arboretum: The arboretum is 2 miles east of the Picketpost Trailhead on US 60. Get there before 5 p.m.

MAPS

USGS Quadrangles: Teapot Mountain, Mineral Mountain, Picketpost Mountain
USFS: Tonto National Forest (South Half)
Other: Arizona Public Lands Information Center, AZT Passage Topo Map 17—
Alamo Canyon

BEGINNING ACCESS POINT

 **White Canyon Wilderness:** On the west edge of the town of Superior, take Mary Road south, passing west of the high school, to FR 4. (Alternatively, take AZ 177 south of Superior about 2 miles to FR 230. Go west on FR 230 for 1.5 miles to FR 4.) Four-wheel drive is needed on FR 4. Follow FR 4 about 7 miles southwest to the AZT, signed with a carsonite post (N33°12'25", W111°08'04"). Park here and follow the very rugged AZT route southeast, often in a wash, for about 2 miles to N33°11'22", W111°08'04". A wooden post with the AZT logo is located east of the wash. Leave the wash and hike east on a good trail approximately 1.25 miles to the western boundary of the White Canyon Wilderness and the beginning of Passage 17.

ENDING ACCESS POINT

 Picketpost Trailhead: See "Beginning Access Point" for Passage 18.

TRAIL DESCRIPTION From the Arizona Trail post and rock cairns just west of the White Canyon Wilderness, follow the good trail and frequent cairns 1.3 miles to a wash and two-track road. A wooden AZT post is there (N33°11'22", W111°08'04"). Turn right (north) in the wash, walk 75 feet, and turn left (west). The AZT follows the rugged wash and old two-track. In about 2.5 miles, the trail/two-track road comes to FR 4.

Turn left (west) to follow FR 4 as it climbs out of the canyon to the north. Stay on the main road as it winds along a ridge, generally trending northwest. After a steep climb (3,740'), the road levels somewhat and then makes a broad turn to the left (south). Partway through this curve, turn right (west) onto a singletrack marked by 4x4 posts (3,720'; N33°12'46", W111°09'56").

 If you start descending abruptly on the road or reach a "T" intersection with another road, you've missed the singletrack turnoff. Backtrack to find it.

Pass through a user-friendly gate in about 80 yards. Frequent cairns mark a clear singletrack that descends along a ridge. The trail is now in the upper reaches of Alamo Canyon, following a small drainage. The trail enters this drainage (3,220'; N33°13'06", W111°10'20") to follow it downstream. Cairns mark the trail as it dodges in and out of this wash. Don't enter washes like this one during periods of heavy rain!

 Southbound Hikers: Look for a 4x4 post with an AZT brand that marks the point where the AZT leaves this drainage to the south on a singletrack.

 A windmill is reportedly a reliable source of water (2,920'; N33°14'00", W111°10'10"). Look for a pond on the north side.

Follow the road up and out of the canyon (west and north) for about 0.75 mile before rejoining Alamo Canyon. Continue to climb in and out of the drainage a few times before reaching Picketpost Trailhead, the end of Passage 17, at mile 11.5 (2,400'; N33°16'22", W111°10'32"). There are bathrooms and parking at this location, but there is no water.

WILDERNESS ALERT

The **White Canyon Wilderness** protects about 5,800 acres of canyon country. Please follow these rules governing wilderness areas:

• Camp out of sight on dry, durable surfaces.

• Use a stove. If you must have a fire, use existing fire rings.

• Bury human waste 6 inches deep and 200 feet from any water. Pack out toilet paper.

• Keep dogs on leashes at all times.

• Do not ride a mountain bike.

• Pack out all trash; don't attempt to burn it.

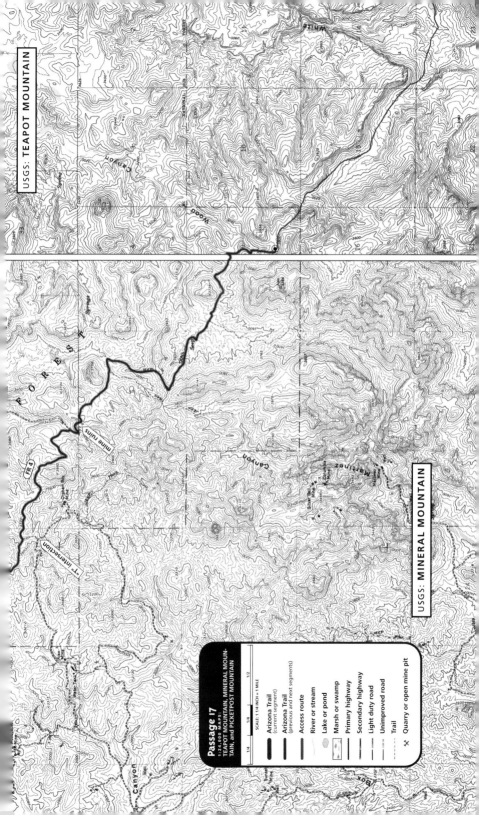

USGS: TEAPOT MOUNTAIN

USGS: MINERAL MOUNTAIN

Passage 17
1:24,000 MAPS:
TEAPOT MOUNTAIN, MINERAL MOUN-
TAIN, and PICKETPOST MOUNTAIN

SCALE: 1 1/4 INCH = 1 MILE

1/4   1/4   1/2

Arizona Trail
(current segment)

Arizona Trail
(previous and next segments)

Access route

River or stream

Lake or pond

Marsh or swamp

Primary highway

Secondary highway

Light duty road

Unimproved road

Trail

Quarry or open mine pit

Passage 18
Reavis Canyon: Picketpost Trailhead to Rogers Trough Trailhead

Saguaro cactus reflected in Happy Camp Creek, Tonto National Forest

TOTAL DISTANCE	18.6 miles
QUALITY HIKING DISTANCE	18.6 miles
DIFFICULTY	Strenuous
TOTAL ELEVATION GAIN	4,047 feet
TOTAL DESCENT	1,608 feet
FROM MEXICO	284.9 miles
TO UTAH	487.0 miles
LAND MANAGERS	Tonto National Forest (Globe Ranger District)
RECOMMENDED MONTHS	September through April. Snow may be present on the second half of the passage in winter.

INTRODUCTION   This passage links the White Canyon Wilderness Area of Passage 17 to the higher elevations of the Superstition Wilderness in Passage 19. The trail features beautiful Sonoran desert landscapes, with panoramic views of the Superstition Mountains to the northwest, Picketpost Mountain to the south, and the Apache Leap formation to the east. Lucky hikers may see a variety of wildlife, including deer, rabbits, javelinas, quail, rattlesnakes, and the elusive Gila monster.

Whitford Canyon and Reavis Trail Canyon are notorious flash-flood paths, so be aware of the weather and don't use them when rain is imminent.

The ATA divides this passage into two segments, with the first running from Picketpost Trailhead to Reavis Trail Canyon Trailhead, and the second completing the passage to Rogers Trough Trailhead.

MOUNTAIN BIKE NOTES

 The terrain on this part of the AZT varies greatly, from flat dirt roads to steep singletrack that is unridable by 99 percent of the population. This passage terminates at the boundary of the Superstition Wilderness, where bikes are prohibited, and more wilderness lies ahead. The best alternative is to cycle the following paved roads to bypass wilderness areas that extend through Passage 20: US 60 east to AZ 88 and AZ 188 north.

WATER

There is no reliable water on this passage, although washes may contain seasonal water. Thru-hikers should resupply at the beginning and carry enough water for the entire passage.

 Whitford and Reavis Trail Canyons: On rare occasions, in early spring and after rainfall, these drainages may contain water, but don't count on it!

MAPS

USGS Quadrangles: Picketpost Mountain, Iron Mountain
USFS: Tonto National Forest (South Half)
Other: Arizona Public Lands Information Center, AZT Passage Topo Map 18—
   Reavis Canyon

BEGINNING ACCESS POINT

  Picketpost Trailhead: From Florence Junction, drive east on US 60 for 9.0 miles. After mile marker 221, continue 0.5 mile and turn right (south) onto FR 231. (This point is 4.0 miles west of the outskirts of Superior on US 60.) Drive 0.4 mile and turn left onto FR 310. Continue 0.6 mile, and then turn right at a sign for Picketpost Trailhead. You will see the large metal AZT sign marking the trailhead in 0.1 mile (N33°16'22", W111°10'32").

ALTERNATE ACCESS POINT

Reavis Trail Canyon Trailhead (Passage 18, Mile 8.9): From Florence Junction, travel east on US 60 for 10.0 miles. After mile marker 222, continue 0.4 mile east, and then turn left (north) onto a dirt road at an unmarked intersection. Continue about 50 yards and turn right (east) onto FR 8, which is poorly marked with an old sign. At mile 1.8 (mileages given from the highway), bear left at a "Y" intersection onto FR 650. At mile 2.1, avoid a left fork and descend to the right on the better road. This road gradually worsens, soon requiring a four-wheel drive. The road jogs in and out of a wash that may be running with water in the spring. At mile 6.2, the road climbs steeply along the right side of the drainage. Just after it tops out, take a left fork down to an AZT marker and a "Road Closed" sign at mile 6.3 (N33°21'11", W111°07'54"). From here, a singletrack trail continues up Reavis Trail Canyon.

ENDING ACCESS POINT

Rogers Trough Trailhead: See "Beginning Access Point" for Passage 19.

TRAIL DESCRIPTION From the metal sign at Picketpost Trailhead (2,400'), look north. You will see a singletrack trail. That is the initial route of Passage 18 of the AZT.

To get there, walk down the dirt road to the northwest 0.1 mile and look for wooden AZT trail markers. Cross a paved road, crest a hill in 100 yards, and continue west on a singletrack marked by cairns. The trail descends to a wash and turns right (north) toward US 60. From here it is 4.6 miles east along US 60 to the center of Superior. (See "Supplies, Services, and Accommodations.")

Follow a culvert under the highway and pass through a fence on the opposite side. Continue 30 yards along the wash, then turn left (west) onto a singletrack trail at a cairn and wooden AZT marker. The trail soon heads north along a hill to a wooden AZT marker at a barbed-wire fence. Descend to cross Queen Creek, a major wash, and head for a wooden AZT sign that marks the trail's continuation on the other side.

In the next 120 yards, the trail curves right and then left before reaching a place where you cross a fence by going through two gates within 6 feet of each other. Be aware of cattle in the area. You should pass a 4x4 post. Continue through heavy vegetation, heading just slightly south of due east. Now follow a faint tread and frequent cairns, generally east and northeast.

When you reach a fence line, turn right (east) and continue 0.1 mile until you pass a fence line perpendicular to the one you're following and on the opposite side. Turn left (north) to pass through the second (easternmost) of two gates, follow the perpendicular fence line 20 yards, and then pick up the trail breaking off to the right (northeast) toward some railroad tracks.

Opposite: South of Picketpost Mountain
Photo courtesy of The Arizona Trail Association

Arizona Trail

Welcome to the Tonto National Forest and the Arizona Trail		USDA Forest Service Tonto National Forest Globe Ranger District

The Arizona Trail is a 790-mile non-motorized trail traversing the entire State of Arizona. The trail is open to hikers, equestrians, and mountain bikers (except where prohibited).

Trail users need to be responsible for their own safety and preparedness. In some cases, route finding skills and the ability to cope with unexpected situations such as weather, natural hazards, venomous creatures and lack of water are essential.

For more information contact the Arizona Trail Association at (602) 252-4794 or visit the web site at www.aztrail.org

 Arizona Trail
a Millennium Legacy Trail

This is your public land. Please join us in its conservation by practicing the following LEAVE NO TRACE ethics:

- Plan Ahead & Prepare
- Travel & Camp on Durable Surfaces
- Dispose of Waste Properly
- Leave What You Find
- Minimize Campfire Impacts
- Respect Wildlife
- Be Considerate of Others

Utah

Mexico

Sponsored By:
Arizona State Parks
Arizona Recreational Trails Program

SUPPLIES, SERVICES, AND ACCOMMODATIONS

SUPERIOR

The businesses in Superior line two main roads: US 60 and Main Street. US 60 runs almost due east from the point where the AZT crosses it (mile 0.6 of this passage). Main Street branches at an angle to the northeast. This "Y" intersection is 4.2 miles east of the AZT crossing on US 60. Because the physical addresses of these businesses don't give you much sense of where they are, I list the US 60 and Main Street businesses separately, and give the distance of each from the point where the AZT crosses US 60.

Distance from Trail 4.6 miles
   Area Code 520
   Zip Code 85273

US 60 Businesses and Services
   ATM Circle K (4.8 miles)
   Camping Superior RV Park, tent sites $10, showers $3, 689-5331 (4.1 miles)
   Dining *Buckboard Restaurant*, 689-5800 (4.1 miles); *Los Hermanos Restaurant*, 689-5465 (4.6 miles, near Circle K)
   Gear None
   Groceries Superior Farmers Market, 689-5845 (4.8 miles)
   Laundry At El Portal Motel (see "Lodging")
   Lodging El Portal Motel, 689-2886 (4.9 miles)
   Medical Claypool Medical Center, 4443 E. Broadway, Claypool, AZ 85532, 473-4441 (24.5 miles)
   Showers See "Camping"
Other Attractions Boyce Thompson Arboretum State Park, 1.5 miles from the trail at mile marker 223 on US 60, open daily 8 a.m. to 5 p.m., 689-2723. In a beautiful natural setting, the arboretum displays many of the plants and trees you may see along the AZT. I highly recommend stopping here to learn more about Arizona flora.

Main Street Businesses and Services
(Bear left from US 60 at a sign that says "Police and Tourist Information.")
   Bank Community First Bank, open 10 a.m. to 3 p.m., except 10 a.m. to 2 p.m. on T, W (no ATM), 689-2431 (5.2 miles)
   Groceries Save Money Discount Center, 689-2265 (5.1 miles)
   Information Town Hall, 689-5752 (4.6 miles)
   Post Office 25 N. High School Ave., general delivery with 30-day maximum, 689-5790 (5.4 miles)

Cross a well-graded dirt road and some parallel railroad tracks (N33°16'57", W111°10'35"). (This rail line is active.) The trail continues northward through generally flat terrain, where it crosses another dirt road with trail markers on both sides. Beyond the dirt road, the trail drops rapidly into a wash and then begins climbing a ridge below high-tension power lines.

The trail tracks northeast up a rough-cut switchback, then up and down a ridgeline with eight crests over the next 2.0 miles. Be cautious on steep, scree-covered sections.

The 360° views from this ridge are excellent. From the sixth crest, you can see the impressive volcanic monolith called Weavers Needle in the Superstition Mountains to the northwest. The AZT begins descending the ridge to the northwest to a stone structure called Barnett Camp and a grave site a short distance to the southeast. The AZT now enters Whitford Canyon, which it follows for the next 1.8 miles. Watch for rattlesnakes and Gila monsters in the canyon's fine riparian habitat.

Cairns mark the trail as it crosses the main wash several times. Pass through a tranquil mesquite forest and look for a small grotto in the rock next to the wash—perfect for a midday break. The trail exits Whitford Canyon and crosses FR 650. This road is heavily used.

After crossing FR 650, continue to follow a singletrack trail up a short hill. Turn north after a couple hundred yards. The trail is easy to follow for the next 3.0 miles, as it parallels FR 650. The trail drops down to a jeep road. Cross the road and follow the tread and rock cairns as the trail winds in and out of washes along easy grades. The trail crosses FR 650 again. Look for a left fork of the road that descends to an AZT sign. The AZT leaves the road here and follows a singletrack trail up Reavis Trail Canyon.

You'll pass through an old ruin that offers some nice, flat camping spots. Follow cairns as the trail weaves in and out of the drainage bed. The canyon and the trail soon bend sharply to the left (northwest). The trail leaves the drainage to the left (northwest), and in another 0.4 mile, it starts switchbacking steeply up the grassy slopes to the northwest. Scratchy brambles frequently reach into the trail here.

You will pass through a gate and reach the top of this long, arduous climb in a saddle (5,460'). Look back almost due south for an interesting perspective on Picketpost Mountain—you are gazing down on the flat top of the mountain that towered over the beginning of this passage.

Follow the trail as it bends right (north), descend slightly for 0.2 mile to a road (FR 650), and bear left (northwest) on it (N33°24'19", W111°09'25"). Stay left (west) on FR 650 as a road forks to the right. You'll see a sign that says "End 650" at a triangular intersection. Turn right (north) onto FR 172A and continue 0.4 mile to the Rogers Trough Trailhead and the beginning of Passage 19 (4,840'; N33°25'20", W111°10'21").

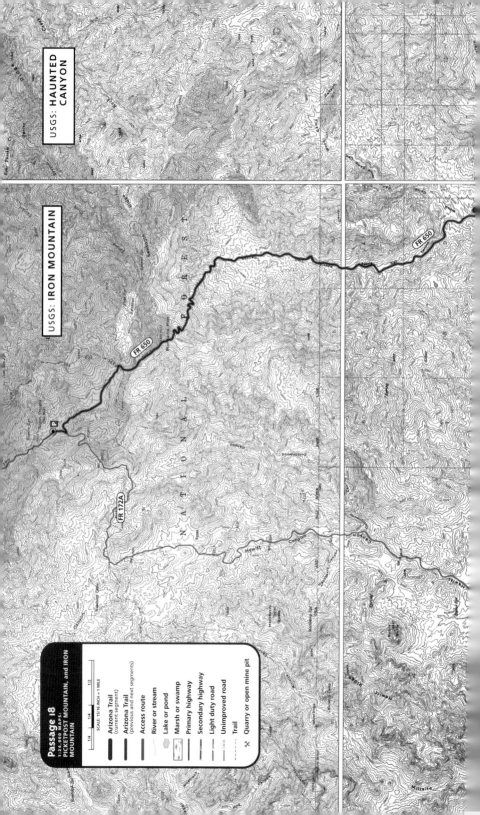

USGS: **HAUNTED CANYON**

USGS: **IRON MOUNTAIN**

FR 650

FR 650

P

FR 172A

Hewitt Canyon

Passage 18
1:24,000 MAPS:
PICKETPOST MOUNTAIN, and IRON
MOUNTAIN

SCALE: 15/16 INCH = 1 MILE

1/4   1/4   1/2

Arizona Trail
(current segment)

Arizona Trail
(previous and next segments)

Access route

River or stream

Lake or pond

Marsh or swamp

Primary highway

Secondary highway

Light duty road

Unimproved road

Trail

✕   Quarry or open mine pit

USGS: SUPERIOR

USGS: PICKETPOST MOUNTAIN

Reavis Trail Canyon

Reavis Trail Canyon TH

FR 650

FR 8

FR 231

FR 310

P

FR 357

60

Passage 19
Superstition Wilderness: Rogers Trough Trailhead to Roosevelt Lake

Looking south over Alchesay Canyon above the Arizona Trail

TOTAL DISTANCE	29.7 miles
QUALITY HIKING DISTANCE	29.7 miles
DIFFICULTY	Strenuous
TOTAL ELEVATION GAIN	5,185 feet
TOTAL DESCENT	7,776 feet
FROM MEXICO	303.5 miles
TO UTAH	468.4 miles
LAND MANAGERS	Tonto National Forest (Mesa Ranger District, Tonto Basin Ranger District)
RECOMMENDED MONTHS	March through November

INTRODUCTION Although the Superstition Wilderness is heavily traveled, thanks to its proximity to Phoenix, this passage still gives a genuine sense of wildness because it traverses the east side of the wilderness area, farthest from the city, and the trailheads require long drives on four-wheel-drive roads. This sense of solitude, which must have been much greater in the 1800s, certainly seems to have appealed to Elisha Reavis, who settled here along a reliable creek around 1874. Rich soil and a favorable climate helped Reavis grow vegetables, which he sold at mining towns in the area. The AZT passes the site of the old Reavis Ranch, still a beautiful spot—Reavis loved it so much he stayed until his death in 1896. Apple trees still bear fruit near the site.

The final few miles of this passage are at low elevations that will be quite hot in summer. The rest of the passage, in the Superstition Wilderness, is pleasant all year except for midwinter, when snow is likely.

Campsites are plentiful on this passage, especially near Walnut Spring at mile 12.3, but there are a few exceptions. Camping is limited before you crest a ridge at mile 4.1. You won't find much camping between mile 18.0 and mile 23.0, and it's limited again during the final few miles, starting at mile 26.6.

MOUNTAIN BIKE NOTES

 Most of this passage is inside the Superstition Wilderness, where bikes are prohibited. Follow US 60, AZ 88, and AZ 188 to bypass the wilderness area. Note that flooding has rendered Cottonwood Canyon unbikable, but trail repairs are slated for the near future.

WATER

 Mile 4.4 to mile 8.0, Reavis Creek: From Reavis Saddle Spring to Reavis Ranch, the water flow seems to be fairly reliable.

 Mile 10.7, Pine Creek: This stream appears to be perennial, but that has not been verified (N33°30'43", W111°07'46").

 Mile 12.3, Walnut Spring: A reliable source of water, but watch out for the spiders (N33°31'29", W111°07'53")

 Mile 20.2, Man-made Pond: (N33°35'55", W111°07'42")

 Mile 21.0, Man-made Pond: (N33°35'51", W111°07'04")

 Mile 22.7, Cottonwood Spring: A trustworthy Forest Service employee reports this source is reliable year-round. A clear sign marks the spring (N33°37'06", W111°07'29").

 Mile 26.6, Cottonwood Creek: The same trustworthy Forest Service employee says this creek also is reliable (N33°39'15", W111°08'00").

MAPS

USGS Quadrangles: Iron Mountain, Pinyon Mountain, Two Bar Mountain, Theodore Roosevelt Dam

USFS: Tonto National Forest (South Half)

Other: Arizona Public Lands Information Center, AZT Passage Topo Maps 19A and 19B—Superstition Wilderness

BEGINNING ACCESS POINT

Rogers Trough Trailhead (from Florence Junction): From Florence Junction, east of Phoenix, travel east on US 60 for 1.8 miles, turn left (north) onto Queen Valley Road, continue 1.8 miles, and turn right (east) on FR 357. Drive 3.0 miles and turn left (north) onto FR 172 at a sign for "Roger's Trough Trailhead." (There is a sign for FR 172 about 20 yards after the turn.) Continue 9.2 miles to a fork and bear right onto FR 172A. Follow this road 3.7 miles, bear left at an intersection with FR 650 (which is also the route of the AZT arriving from Passage 18), and continue 0.4 mile to a very large parking area (N33°25'20", W111°10'21"). The trail departs from the north end of the parking lot.

Rogers Trough Trailhead (from Superior): About 3.0 miles west of Superior on US 60, 0.6 mile west of mile marker 223 (or 0.4 mile east of mile marker 222), turn north at an unmarked intersection onto a dirt road. This is FR 357. Follow it 5.0 miles to a right turn onto FR 172, which is only marked as such about 20 yards after the turn. (A sign on FR 357, facing the opposite direction, indicates this is the turn for "Roger's Trough Trailhead.") Join the directions from Florence Junction at "Continue 9.2 miles…"

ALTERNATE ACCESS POINT

Two Bar Ridge Trailhead (Passage 19, Mile 20.1): This is an ideal parking spot for purists who only want to traverse the Superstition Wilderness. From the suspension bridge near Roosevelt Dam, follow AZ 88 east 5.5 miles and turn right onto a dirt road, which is marked as FR 83 a short distance off the highway. The following mileages are from the highway turnoff. Drive 2.8 miles to a gate at Black Bush Ranch and bear left, continuing on FR 83. At a gate and fork at mile 3.9, take the left fork, go about 30 yards to another fork, and bear right. At mile 4.1, you'll see Trail #120 on the right (north). This is the path of the AZT along Cottonwood Creek. Continue southwest on the "main" road (and the AZT), which gradually becomes quite steep. Make a left turn at mile 5.6, just before the road crosses an earthen dam. Drive the final steep 0.1 mile to the trailhead (N33°35'55", W111°07'33").

Frasier Trailhead (Passage 19, Mile 26.6): This trailhead is recommended for horse trailers. From the suspension bridge near Roosevelt Dam, follow AZ 88 for 2.0 miles east and turn right into the trailhead parking area. The AZT is 1.2 miles up the trail.

Cemetery Trailhead (Passage 19, Mile 27.7): From the suspension bridge by Roosevelt Dam, follow AZ 88 for 1.4 miles east and turn right into an RV park across the highway from the Roosevelt Marina and Visitor Center. Make another immediate right into the Cemetery Trail parking area. The AZT is 0.25 mile up the trail.

ENDING ACCESS POINT

Roosevelt Lake: See "Beginning Access Point" for Passage 20.

TRAIL DESCRIPTION

Follow the trail out of the north end of the parking lot (4,840') and immediately enter the Superstition Wilderness. At mile 0.1, turn left (west) on the Reavis Ranch Trail (#109) toward Reavis Ranch. The trail forks at mile 1.0 but soon converges back into a single trail. Continue downstream to a junction at mile 1.8 (4,365'; N33°26'23", W111°11'04"), and go straight (northeast) into a gradual climb up a side drainage.

At mile 2.5, the trail climbs out of the drainage via a series of switchbacks trending west. At mile 4.1, the trail reaches flat ground and good campsites, although there is no water.

WILDERNESS ALERT

The **Superstition Wilderness** was designated in 1964 to be "an area where the earth and its community of life are untrammeled by man, where man himself is a visitor who does not remain." It protects approximately 160,200 acres of land ranging in elevation from 1,980 feet to 6,265 feet and encompasses ecosystems from Sonoran Desert to cool ponderosa pine forests.

Please remember and practice these rules governing wilderness areas:

- Camp out of sight, at least 200 feet from lakes and streams, on dry, durable surfaces.
- Use a stove instead of building a fire; use existing fire rings if you must have a fire.
- Keep water sources clean by washing at least 200 feet from them.
- Bury human waste 6 inches deep and 200 feet from lakes and streams; pack out toilet paper.
- Hobble or picket livestock at least 200 feet from lakes and streams, and use only treated, weed-free feed and grain.
- All dogs must be on a leash.
- No mountain bikes.
- Pack out all trash; don't attempt to burn it.

As you begin the descent on the north side of the ridge, you'll notice a much different vegetation zone. The moister environment here encourages beautiful stands of ponderosa pines, which provide a soft carpet of fallen needles on the trail.

 Reavis Creek is generally reliable, but you should check with the Forest Service or AZT stewards before counting on water from this creek.

Around mile 6.5, there are some nice, flat spots to camp (N33°28'43", W111°09'30"). The AZT continues to descend along the creek. There are numerous crossings, which can be confusing—just remember that the trail never strays far from the streambed.

Avoid a sharp right turn onto the Fire Line Trail at mile 7.3 and continue descending straight (north) toward the creek on the Reavis Trail (#109). After you cross the creek and climb the short bank on the other side, you'll find yourself in the flat, grassy fields that surround Reavis Ranch. Near this creek crossing is the last place you can camp legally until after you leave the ranch area at mile 8.0. Don't forget to camp at least 200 feet from the stream.

Bear right at a fork at mile 7.5 and pass near the ruins of the ranch. Around mile 7.9, you may notice two trails that parallel one another; stay on the one on the right. At mile 8.0 (4,795'), the trail forks just before a fence. Avoid going straight through the fence and take the fainter right (east) fork to the Reavis Gap Trail (#117). Cross the stream, climb a stair-stepped red rock wall on the opposite bank, and pick up the trail as it angles up to the right (southeast).

Now the trail climbs steadily along the southern flanks of Boulder Mountain until it tops out on a shoulder of the mountain at mile 9.2 (5,280'; N33°30'01", W111°08'26").

 A moderate descent into the Pine Creek drainage leads to a tributary crossing at mile 10.5, followed by the creek itself at mile 10.7 (N33°30'43", W111°07'46").

Climb north-northeast to a saddle and cross into another drainage at mile 11.2 (4,880'). Continue around the top of the drainage to an obscure trail intersection at mile 11.7. Turn left (west) onto the Two Bar Ridge Trail (#119)(4,760'; N33°31'13", W111°07'32"). There's not much of a tread as you descend here, but frequent cairns mark the way.

The trail improves, and you soon reach the dense vegetation, large clumps of grass, and ubiquitous spiders that mark Walnut Spring at mile 12.3 (N33°31'29", W111°07'53"). You'll find a nice camping area about 100 yards past the spring on the west side of the trail.

Follow a gradual climb to the north to cross a ridge at mile 13.0 (4,765'). The trail fades here, but cairns show the way across the ridge to the north-northwest. A clear trail descends the other side. The trail is occasionally overgrown, so have some long pants and a long-sleeved shirt ready. After 0.2 mile trending east-southeast, the AZT veers left for a very steep, rocky descent to the north-northeast, sometimes with switchbacks, sometimes without. As you descend, look across the valley for the faint trace of the trail marching back up the other side. You will reach the valley bottom at mile 14.1 (4,000').

Cairns soon mark a strenuous climb through a healthy population of prickly pear cactus. Crest the ridge at a saddle at mile 15.0 (4,810'; N33°32'58", W111°07'42"). There are great views from here, including Apache Lake in the valley to the northwest. The scenery only improves as the route turns right (north) to follow the trail's namesake land formation, Two Bar Ridge. At a trail fork at mile 16.4, avoid Tule Canyon Trail (#122) by continuing on the ridge to the north (4,760'; N33°34'02", W111°07'41"). In about 0.2 mile, you can see Roosevelt Lake to the north-northeast from a saddle.

The AZT's due-north trend continues atop this ridge to mile 16.8, then veers left (west) to descend gradually along the ridge before making an abrupt turn to the right (north) at mile 17.4. The trail descends into a pleasant pine forest with some nice camping spots but no water. After a low point at mile 18.2 (4,315'), the AZT climbs steeply and peaks on a southwest ridge of Pinyon Mountain at mile 18.9 (4,945'; N33°35'25", W111°08'20"). Trend north and east along the rugged gyrations of the mountain and exit the wilderness at mile 19.8. After walking all the way around to the northeast slopes, drop abruptly to the south edge of the parking area for Two Bar Ridge Trailhead at mile 20.1 (4,520'; N33°35'55", W111°07'33").

 Turn left (north) and follow a very clear dirt road steeply down past a man-made pond at mile 20.2. This had ample water when I was here in April (N33°35'55", W111°07'42"). Avoid the road to the left over an earthen dam and continue a steep descent along FR 83.

 You'll pass another man-made pond at mile 21.0 (3,960'; N33°35'51", W111°07'04").

At mile 21.7, turn left (north) onto a road labeled "Trail No. 120" (3,760'; N33°36'18", W111°06'49"). Follow this old roadbed 0.2 mile to a wide clearing. Avoiding some decoy trails as you cross to the north side of the clearing, find the singletrack AZT behind a carsonite post.

Southbound Hikers: Hikers going in the opposite direction will arrive at this clearing and pick up the roadbed on the north side, then continue 0.2 mile to FR 83 and turn right.

Descend the singletrack into a small gully and continue north-northwest along the beautiful drainage of Cottonwood Creek, following cairns where the trail becomes obscure. *Note:* Recent flooding in Cottonwood Canyon has caused extensive damage to the AZT. Hikers can get through the damaged area but horses and mountain bikers can't. Repairs are planned in the near future.

 You'll find Cottonwood Spring, marked by a clear sign, at mile 22.7 (3,420'; N33°37'06", W111°07'29"). A trustworthy Forest Service employee says this spring is perennial.

At mile 24.4, a sign marks your arrival at FR 341. Turn right (north) on this road. Here the AZT returns to the low Sonoran Desert ecosystem, complete with saguaro cactus, paloverde trees, and nice stands of ocotillo.

SUPPLIES, SERVICES, AND ACCOMMODATIONS

ROOSEVELT

A small community of businesses supports tourism on the lake. Some services are found near the trail, while others are several miles away, as indicated. The best way to reach this area from the AZT is to walk 0.25 mile to the Cemetery Trailhead from mile 26.8 of Passage 19 and then cross AZ 88 to the Roosevelt Lake Marina.

Distance from Trail 0.4 mile

Area Code 928

Zip Code 85545

ATM Butcher Hook Restaurant & Store, 479-2712, 14.5 miles north of Roosevelt suspension bridge on AZ 188

Bank None

Bicycle Shop None

Bus None

Camping Windy Hill Campground. Go 2.6 miles east of Roosevelt Lake Marina on AZ 88, then turn left (north) at a sign for the campground. Go 0.2 mile to a "T" intersection and turn right onto Road 82. Continue 1.5 miles and turn left into campground.

Dining *Roosevelt Lake Marina* offers limited breakfast and lunch (see "Groceries"); *Roosevelt Lake Resort,* 467-2276, is 9.5 miles east of Roosevelt Lake Marina on AZ 88. Turn left on Roosevelt Lake Resort Road and continue 0.5 mile to the motel and restaurant on the left.

Gear Roosevelt Lake Marina (see "Groceries")

Groceries Roosevelt Lake Marina, 467-2245, basic supplies including white gas. It is 1.4 miles east of the Roosevelt suspension bridge on AZ 88, across from the Cemetery Trailhead.

Information Roosevelt Lake Visitor Center and Tonto Basin Ranger District office, 467-3200, 0.2 mile behind Roosevelt Lake Marina

Laundry Roosevelt Lake Marina (see "Groceries")

Lodging: Roosevelt Lake Resort, starts at $30 (see "Dining")

Medical None

Post Office On AZ 88, 9.0 miles east of the Roosevelt Lake Visitor Center

Showers Windy Hill Campground (see "Camping")

Other Attractions Tonto National Monument (467-2241) allows you to explore well-preserved ruins of structures from this area's early inhabitants, the Salado people. It is 1.9 miles east of Roosevelt Lake Marina on AZ 88; turn right and continue 0.8 mile.

The road climbs above the Cottonwood Creek drainage and reaches a high point at mile 25.1 (2,940') with nice views of Theodore Roosevelt Lake to the north, as well as the blue-roofed buildings of the visitor center.

 At mile 25.5, the road dives to cross Cottonwood Creek at mile 26.6 (2,340'; N33°39'15", W111°08'00").

 Before the creek crossing, a sign seems to indicate that the AZT continues downstream on the Lower Cottonwood Trail. This is incorrect. That trail is the 1.2-mile spur to the Frasier Trailhead (see "Alternate Access Point"). Instead, turn left (west) and cross the stream. The road ascends steadily to a junction with FR 1080 at mile 26.4 (2,540'). Cross this road and pick up a singletrack, the Thompson Trail (#121), which will trend to the west and north.

This pleasant singletrack, with continuous views of Roosevelt Lake, is a popular day-hiking trail. At mile 26.8 (2,330'), the trail reaches an intersection with the so-called Cemetery Trail, which leads through a fence to the right (north) 0.25 mile to the Cemetery Trailhead, across the highway from the Roosevelt Lake Marina store and the visitor center. This is the best access to the services in this area. (See "Supplies, Services, and Accommodations.") Markers indicate the AZT follows both forks. To reach the end of Passage 19, continue along the left fork to the northwest.

At mile 27.2, the trail splits as an equestrian bypass takes off to the left (south). Hikers should stay on the main trail to the north. This trail seems to fork again at a water trough at mile 27.8; this is actually the return of the equestrian bypass, so take the right fork (northwest).

The AZT climbs to a saddle at mile 28.2 (2,530') with a great view of the suspension bridge you'll soon cross. Descend to reach AZ 88 at mile 29.0. Turn left (southwest). Follow a bend to the north and cross the suspension bridge by walking on the far left side, against the traffic, and be careful!

Reach the end of both the bridge and Passage 19 at mile 29.7 (2,220'; N33°40'36", W111°09'39"). Right where the cement guardrail ends on the left-hand side, a single-track trail, the Vineyard Trail, leads into Passage 20. There is a large parking area on the right (east) side of the highway.

Sundown, Superstition Mountains, along the Arizona Trail near Two Bar Ridge

USGS: WINDY HILL

USGS: THEODORE ROOSEVELT DAM

88

FR 83

TR 120

Cottonwood Spring

Two Bar Ridge TH

FR 83

ponds

FR 341

water

TR 121

Frazier TH

Cemetery TH

Theodore Roosevelt Bridge

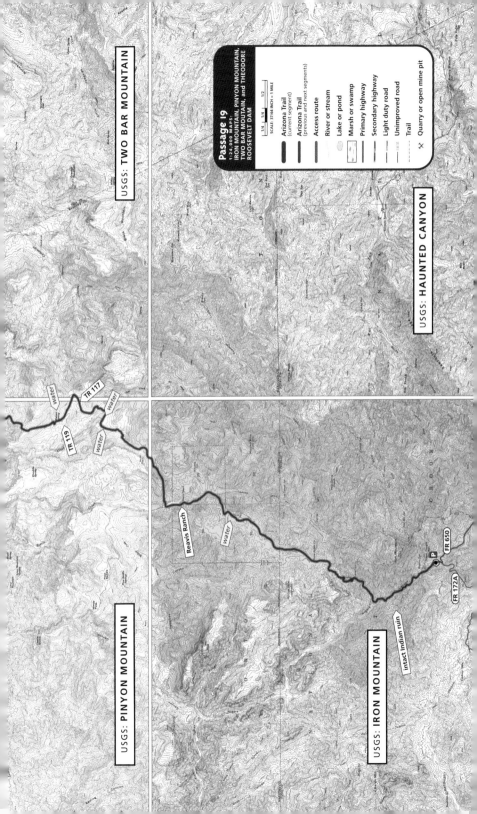

USGS: TWO BAR MOUNTAIN

USGS: HAUNTED CANYON

USGS: PINYON MOUNTAIN

USGS: IRON MOUNTAIN

Passage 19
1:74,000
IRON MOUNTAIN, PINYON MOUNTAIN,
TWO BAR MOUNTAIN, and THEODORE
ROOSEVELT DAM

SCALE 37/64 INCH = 1 MILE

1/4   1/4   1/2

Arizona Trail
(current segment)

Arizona Trail
(previous and next segments)

Access route

River or stream

Lake or pond

Marsh or swamp

Primary highway

Secondary highway

Light duty road

Unimproved road

Trail

Quarry or open mine pit

water

TR 117

TR 119

water

water

Reavis Ranch

water

FR 650

P

FR 172A

intact Indian ruin

Passage 20
Four Peaks: Roosevelt Lake to Lone Pine Saddle

Four Peaks along the Arizona Trail

TOTAL DISTANCE	18.3 miles
QUALITY HIKING DISTANCE	17.5 miles
DIFFICULTY	Strenuous
TOTAL ELEVATION GAIN	7,026 feet
TOTAL DESCENT	3,645 feet
FROM MEXICO	333.2 miles
TO UTAH	438.7 miles
LAND MANAGERS	Tonto National Forest (Tonto Basin Ranger District)
RECOMMENDED MONTHS	March through May, September through November. The lower elevations will be quite hot in the summer months, but you may encounter snow up high during winter.

INTRODUCTION This passage has several striking aspects, including great views of Theodore Roosevelt Lake and the dam that created it, close-up views of the magnificent Four Peaks, and the startling effects of a massive forest fire.

Roosevelt Dam was completed in 1911, following President Theodore Roosevelt's 1902 edict to divert and store water to spur development of the West. In 1984, engineers determined that the dam might be inadequate to withstand the greatest possible earthquake that could occur in the area, and also that a large flood could overwhelm the dam. A $410 million project to reconfigure the dam began in 1989 and was completed in 1996. The dam's height increased from 280 to 357 feet; the length of the crest grew from 723 to 1,210 feet; and the lake's surface gained 1,862 acres, an increase of almost 10 percent.

Another man-made feature that defines this passage was not so carefully planned and executed. This was a wild conflagration called the Lone Fire, started by careless campers near Pigeon Spring on April 28, 1996. In a week, this fire consumed 60,000 acres, making it the largest fire in Arizona history at that time. The AZT goes through the heart of this burn area, presenting some unique challenges to the hiker. The trail is impossible to see in some areas, because the vegetation that surrounded it was destroyed. Cairns mark the trail in these areas, but frequently they are inadequate. Therefore, map and compass skills are imperative, and it doesn't hurt to have a GPS unit. Adding to the peril are burned-out snags that can topple at any time. Keep your eyes peeled, and be mindful when choosing a campsite. Call the Forest Service for the latest conditions.

This passage traverses some high ridges and crosses slopes made slippery by loose rock. It is not recommended for pack stock or for the weak of heart.

MOUNTAIN BIKE NOTES

 Most of this passage is inside the Four Peaks Wilderness, where bikes are prohibited. The first 6 miles are not in wilderness, but they would be very difficult for all but the most accomplished riders. It's best to take AZ 188 north, and then follow directions to the beginning of Passage 20.

WATER

 Shake Spring: (N33°42'05", W111°19'13")

 Pigeon Spring: The Forest Service describes this source as intermittent, but it had a strong flow when I passed here in May (N33°42'48", W111°20'06").

MAPS

USGS Quadrangles: Theodore Roosevelt Dam, Four Peaks
USFS: Tonto National Forest (South Half)
Other: Arizona Public Lands Information Center, AZT Passage Topo Map 20—
Four Peaks

BEGINNING ACCESS POINT

 Smooth road to Trailhead **Roosevelt Lake:** This is near Theodore Roosevelt Dam, where AZ 88 and AZ 188 meet. The parking area is at the north end of the suspension bridge, on the east side of the highway (N33°40'36", W111°09'39").

ALTERNATE ACCESS POINT

  Bumpy road to Trailhead 4.9 miles **Mills Ridge Trailhead:** From the Roosevelt suspension bridge, drive 2.5 miles northwest on AZ 188 and cross a bridge. Turn left (west) onto an unmarked dirt road. (The following mileages are from AZ 188.) Follow the road's curve to the right, then turn left (west) onto FR 429 at mile 0.4. Stay on FR 429 until you reach a parking area and trailhead at mile 4.9 (N33°40'19", W111°14'28"). The AZT arrives from the east on the Vineyard Trail and departs to the west on Trail #130.

ENDING ACCESS POINT

  Bumpy road to Trailhead 10.5 miles **Lone Pine Saddle:** See "Beginning Access Point" for the next passage.

TRAIL DESCRIPTION

 From the parking area on the east side of AZ 188 (2,200'), walk southwest across the highway by the suspension bridge and you'll see a singletrack trail that climbs to the southwest. The trail is marked by a brown carsonite post with an AZT sticker on it. Wind up the ridge, and after 0.5 mile make a sharp turn to the right as another spur continues straight to the south. (This spur leads a short distance to a bird's-eye view of Roosevelt Dam.)

The trail's initial climb soon gives way to rolling ups and downs along a prominent ridge, with stunning views of Apache Lake to the south. Soon you'll reach an old two-track road that is marked by AZT stickers on carsonite posts (3,145'; N33°40'11", W111°12'27"). Turn right (west) and follow a slight descent.

Southbound Hikers: The posts here may be somewhat confusing. Be sure to turn left (northeast) onto the somewhat overgrown singletrack trail.

When you reach a better road in 0.3 mile, turn left (south) onto it (3,120'; N33°40'13", W111°12'45"). Over the next 0.1 mile, the road switchbacks across a drainage to a "Road Closed" sign and an AZT marker indicating you should follow this closed road along the crest of the ridge to the west. The road is overgrown but clearly visible.

The ridge (3,250'; N33°40'11", W111°13'20") dwindles away and the trail fades somewhat as it bends right (northwest) to climb pretty steeply onto another ridge. As you walk due west along this ridge, you'll feel like you're near the top of the world, with astounding views in all directions, even though you're only about 3,400 feet above sea level. Reach a parking area at Mills Ridge Trailhead (3,720'; N33°40'19", W111°14'28").

Walk west across the parking area to pick up the AZT at a sign for Trail #130. A relatively steep climb leads to a ridge crest in 0.5 mile, followed by a knob (4,590'; N33°39'57", W111°15'09"). From here, the effects of the fire that ravaged this area are very clear, and the erosion damage to the trail is significant. The trail is frequently unclear

Opposite: "Brown's Peak," highest of the Four Peaks, covered with a dusting of snow

WILDERNESS ALERT

The **Four Peaks Wilderness** was designated in 1984 to be "an area where the earth and its community of life are untrammeled by man, where man himself is a visitor who does not remain." It protects approximately 60,740 acres of land surrounding the craggy Four Peaks, which rise to 7,657 feet.

Please remember and practice these rules governing wilderness areas:
- Camp out of sight, at least 200 feet from lakes and streams, on dry, durable surfaces.
- Use a stove instead of building a fire; use existing fire rings if you must have a fire.
- Keep water sources clean by washing at least 200 feet from them.
- Bury human waste 6 inches deep and 200 feet from lakes and streams. Pack out toilet paper.
- Hobble or picket livestock at least 200 feet from lakes and streams, and use only treated, weed-free feed and grain.
- Keep all dogs on a leash.
- No mountain bikes.
- Pack out all trash; don't attempt to burn it.

---

because there's no way to distinguish between the tread from the denuded ground that surrounds it. Cairns mark the difficult sections, but they're not always adequate.

Look southwest for the trace of a trail ascending a hill. That is your immediate destination. To get there, the AZT descends 0.3 mile to a low point in the ridge, bends left (southwest), and bottoms out in a rocky drainage (4,295'). About 20 yards downstream, a cairn indicates that the trail climbs out of the drainage and up the hillside to the southeast. The steep trail and switchbacks lead to a flat area with camping possibilities (4,910'; N33°39'32", W111°15'31"). The trail bends to the left (south), 0.3 mile farther and enters the Four Peaks Wilderness, but no sign indicates this.

Soon the trail arrives at Granite Spring (N33°39'20", W111°16'13"). From there, a new section of Trail #130, constructed in 2003–2004, heads north and then west. The approximately 2.5 miles of new trail pass easily through thick vegetation (N33°39'44", W111°16'42") and cross Trail #132 as it heads west-northwest. The views to the east (N33°40'33", W111°18'38") into the large drainage are awesome.

It is reassuring to see some ponderosa pines that are still alive. Hiking north, you'll reach an intersection with the Alder Creek Trail (#82) (5,835'; N33°41'08", W111°18'37"). Stay on Trail #130 to the right (west) for about 10 yards, and then follow it as it makes a right (north) turn to continue contouring along this steep hillside. The trail becomes very clear. At the intersection with Oak Flat Trail (#123) (5,400'), turn left (northwest).

 You'll cross a possible flow of water at Shake Spring (N33°42'05", W111°19'13").

At the intersection with the Pigeon Trail (#134), thru-hikers should turn right (northwest). (To go to the popular trailhead at Lone Pine Saddle, continue straight up the trail to the south, and later west-northwest, about 2.0 miles.) After crossing a streambed, the trail fades near some unusually flat terrain. Bear right (east) of the flat point, and the trail is soon apparent. For those with a GPS, the next waypoint is N33°42'15", W111°19'39".

In less than a mile, you'll crest a small ridge and exit the Four Peaks Wilderness at a marker. Descend into the heart of a burn area, where the ghosts of trees are all charred to black.

 Next you'll reach Pigeon Spring (5,510'; N33°42'48", W111°20'06"). From the sign for Pigeon Spring, the trail climbs southwest on an old roadbed.

The trail reaches Pigeon Trailhead on FR 648, and the end of Passage 20 (5,620'; N33°42'38", W111°20'08"). Thru-hikers will turn right (west) and follow the road.

El Oso Road

FR 648

Pigeon Spring
Pigeon Spring

one Pine Saddle

TONTO

Shake Spring
Shake Spring

NATIONAL   FOREST

Four Peaks

MOUNTAINS

BUCKHORN RIDGE

Passage 20
1:24,000 MAPS:
THEODORE ROOSEVELT DAM
and FOUR PEAKS

SCALE: 31/32 INCH = 1 MILE

▬▬▬ Arizona Trail
(current segment)

▬▬▬ Arizona Trail
(previous and next segments)

▬▬▬ Access route

— River or stream

⬭ Lake or pond

Marsh or swamp

— Primary highway

Secondary highway

Light duty road

Unimproved road

Trail

✕ Quarry or open mine pit

USGS: FOUR PEAKS

USGS: **THEODORE ROOSEVELT DAM**

Passage 21
Pine Mountain/Boulder Creek:
Lone Pine Saddle to Sunflower

Wash running with meltwater from recent snow in the Mazatzal Mountains

INTRODUCTION This passage is essentially a link from the Four Peaks Wilderness of Passage 20 to the Mazatzal Wilderness of Passage 22. About 13 miles are open to motorized vehicles, and the roads near the end are very popular with ATVs and motor-bikes. Consider avoiding the developed campsites in this area—because of its proximity to Phoenix and easy access by passenger car, it has been the site of urban-style crime.

In spite of this passage's accessibility, it has a remote feel, and the singletrack trails in the Boulder Creek drainage offer beautiful views. The trailhead in the Sunflower

TOTAL DISTANCE	20.0 miles
QUALITY HIKING DISTANCE	18.4 miles
DIFFICULTY	Moderate
TOTAL ELEVATION GAIN	2,214 feet
TOTAL DESCENT	4,397 feet
FROM MEXICO	351.5 miles
TO UTAH	420.4 miles
LAND MANAGERS	Tonto National Forest (Tonto Basin Ranger District, Mesa Ranger District)
RECOMMENDED MONTHS	March through May, September through November. The lower elevations of this passage will be quite hot in the summer; you may encounter snow up high during winter.

area, at the end of this passage, may change while this book is in print. Check with the Arizona Trail Association (602-252-4794 or ata@aztrail.org) for the latest information.

MOUNTAIN BIKE NOTES

Most of this passage is ridable, but the Boulder Creek Trail is only about 20 percent ridable—the other 80 percent resembles a bobsled run filled with softball- to volleyball-sized rocks. In addition, the final 0.8 mile of this passage is not ridable. To avoid this portion, leave the AZT at mile 18.0 where it crosses a creek and leaves a road, and stay on the road out to the highway. Turn left to pedal a short distance to the parking area at the "Ending Access Point" near Sunflower.

WATER

The only known reliable sources of water in this passage are near the endpoints. You may want to cache water somewhere along FR 422, which the AZT follows for 9 miles and is drivable by four-wheel-drives.

The Arizona Trail Association reports that Circle M Spring sometimes has water. The Boulder Mountain USGS map shows it about 0.4 mile off FR 422.

Sycamore Creek: This is the most reliable source of water on this passage (N33°51'49", W111°27'42").

MAPS

USGS Quadrangles: Four Peaks, Mine Mountain, Boulder Mountain
USFS: Tonto National Forest
Other: Arizona Public Lands Information Center, AZT Passage Topo Map 21—
    Pine Mountain/Boulder Creek

BEGINNING ACCESS POINT

Lone Pine Saddle: From the suspension bridge near Roosevelt Dam, drive north on AZ 188 for 11.0 miles and turn left (west) at mile marker 255 onto El Oso Road. At 4.4 miles from the highway, the road appears to fork. Take the sharp right turn and follow the road as it climbs. Continue another 4.2 miles to an intersection with FR 422, which is the path of the AZT to the north. The AZT arrives from the southeast (left) on FR 143. Drive 1.0 mile on FR 143 to an intersection, bear left onto FR 648, and continue almost another mile to Pigeon Spring Trailhead on the left (N33°42'38", W111°20'08").

Alternatively, to reach a larger, more developed parking area and trailhead at Lone Pine Saddle, continue 0.5 mile ahead. Parking here allows you to hike on a singletrack trail into the Four Peaks Wilderness and meet the AZT in about 2.0 miles.

ENDING ACCESS POINT

Sunflower: See "Beginning Access Point" for Passage 22.

TRAIL DESCRIPTION   From the Pigeon Spring Trailhead (5,620'), walk northwest on FR 648. After 1.0 mile, you'll reach an intersection with FR 143. Turn right (north) and descend another mile, where you'll take a left (northwest) fork onto FR 422 (5,685'; N33°43'51", W111°20'52"), following AZT stickers on carsonite posts. Stay on FR 422 for approximately 9.0 miles.

Bear right (east) at a fork (N33°45'33", W111°22'51") and make your way through a pretty ponderosa pine and oak forest. Campsites are plentiful along this part of the passage.

In 0.5 mile, the road reaches a high north-facing slope and bends to the left (west), offering great 180-degree views. Continue on the primary road, avoiding the occasional faint fork. The road begins a sharp, rocky descent and bottoms out in a saddle (5,140'; N33°48'46", W111°23'09"). Climb 0.1 mile northeast on the road (5,260'), descend another 0.1 mile, and look for a singletrack climbing away from the road on the left (west) side (5,220'; N33°48'53", W111°22'57"). After a brief climb, the trail begins a descent (4,760'; N33°48'51", W111°23'24"). Turn right (west) onto the trail in the drainage and continue to descend.

Four Peaks

Arizona Trail Association

Southbound Hikers: To avoid missing this turnoff, look for a clear trail through the dense vegetation on the left (north). If you do miss it, continuing up the Boulder Creek drainage will deposit you on FR 422, the route of the AZT. Once there, turn right (south) and continue.

The trail follows the valley through thick manzanita and other vegetation crowding the trail. Descend steadily until the AZT climbs gradually out of the drainage to the right, north (4,000'; N33°49'45", W111°24'24"). Undulations through side washes lead to a 0.2-mile climb. During the steep descent that ensues, the trail becomes a primitive, two-track road.

Follow this two-track road due west along the crest of a ridge for the next 1.3 miles. Then you will pass a junction with FR 1451 on your left, but continue straight west. In 1.0 mile, you reach the junction of a second two-track road (FR 1452), which crosses this east-west ridge perpendicularly from north to south. Turn left (south) to follow this two-track road, which drops steeply into the valley floor of Boulder Creek. Before reaching Boulder Creek, the road levels where a carsonite post marks the return of the AZT to singletrack. Watch on your right (west) for the brown post where the AZT leads directly west.

The trail begins a gradual but long westward climb to cross a saddle. Continue west as the trail gradually drops into the valley of Sycamore Creek and reaches the stream crossing. A cairn and carsonite post mark the trail access to the crossing on each side of the floodplain. Look directly west for a cairn that marks a short, steep ramp leading up and out of the streambed.

Water usually flows in Sycamore Creek at low levels during normal years (N33°51'49", W111°27'42").

After a brief climb south out of Sycamore Creek, the trail turns west again, passes into a shallow valley, and then begins a long, gradual ascent. Soon the trail levels out and begins following midslope contour as it parallels the valley formed by Sycamore Creek. There are many good campsites along Sycamore Creek below, but keep in mind that much of this area receives high use from car campers and ATV users.

Look carefully where the trail appears to die out as it meets a two-track ATV road. The trail has intentionally been left incomplete for about 20 yards on both sides of this road to hide the trail and prevent ATV use on the AZT. However, look directly across the road to the west for a faint footpath. The well-marked AZT continues past some thick brush, just out of view from the ATV road.

Follow the trail to a large AZT trailhead sign. At this point, the AZT continues west to Passage 22, or look to your right for a wire gate leading to the Sunflower trail access.

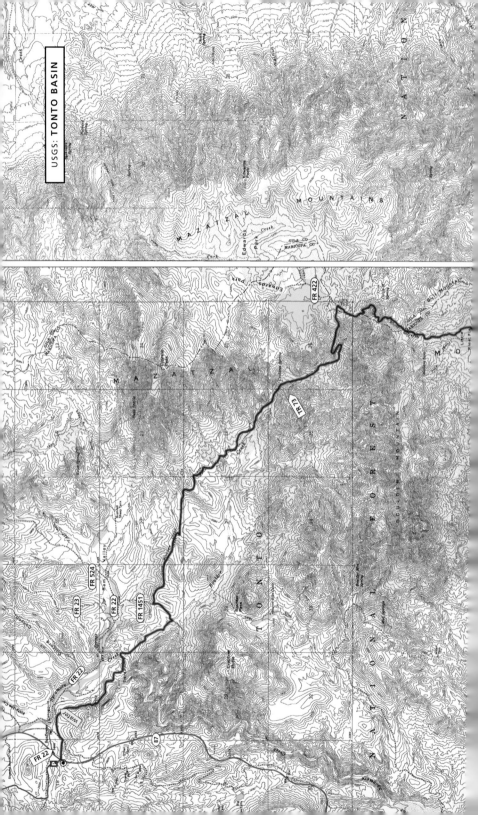

USGS: TONTO BASIN

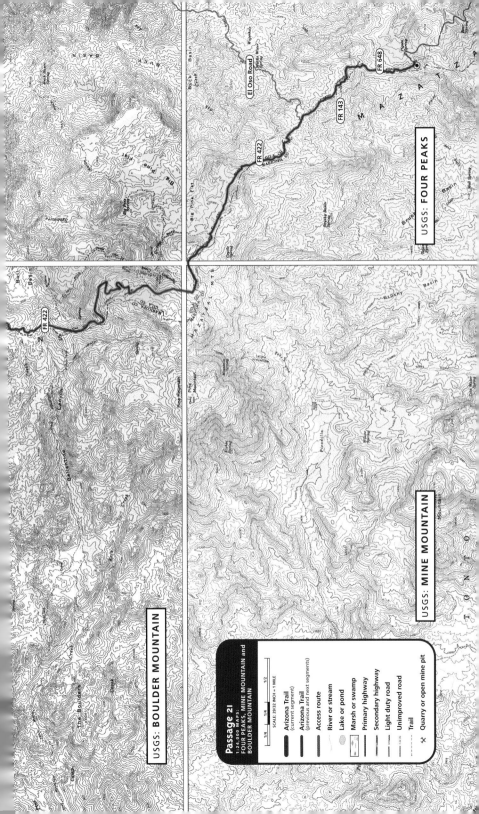

USGS: BOULDER MOUNTAIN

USGS: FOUR PEAKS

USGS: MINE MOUNTAIN

FR 422

FR 422

El Oso Road

FR 143

FR 648

Passage 21
1:24,000 Maps.
FOUR PEAKS, MINE MOUNTAIN and
BOULDER MOUNTAIN

SCALE 2932 INCH = 1 MILE

1/4   1/4   1/2

Arizona Trail
(current segment)

Arizona Trail
(previous and next segments)

Access route

River or stream

Lake or pond

Marsh or swamp

Primary highway

Secondary highway

Light duty road

Unimproved road

Trail

Quarry or open mine pit

Passage 22
Saddle Mountain: Sunflower to Mount Peeley

Near Mount Peeley

TOTAL DISTANCE	16.0 miles
QUALITY HIKING DISTANCE	15.0 miles
DIFFICULTY	Strenuous
TOTAL ELEVATION GAIN	3,958 feet
TOTAL DESCENT	1,642 feet
FROM MEXICO	371.5 miles
TO UTAH	400.4 miles
LAND MANAGERS	Tonto National Forest (Mesa Ranger District)
RECOMMENDED MONTHS	March through November. The summer months will be uncomfortably hot over the first 9.0 miles of the passage, but the second half is much cooler. Snow is likely in the higher elevations in winter.

INTRODUCTION This inconspicuous passage traverses some of the most beautiful places on the entire AZT and offers a stunning variety of landscapes over a relatively short distance. The quiet stream valley 5 miles from Sunflower is sublime, and the canyon soon rivals some of the Grand Canyon's tributaries. Outdoor enthusiasts must be overlooking this rugged pocket of the state, for you're not likely to see many people here and portions of the trail are overgrown.

This passage begins a long stint (Passages 22–25) in the Mazatzal Wilderness, a varied land marked by serpentine canyons and rocky peaks in this passage, a perennial river farther ahead, and surreal high desert in the north. Bring protective clothing (long-sleeves and long pants) and keep it accessible, as Arizona's forbidding flora often reaches over the trail.

Water is not guaranteed, although there are many sources that seem reliable in early spring. You may want to cache water at various access points. Also, note that many of the signs along this passage bear the AZT brand on their back side, where you can't see the markings.

Note: The 2004 Willow Fire severely burned many areas in the Mazatzal Mountains, including some areas in this passage.

MOUNTAIN BIKE NOTES

 Most of this passage is in the Mazatzal Wilderness, where bikes are prohibited. Thru-bikers should follow AZ 87.

WATER

 Unnamed spring: N33°52'59", W111°29'00"

 Unnamed stock pond: N33°53'52", W111°29'33"

 Unnamed stream in gorgeous valley: N33°54'36", W111°29'37"

MAPS

USGS Quadrangles: Boulder Mountain, Reno Pass, Lion Mountain, Mazatzal Peak
USFS: Tonto National Forest (North Half)
Other: Arizona Public Lands Information Center, AZT Passage Topo Map 22—
    Saddle Mountain

BEGINNING ACCESS POINT

 Sunflower: From Phoenix, take AZ 87 north to FR 22 (Bushnell Tanks Rd.). Turn right (east) and follow FR 22 for 0.5 mile. Turn right onto a two-track road just before you reach the first cattleguard. Follow the two-track road about 300 yards to a grove of large sycamore trees. Look for the AZT marker at the southwest corner of this grove. A short spur access trail crosses Sycamore Creek and leads to the AZT in about 200 yards. A large AZT sign marks the connection with the AZT. Follow the trail west of the sign through a tunnel under AZ 87 to hike north on the Sunflower Trail. Southbound hikers follow the trail east of the sign to travel the Boulder Creek Trail.

ALTERNATE ACCESS POINT

Mormon Grove Trailhead: Drive 6.8 miles north of Sunflower on AZ 87 to mile marker 225. (This is approximately 10 miles south of the AZ 87–AZ 188 intersection.) Turn left (west) onto FR 201, which is only marked by a sign once you're off the highway. Make an immediate left onto FR 25. After 2.7 miles, turn left, staying on FR 25 toward Mormon Grove Trailhead. Continue 2.0 miles to a parking area at a corral and a couple of wilderness signs (N33°56'21", W111°30'06"). Walk up the road 0.5 mile to reach the AZT at a sign for Saddle Mountain Trail (#91) (N33°56'23", W111°30'29"). Turn right to head northbound on the AZT and pick up the trail description at the "T" intersection with the Saddle Mountain Trail (#91).

ENDING ACCESS POINT

Mount Peeley: See "Beginning Access Point" for Passage 23.

TRAIL DESCRIPTION   From the sycamore grove described in the "Beginning Access Point" section of this passage, follow the access trail about 0.25 mile to the AZT trailhead sign. Turn right (west) onto the AZT, where a carsonite post marks the trail about 30 yards away. The trail soon crosses an abandoned road; look for cairns on the opposite side and continue west. At this point, a tunnel (3,445'; N33°51'45", W111°28'18") below AZ 87, 100 yards south of mile marker 218, becomes visible. Follow the trail through the tunnel and pass through a wire gate on the west side of the highway. Specifically designed for the AZT, this tunnel is tall and wide enough to accommodate stock.

Continue west from the tunnel along the fenceline for about 50 yards to where a cairn marks a right-hand (north) turn (N33°51'45", W111°28'26"). A carsonite post marks a singletrack trail that soon climbs over a small ridge to the north. The trail veers left (northwest) to drop into a small wash. Pass through a gate in 0.1 mile and follow cairns west along a somewhat fainter trail. Stay off the dirt road on your right and follow Trail #344, the faint remnant of a two-track road. Shortly, pass through a gate to the south side of a fence. You'll soon be on a very clear singletrack.

Crest a small hill (3,640'; N33°52'13", W111°28'39") and start down the other side. Next, cross a wash. Cattle trails create multiple forks here, but large cairns will keep you on the right path. In 0.4 mile, pass through a gate in a fence. Look due north (a little left as you come through the gate) for carsonite posts marking a clear, two-track road.

The AZT follows a left (west) fork in the road (3,555'; N33°52'59", W111°29'00"). The right fork leads about 80 yards to a spring that seems to be reliable. (To find the spring, make a 90-degree turn to the right when you reach a fence.)

Take the right (north) fork (3,750'; N33°53'33", W111°29'52") and stay on Trail #344. Follow the very faint singletrack that breaks off to the left (north) of the road, as marker posts indicate.

WILDERNESS ALERT

The **Mazatzal Wilderness** was designated in 1964 to be "an area where the earth and its community of life are untrammeled by man, where man himself is a visitor who does not remain." It protects more than 252,000 acres of land, including its crown jewel, 7,903-foot Mazatzal Peak. Please remember and follow these rules governing wilderness areas:

• Camp out of sight, at least 200 feet from lakes and streams, on dry, durable surfaces.
• Use a stove instead of building a fire; use existing fire rings if you must have a fire.
• Keep water sources clean by washing at least 200 feet from them.
• Bury human waste 6 inches deep and 200 feet from lakes and streams. Pack out toilet paper.
• Hobble or picket livestock at least 200 feet from lakes and streams, and use only treated, weed-free feed and grain.
• All dogs must be on a leash.
• No mountain bikes.
• Pack out all trash; don't attempt to burn it.

 In 0.1 mile, you'll pass through a gate and pass a stock pond (N33°53'52", W111°29'33").

Cairns guide you north-northwest. Cross under power lines and head across a grassy field to the north-northeast. At the northern edge of the grassy field, reach a road (FR 393, not marked). Walk straight across the road to the northeast. Look for an AZT sign between a tall pine on the right and a healthy juniper on the left. In the scrub oak straight ahead, you can pick up the trail at some cairns. The trail immediately bends left (west) and follows cairns through more fields.

The trail crosses a streambed (N33°54'36", W111°29'37") in a charming valley under idyllic white cliffs. This stream had water in June 2000, but is marked as intermittent on the map.

At a trail intersection (N33°54'44", W111°29'31"), take the left fork to wind north-northwest, following Little Saddle Mountain Trail (#244). Pass through a gate and then turn to the right (north-northwest) to climb along a canyon that leads toward the stunning Mazatzal Wilderness. In less than a mile, (4,275'), the trail turns left (west) into a side canyon. Long pants and a long-sleeved shirt are useful here. Although no signs indicate it, you will enter the Mazatzal Wilderness.

After a good climb to the ridge above the canyon (4,840'), the trail rolls to a "T" intersection (5,040'; N33°56'26", W111°30'27") with the Saddle Mountain Trail (#91). Turn left to stay on the AZT. A right turn leads down 0.5 mile to the Mormon Grove Trailhead (see "Alternate Access Point" above).

Now the AZT follows an old roadbed that has been turned into a very clear singletrack. The trail passes through a flat saddle called Potato Patch (5,445'). Rising to the northwest is Saddle Mountain at 6,535 feet. At the intersection with the trail to Story Mine (5,260'; N33°57'48", W111°30'29"), turn left (north-northeast) onto the singletrack Sheep Creek Trail (#88). The trail is frequently overgrown for the next several miles, so you may want to wear protective clothing.

The AZT soon begins a descent into McFarland Canyon and reaches the bottom at an intersection with Thicket Spring Trail (#95), a great spot to take a break.

 It's a bit confusing here, but turn right (east) and continue downcanyon through prolific stands of ponderosa and oak trees.

There is sometimes good water in this canyon. Pass a wilderness sign and continue about 20 yards. Follow cairns across the bottom of the drainage, then take an overgrown trail that descends along the left side of the drainage for about 50 yards, and follow a clear singletrack that climbs out of the drainage to the northeast.

The trail then reaches a low saddle, descends into the next drainage, and climbs to the right (east-northeast) above yet another side drainage on a rugged trail. At an intersection with the West Fork Trail (#260) on the right, the AZT continues straight (northeast) on the Thicket Spring Trail (#95).

This is not much of a trail—just stay in the bottom of the drainage for a short distance as the trail reaches a small saddle, leaves the drainage bed, and climbs steeply along a ridge to the north. Stay on the spine of the ridge if the trail becomes obscure. Bypass the overgrown ridgetop on its left (west) side (5,670'; N33°58'59", W111°29'41"). The trail rambles northeast, dipping in and out of drainages to bypass majestic, rocky Mount Peeley.

Finally, the trail reaches an intersection with the Cornucopia Trail (#86). To stay on the AZT, follow the sign toward Peeley Trailhead and Mazatzal Divide Trail (#23) by taking the left fork on the other side of the drainage. Many of the signs are marked with the AZT brand on the back, where you can't see them.

At a wide-open, rocky area, turn left and follow a clear swath through the vegetation to the west. In about 50 yards the trail switchbacks right to angle northeast up the steep slopes of Mount Peeley. The trail levels in 0.5 mile and reaches an intersection (5,760'; N34°00'09", W111°28'35") with the Mazatzal Divide Trail (#23). This is the end of Passage 22. To continue on the AZT, climb a sharp switchback to the left (southwest). To reach the parking area at the Mount Peeley Trailhead, continue straight ahead on the Cornucopia Trail.

Opposite: Postburn growth near the Vineyard Trailhead
Photo by Tom Jones

trail access

Saddle Mtn. Trail #91

FR 201

FR 25

87

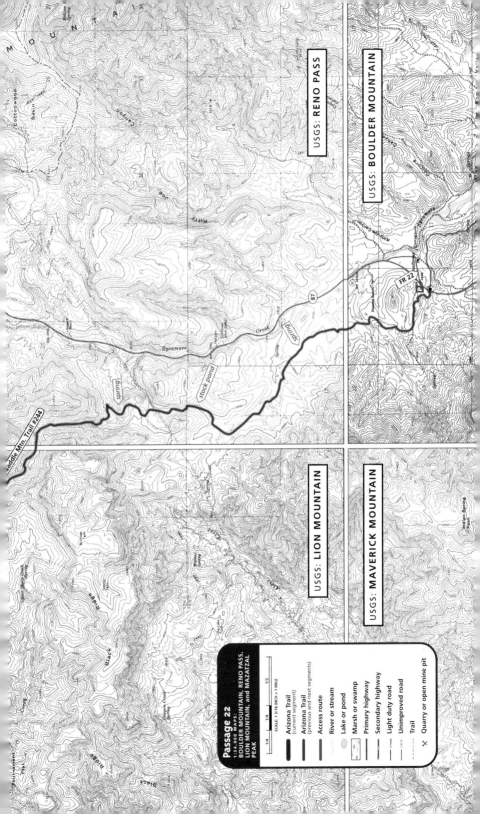

USGS: RENO PASS

USGS: BOULDER MOUNTAIN

USGS: LION MOUNTAIN

USGS: MAVERICK MOUNTAIN

Passage 22
1:24,000 MAPS:
BOULDER MOUNTAIN, RENO PASS,
LION MOUNTAIN, and MAZATZAL
PEAK

SCALE 1 3/16 INCH = 1 MILE

1/4   1/4   1/2

Arizona Trail
(current segment)

Arizona Trail
(previous and next segments)

Access route

River or stream

Lake or pond

Marsh or swamp

Primary highway

Secondary highway

Light duty road

Unimproved road

Trail

×   Quarry or open mine pit

FR 22

87

Saddle Mtn. Trail #244

spring

stock pond

Sycamore   Creek

Spring   Creek

Passage 23
Mazatzal Divide: Mount Peeley to The Park (Junction of Trails 23 and 24)

Looking north at sunset along Trail #23 south of Mazatzal Peak

TOTAL DISTANCE	22.0 miles
QUALITY HIKING DISTANCE	22.0 miles
DIFFICULTY	Strenuous
TOTAL ELEVATION GAIN	3,729 feet
TOTAL DESCENT	3,595 feet
FROM MEXICO	387.5 miles
TO UTAH	384.4 miles
LAND MANAGERS	Tonto National Forest (Payson Ranger District)
RECOMMENDED MONTHS	March through November. Snow may last well into spring and start falling in early autumn. Check current conditions before setting out.

INTRODUCTION Before the 2004 Willow Fire, this passage may have been the single most beautiful segment of the AZT. It winds near the top of the Mazatzal Mountains, including Mazatzal Peak, whose impressive west face towers 1,700' above the trail. The cool, thin air encourages the growth of some beautiful trees, especially stands of ponderosa pines that are hundreds of years old. Farther north in the passage, red-rock canyons reflect sunset colors that no human artist could re-create.

This is the middle of the AZT's longest sojourn in a designated wilderness area, and you can feel it. Humans are infrequent visitors to these lonely ridges, and the land is much the same as it was hundreds of years ago when it was the domain of the Yavapai and Apaches. Oddly, the name Mazatzal, meaning "land of deer," is traced to the Aztec language, even though the Aztecs never lived this far north.

Late spring is an ideal time to hike here, although summer temperatures are generally not unbearable. Snow is likely in the winter, making most of the Mazatzal Mountains impassable. Campsites are rare because of the precipitous terrain, but there are some nice spots at miles 6.7, 9.4, 19.4, and 22.0. Keep protective clothing handy around mile 12.0 because of thick brush.

Note: The 2004 Willow Fire severely ravaged this passage, so the area might be restricted. Please contact the Arizona Trail Association or Tonto National Forest for updates.

MOUNTAIN BIKE NOTES

This passage lies entirely within the Mazatzal Wilderness, where bikes are prohibited.

WATER

There are many springs and seeps marked on the maps near the trail, and signs indicate the turnoffs to most of them. However, I have not verified their reliability, with the exception of Horse Camp Seep and Hopi Spring, which have had water on several visits in the spring.

 Hopi Spring: N34°07'13", W111°29'13"

MAPS

USGS Quadrangles: Mazatzal Peak, North Peak
USFS: Tonto National Forest (North Half)
Other: Arizona Public Lands Information Center, AZT Passage Topo Map 23—
    Mazatzal Divide

BEGINNING ACCESS POINT

Mount Peeley: Drive 6.8 miles north of Sunflower on AZ 87 to mile marker 225 and turn left (west) onto FR 201, which is only marked by a sign once you're off the highway. Drive 8.5 miles from the highway to the trailhead, where there is a moderate-sized parking area (N34°00'15", W111°28'12"). The sign here says

Cornucopia Trail (#86) and indicates a 0.5 mile walk to the Mazatzal Divide Trail, which the AZT follows.

ENDING ACCESS POINT

The Park (Junction of Trails 23 and 24), via Mineral Creek Trailhead: See "Beginning Access Point" for Passage 24.

TRAIL DESCRIPTION From the parking area, walk 0.5 mile up the Cornucopia Trail (#86) to reach the AZT at an intersection with the Mazatzal Divide Trail (N34°00'09", W111°28'35"). To walk southbound on the AZT, toward Sunflower, stay on Trail #86 as it turns left. To follow this trail description toward The Park and the East Verde River, turn right (southwest) and start up the Mazatzal Divide Trail (#23) toward Mount Peeley.

The switchbacks seem endless as the trail climbs along the east side of Mount Peeley, but the AZT levels after 1.5 miles (6,400') as it bends west to pass under the north slopes of the mountain. You'll soon enter the Mazatzal Wilderness (6,490'). The views from here are incredible.

> **WILDERNESS ALERT**
>
> Please review the regulations governing travel in the **Mazatzal Wilderness** on p. 183.

After 5.0 miles, the trail skirts very deep canyons across steep slopes. A saddle offers a rare place to camp, near the higher reaches of this long ridge (6,965'; N34°01'50", W111°29'46"). This elevated perch provides awesome views to the west. There is no water.

The trail descends via sharp switchbacks, and Mazatzal Peak's intimidating west face dominates the immediate horizon. A second broad saddle adorned with peaceful stands of ponderosa pines provides another nice place to camp (6,580'; N34°02'26", W111°28'35").

In the next 0.1 mile, signs indicate two springs lying a short distance off the trail: Bear Spring, 0.25 mile from the AZT to the south (right); and Fisher Spring, 0.5 mile off the trail to the northwest (left). Their reliability has not been confirmed.

After 10.5 miles from the Mount Peeley parking lot, the trail switchbacks through a beautiful forest of old-growth ponderosa pine, alligator juniper, and oak trees. The AZT reaches a saddle 0.5 mile farther (6,660') and crosses to the east side of the Mazatzal Divide.

From the saddle, a singletrack trail trends north-northeast over gentle terrain. At an intersection (6,540') with the Y Bar Trail (#44), turn left (north) to stay on the Mazatzal Divide Trail (#23). After passing under the steep cliffs of Mazatzal Peak, the trail climbs through thick manzanita, making protective clothing helpful.

Signs indicate turnoffs to several springs and seeps along the next 8 miles of the AZT. Horse Camp Seep and Hopi Spring have had water on several occasions in the spring. At each of these junctions, clear signs indicate the direction of the AZT as it continues north along the Mazatzal Divide Trail, through some of the most beautiful country you'll ever see. Avoid turnoffs for the Brody Seep Trail, the Barnhardt Trail, Chilson Spring, and the Sandy Saddle Trail (#231).

 Note that the 1972 Mazatzal Peak USGS map is inaccurate from mile 13.9 to 16.6. Follow the AZT and Mazatzal Divide Trail signs.

 You'll pass the turnoff to Horse Camp Seep on the left. This has been a reliable source of water, but the area is showing wear and tear as a popular campsite.

For a somewhat nicer watering hole and campsites, continue another mile to Hopi Spring (6,430'; N34°07'13", W111°29'13"). This is also the turnoff to the Rock Creek Trail (#42). Avoid this trail and continue north along the Mazatzal Divide Trail.

A mile past Hopi Spring, cairns guide you through a rocky section, and soon a high, rocky point offers expansive views of the valleys to the west and the low country by the East Verde River to the north-northwest. On a clear spring day, you can see snowcapped Mount Humphreys about 75 miles to the north. From this point, turn right (northeast), walk about 50 yards, and follow a switchback that descends to the left (south) underneath the rocky escarpment. Another switchback soon points you back to the north.

A long, gradual descent leads to a "T" intersection (5,870'; N34°08'50", W111°30'00") with the Willow Spring Trail (#223). Turn right (north-northeast), as the signs indicate. There's a lovely campsite about 100 yards northeast of this "T" intersection.

In 0.1 mile, watch for cairns marking the trail's crossing of a rocky streambed. Then, in the natural open area called The Park (5,925'; N34°09'00", W111°29'57"), the North Peak Trail (#24) breaks off to the right. Thru-hikers should continue straight ahead (north) on the AZT. Passage hikers with vehicles parked at the Mineral Creek Trailhead should turn right on the North Peak Trail and descend 5.0 miles to the trailhead.

USGS: NORTH PEAK

USGS: MAZATZAL PEAK

USGS: CYPRESS BUTTE

USGS: TABLE MOUNTAIN

trail access

water

water

follow trail signs

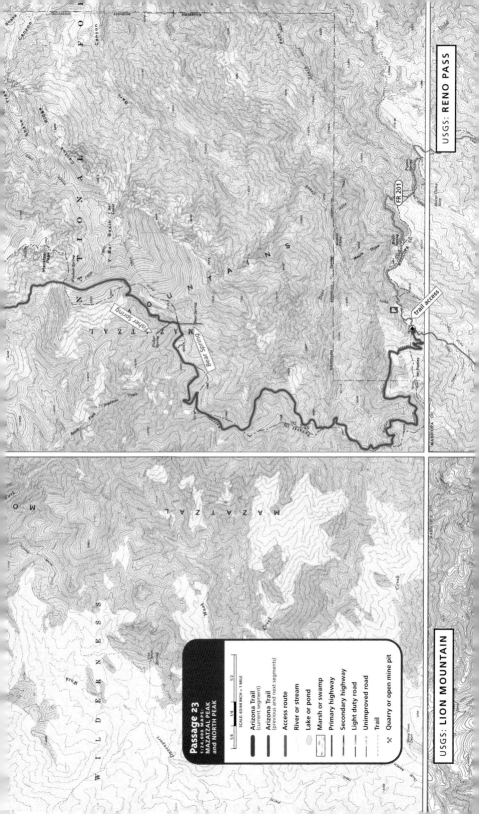

FR 201

trail access

FISHER TRAIL

Bear Spring

MAZATZAL TRAIL

MOUNTAINS

NATIONAL

WILDERNESS

MAZATZAL

MARICOPA CO.

Passage 23
1:24,000 MAPS:
MAZATZAL PEAK
and NORTH PEAK

SCALE: 63/64 INCH = 1 MILE

1/4   1/4   1/2

Arizona Trail
(current segment)

Arizona Trail
(previous and next segments)

Access route

River or stream

Lake or pond

Marsh or swamp

Primary highway

Secondary highway

Light duty road

Unimproved road

Trail

Quarry or open mine pit

Passage 24
Red Hills: The Park (Junction of Trails 23 and 24) to East Verde River

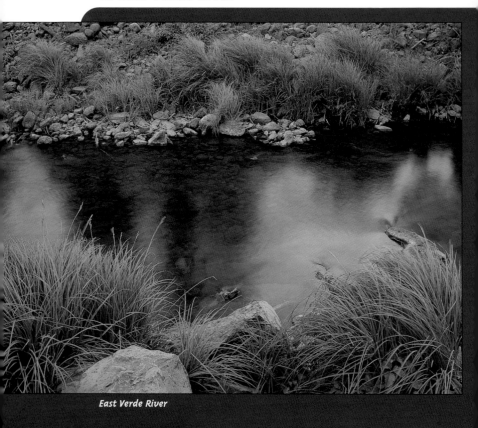

East Verde River

TOTAL DISTANCE	14.3 miles
QUALITY HIKING DISTANCE	14.3 miles
DIFFICULTY	Moderate
TOTAL ELEVATION GAIN	2,265 feet
TOTAL DESCENT	4,863 feet
FROM MEXICO	409.5 miles
TO UTAH	362.4 miles
LAND MANAGERS	Tonto National Forest (Payson Ranger District)
RECOMMENDED MONTHS	March through November. The summer months may be uncomfortably hot in the lower elevations near the end of this passage. Snow is likely in the higher reaches during winter.

INTRODUCTION   The AZT's longest stretch entirely within designated wilderness areas continues as the trail bends even deeper into this pristine, remote landscape. It's 5.0 miles from the nearest parking area to the beginning of this passage and 4.0 miles to the nearest parking at the end.

Thru-hikers will lose much of the elevation they gained over the last few passages as the trail drops into the valley of the East Verde River. The elevation ranges from 6,300' on Knob Mountain to 3,380' at the passage's end near the river.

This elevation change offers the opportunity to see a variety of Arizona's life zones, from majestic stands of ponderosa pines to a lush riparian zone whose denizens include turtles and rare birds. A harmless Arizona whip snake had me jumping about 3 feet in the air here. The flora is so thick in places that it overgrows the trail, so you'll want to have a long-sleeved shirt and long pants handy.

Note: A huge forest fire swept through much of this area in June and July 2004. As of this printing, damage to the AZT was extensive.

MOUNTAIN BIKE NOTES

Bikes are not allowed on this passage, which lies entirely within the Mazatzal Wilderness.

WATER

Red Hills Trail: Springtime pools are likely in a wet year.

Brush Spring: Hikers have found water here on several occasions, but it is usually dry (N34°11'11", W111°32'28").

East Verde River: Reached at the beginning of Passage 25, this is a perennial source of water.

MAPS

USGS Quadrangles: North Peak, Cypress Butte
USFS: Tonto National Forest (North Half)
Other: Arizona Public Lands Information Center, AZT Passage Topo Map 24—
Red Hills

BEGINNING ACCESS POINT

The Park (Junction of Trails 23 and 24), via Mineral Creek Trailhead: About 9.0 miles south of Payson on AZ 87, turn right (west) onto FR 414. Continue 9.0 miles to the Mineral Creek Trailhead on the left (N34°10'39", W111°26'50"). From here, walk 5.0 miles on the North Peak Trail (#24), with 2,500 feet of elevation gain, to reach the AZT (N34°09'00", W111°29'57") as it follows the Mazatzal Divide Trail (#23).

ENDING ACCESS POINT

East Verde River, via Doll Baby Trailhead: See "Beginning Access Point" for Passage 25.

TRAIL DESCRIPTION If you're coming up the North Peak Trail (#24) from the Mineral Creek Trailhead, turn right (north) onto the Mazatzal Divide Trail (#23), the route of the AZT (5,925'). You'll soon bend northwest and climb to 6,170', then descend to cross two tributary canyons of City Creek at 6,000' before turning back to the northeast and climbing again.

From a high point on indistinct Knob Mountain (6,300'; N34°10'07", W111°30'30"), you can look northeast for a clear view of the Mogollon Rim, the geographical dividing line between Arizona's lower-elevation southern half and cooler, higher-elevation north. Thru-hikers will be climbing onto the rim within a few days.

WILDERNESS ALERT

Please review the regulations governing travel in the **Mazatzal Wilderness** on p. 183.

You'll reach an important trail intersection (6,080'; 34°10'43", 111°30'14"), at which the Mazatzal Divide Trail makes a hard right turn to head east. (Staying on the Mazatzal Divide Trail leads you to the City Creek Trailhead on the East Verde River.) The AZT goes straight (north) on one trail that bears three names: Red Hills, Brush, and Midnight.

The Park in the Mazatzal Wilderness

Note that the 1967 Cypress Butte USGS map does not show the next 2.7 miles of the AZT.

After a few quick switchbacks, the trail turns left at a cairn-marked junction, descends to the west along a small drainage, and passes through an idyllic ponderosa pine forest. In the springtime, water is often present through here. In a confluence of drainages (5,610'; N34°10'48", W111°31'07"), follow large cairns as the trail turns left and climbs to the southwest.

This occasionally steep climb levels just before a trail intersection (6,085'; N34°10'20", W111°32'03"). Turn right (northwest) onto the Brush Trail.

As the trail descends to the west and northwest, you'll find more nice views of the East Verde River Valley. The trail drops sharply on a rocky, red path. Thick plants occasionally obscure the trail, but cairns show the way. Pull out the long pants here to fend off the spiny branches.

The trail reaches a sign (5,200'; N34°11'11", W111°32'28") for the usually dry Brush Spring, which is about 50 yards to the northwest. There is a slightly overused place to camp here, the last site for 5 miles.

From this sign, the trail bends right (east) to go upstream along an adjoining drainage. In 0.1 mile, the AZT climbs northwest out of the drainage and follows switchbacks along a swath cut through thick vegetation to reach the top of a steep hill. A brief descent leads through heavy brush—protective clothing will help you fight the thick vegetation.

The trail crosses a fence in a saddle (5,300'; N34°11'46", W111°32'27") and climbs northwest 0.1 mile to an important but obscure trail junction. Make a sharp left (southwest) and climb a bit more. You'll top out in a saddle (5,455') before beginning a steep descent, from which you can see the East Verde River in the valley bottom.

The AZT starts climbing again in less than a mile and reaches the remnant of an old road that's in much better shape than the last few miles of trail. Pass through a gated fence, turn right, and descend to the northeast.

Southbound Hikers: If you are heading toward the beginning of this passage, follow a sign at this intersection toward Brush Spring. Make a left turn through the gate and onto the overgrown path.

From the road headed northeast, you'll soon see the buildings of LF Ranch, near this passage's end, in the valley below. The Mogollon Rim defines the horizon far behind the ranch. The trail descends all the way to a "T" intersection (3,425'), turns right, and starts looking more like a trail again. Ramble on gentler terrain to the east, occasionally following cairns and avoiding cow trails. You'll reach a road that indicates the end of this passage (3,380'; N34°13'26", W111°30'56"). AZT signs mark the northeast side of the road.

To exit the wilderness and reach the parking area at Doll Baby Trailhead, turn right (south) on the road and continue 4.0 miles. Thru-hikers should turn left (northeast) on this road, walk 70 yards, and look for a sign on the right for the next passage of the AZT. The East Verde River awaits you and your water bottles.

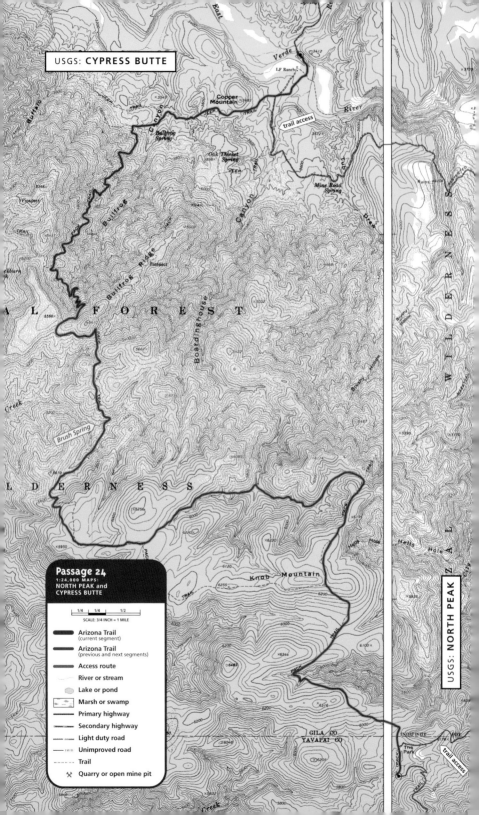

USGS: **CYPRESS BUTTE**

Copper Mountain

Bullfrog Spring

Oak Thicket Spring

Mine Road Spring

trail access

LF Ranch

Verde

River

Brushy Canyon

Prospect

Bullfrog Ridge

Boardinghouse Canyon

FOREST

WILDERNESS

Brush Spring

Creek

Knob Mountain

Hells Hole

Hells Hole

GILA CO
YAVAPAI CO

trail access

Passage 24
1:24,000 MAPS:
NORTH PEAK and
CYPRESS BUTTE

| 1/4 | 1/4 | 1/2 |

SCALE: 3/4 INCH = 1 MILE

━━━ **Arizona Trail**
(current segment)

━━━ **Arizona Trail**
(previous and next segments)

━━━ **Access route**

⌇⌇⌇ **River or stream**

◯ **Lake or pond**

▬ **Marsh or swamp**

━━━ **Primary highway**

━━━ **Secondary highway**

─ ─ ─ **Light duty road**

─ ⋅ ─ **Unimproved road**

─ ─ ─ **Trail**

✕ **Quarry or open mine pit**

USGS: **NORTH PEAK**

Passage 25
Whiterock Mesa: East Verde River to Twin Buttes (FR 194)

Arizona Trail Association

Looking toward Hardscrabble Mesa

INTRODUCTION   This passage makes a consistent, gradual climb out of the East Verde River Valley through high desert terrain characterized by juniper and piñon pine. The climb is constant—you will gain 2,661 feet while losing only 87 feet over the next 11.4 miles. Keep an eye out for the animals that inhabit this ecosystem—my father and I saw javelina and wild turkeys when we did this stretch.

Because the climb away from the East Verde River and the mesa top are so rocky, it is wise to camp near the river or somewhere prior to the turnoff to Polk Spring. There is a nice meadow southeast of the spring. There's also a nice spot in a drainage between

TOTAL DISTANCE	Approximately 11.4 miles
QUALITY HIKING DISTANCE	Approximately 11.4 miles
DIFFICULTY	Easy
TOTAL ELEVATION GAIN	2,661 feet
TOTAL DESCENT	87 feet
FROM MEXICO	423.8 miles
TO UTAH	348.1 miles
LAND MANAGERS	Tonto National Forest (Payson Ranger District)
RECOMMENDED MONTHS	September to April. You may encounter snow in winter, and the summer heat is too much for most hikers.

Whiterock Mesa and Saddle Ridge. From there, the terrain is incredibly rocky again until near the end of the passage.

Instead of stopping at the end of this passage, consider hiking all the way to the Pine Trailhead to get the complete experience of this area. The tall pines and lush wetlands as you approach Pine in Passage 26 provide a nice balance to the drier country on this passage.

MOUNTAIN BIKE NOTES

Bikes are not permitted on this passage because it lies almost entirely within the Mazatzal Wilderness.

WATER

East Verde River: This is a perennial river (N34°13'45", W111°30'45").

Polk Spring: If you choose to bypass the water in the East Verde River, you might find fresher water here (N34°14'10", W111°30'34").

Red Saddle Tank: This is usually dry (N34°15'26", W111°31'05").

Whiterock Spring: N34°16'21", W111°30'48"

Saddle Ridge Pasture Tank: N34°21'05", W111°33'09" (5,765')

MAPS

USGS Quadrangles: Cypress Butte, Cane Springs Mountain
USFS: Tonto National Forest (North Half)

East Verde River, via Doll Baby Trailhead: In the town of Payson, drive west 2.0 miles on Main Street, which turns into Country Club Drive. At the end of Country Club Drive, continue on the dirt FR 406. Drive 9.3 miles, following signs to stay on the bumpy but accessible FR 406, to a parking area right next to the East Verde River, at Doll Baby Trailhead (N34°12'46", W111°29'02"). You may camp here. Leave your car and enter the Mazatzal Wilderness by walking southwest along an old jeep road. It is 4.0 miles from here to the AZT. The jeep road winds into the hills, climbing almost 600 feet before bending north to give up all of that elevation as it returns to the river valley. When the road has leveled in the valley, the AZT comes in as a faint singletrack trail from the west (N34°13'26", W111°30'56").

Twin Buttes (FR 194): See "Beginning Access Point" for Passage 26.

From the junction of the jeep road coming from Doll Baby Trailhead and the AZT singletrack (3,380'; N34°13'26", W111°30'56"), follow the road northeast 70 yards to a sign on the right with an AZT marker. This sign also indicates Polk Spring and Whiterock Spring. Leave the road here and follow a singletrack east on an old roadbed.

Use cairns to follow the old roadbed through a bend to the left (northeast) and pass through a gate. In another 0.2 mile, avoid a singletrack trail cutting off toward the ranch to the left (northwest), continue about 10 yards to a rocky streambed on the left (due north), and turn to follow it.

> **WILDERNESS ALERT**
>
> Please review the regulations governing travel in the **Mazatzal Wilderness** on p.183.

If you miss this turn and continue straight ahead, you will run into the river within about 100 yards, and you will know you have gone too far.

Immediately after you cross through another drainage, the trail bends left (northwest) to parallel the river, which is 40 yards to the right.

In less than 0.25 mile, several large cairns lead out of the right side of the drainage and over to the bank of the East Verde River (3,275'; N34°13'45", W111°30'45"). As you pass by a painted wooden sign for the ranch (which may be missing), look across the river for a trail climbing the opposite bank, just downstream from a solid-rock streambed where spring water flows into the river. The depth of the water here varies depending on the season and recent weather. Wade across at your own risk.

Climb the bank on the north side of the river, pass through a fence, and follow the trail as it climbs to the north-northeast.

Soon you'll find a sign for Polk Spring (N34°14'10", W111°30'34"). It's about 30 yards to the spring, which is behind a gigantic tree. (The 1967 Cypress Butte USGS map does not name Polk Spring.) If you walk a couple hundred yards southeast from here, you will find an open meadow that provides good camping, the last for at least 3 miles. Just make sure to camp well away from the water.

From the sign for the spring, follow a singletrack trail to the left (northwest). This faint trail soon becomes much clearer; if you get confused, head for the high, rocky butte to the northwest. A very rocky road leads to and ascends Polles Mesa.

The grade steepens considerably as the AZT climbs through loose volcanic rock, then flattens on Polles Mesa (4,090'). The trail virtually disappears here; bear north-northeast and look for the occasional cairn. They are there—often just below the high vegetation. The ground is so rocky that it would be difficult to find a place to camp.

The trail passes by the west side of Red Saddle Tank (4,220'; N34°15'26", W111°31'05"), which is usually dry.

Cairns mark the trail as you continue north. In 1.0 mile, pass through a gate, then take a 90-degree turn to the right (east) in 0.1 mile at the base of Whiterock Mesa.

The javelina is the only wild piglike animal native to the U.S. —Photo by Tom Jones

At Whiterock Spring, you'll reach a sign. Whiterock Spring is misplaced on the 1967 Cane Springs Mountain USGS map (4,400'; N34°16'21", W111°30'48"). From here, the AZT makes a sharp turn to the left (northwest) for the brief, steep climb onto Whiterock Mesa (4,565').

You'll see that Whiterock Mesa is aptly named as you make your way along the obscure trail—there is ample raw material here for cairns! As you slowly gain elevation, a few pine trees start to make an appearance. Climb along the mesa to where the trail descends briefly to a drainage (usually dry) between Whiterock Mesa and Saddle Ridge. There is a nice place to camp here.

The climbing resumes as you make your way up Saddle Ridge, a spit of land above Rock Creek on the east and The Gorge on the west. This terrain is so rocky that it makes the first half of the passage look like a carefully manicured golf course.

After 47 nonstop miles in the Mazatzal Wilderness, the AZT leaves this wilderness area (5,562'; N34°20'03", W111°32'22"). Cairns lead to a crossing of two fences. From there, enter Saddle Ridge Pasture, a broad expanse sparsely covered with small trees.

The trail passes just to the right (east) of Saddle Ridge Pasture Tank (5,765'; N34°21'05", W111°33'09").

Finally, the trail reaches FR 194 at a "T" intersection. This is the end of Passage 25 (5,840'; N34°21'36", W111°33'26"). Thru-hikers will turn right (east) and walk along FR 194.

Opposite: *Sunset near Hardscrabble Mesa*
Photo courtesy of the Arizona Trail Association

USGS: CANE SPRINGS MOUNTAIN

FR 194

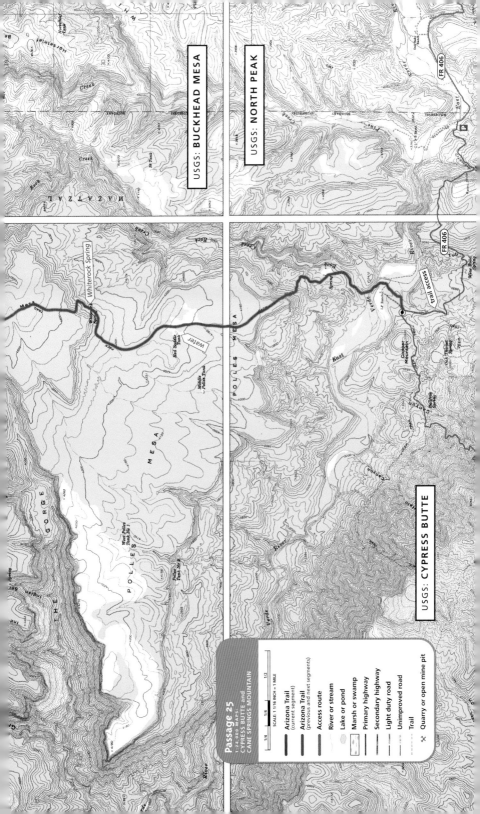

USGS: BUCKHEAD MESA

USGS: NORTH PEAK

USGS: CYPRESS BUTTE

Passage 25
1:24,000 MAPS,
CYPRESS BUTTE and
CANE SPRINGS MOUNTAIN

SCALE: 1 11/16 INCH = 1 MILE

1/4   1/2

Arizona Trail
(current segment)

Arizona Trail
(previous and next segments)

Access route

River or stream

Lake or pond

Marsh or swamp

Primary highway

Secondary highway

Light duty road

Unimproved road

Trail

✕ Quarry or open mine pit

Whiterock Spring

water

MESA

POLLES MESA

POLLES

THE GORGE

East Verde River

Bull Spring

Cottbont Mountain

trail access

FR 406

FR 406

Passage 26
Hardscrabble Mesa: Twin Buttes (FR 194) to Pine Trailhead

Hardscrabble Mesa Trail Sign

Arizona Trail Association

INTRODUCTION This passage uses existing roads and trails to convey hikers from the north end of the Mazatzal Wilderness to the Pine Trailhead on AZ 87. Its relatively short length and easy to moderate trails provide a nice setting for a long day hike or a quick overnighter. Although this passage is entirely outside of designated wilderness, portions of it feel quite remote, and the brief passage through Oak Spring Canyon is beautiful. Hikers also will enjoy frequent views of the Mogollon Rim, the massive escarpment that rises 1,500 feet above the Pine Valley.

TOTAL DISTANCE	12.0 miles
QUALITY HIKING DISTANCE	12.0 miles
DIFFICULTY	Moderate
TOTAL ELEVATION GAIN	1,284 feet
TOTAL DESCENT	1,750 feet
FROM MEXICO	435.2 miles
TO UTAH	336.7 miles
LAND MANAGERS	Tonto National Forest (Payson Ranger District)
RECOMMENDED MONTHS	March through October. The summer months can be quite hot, but there is ample shade. Snow is likely in winter.

MOUNTAIN BIKE NOTES

Most of this passage consists of intermediate riding over rocky terrain, with one very important exception. Only the most skilled riders will be able to negotiate the drop into and subsequent climb out of Oak Spring Canyon. This is a 2-mile stretch in the second half of the passage. Most riders will have to do some pushing or carrying through here.

WATER

Headwaters of Rock Creek: Finding water here depends on recent weather and seasonal moisture (N34°21'49", W111°31'58").

East Tank: N34°20'03", W111°29'10"

Tank Gulch: As with Rock Creek, finding water here depends on recent weather and seasonal moisture (N34°20'24", W111°28'52").

Oak Spring: This spring appears to be perennial (N34°21'04", W111°28'21").

Pine Creek: No GPS coordinates are available for this perennial creek, but you'll know it when you've found it.

MAPS

USGS Quadrangles: Cane Springs Mountain, Buckhead Mesa
USFS: Tonto National Forest (North Half)
Other: Arizona Public Lands Information Center, AZT Passage Topo Map 26—
Hardscrabble Mesa

Bumpy road to Trailhead 5.3 miles

Twin Buttes (FR 194): From AZ 87, turn west into the town of Strawberry. Drive through town and turn left (south) onto FR 428. Continue a short distance then turn right onto FR 194. Follow this road 4.6 miles. AZT markers indicate the arrival of Passage 25, following Trail #14, on the left side of the road (N34°21'36", W111°33'26").

Smooth road to Trailhead

Pine Trailhead: See "Beginning Access Point" for Passage 27.

TRAIL DESCRIPTION   From Trail #14's intersection with FR 194 (5,840'), walk east on the road. (If you just drove to this trailhead from Strawberry, you'll be back-tracking.) Walk 1.2 miles and turn right (southeast) to follow a faint malpais rock–laden roadbed along a power line, as indicated by a brown carsonite post.

 The power-line trail crosses the headwaters of Rock Creek (5,935'; N34°21'49", W111°31'58"), where you might find a moderate flow of water. A calm grove of ponderosa pines makes an inviting campsite.

SUPPLIES, SERVICES, AND ACCOMMODATIONS

PINE

Pine is a small town with a variety of services. Turn left when you reach AZ 87 at mile 11.9 and walk about 1.0 mile into town. Or, finish Passage 26 at the Pine Trailhead, then follow the access road 0.1 mile to the highway, turn right, and you will be 0.3 mile closer to town than if you had turned off the AZT at mile 11.9 as described above. The distance of each business from the AZT's crossing of AZ 87 is listed in parentheses.

Distance from Trail   About 1.0 mile

Area Code	928
Zip Code	85544
ATM	Texaco Food Court (1.6 miles)
Bank	None (closest bank is in Payson)
Camping	Pine Creek RV Park, tent sites $15, 476-4595 (1.0 mile)
Dining	The Ponderosa Market has hot, fresh pizza (see "Groceries").
Gear	Texaco Food Court has basic camping supplies (1.6 miles).
Groceries	Ponderosa Market, grocery with basic camping supplies and white gas, 476-3590 (1.0 mile)
Information	Chamber of Commerce, open 11 a.m. to 1 p.m., 476-3547 (0.9 mile)
Laundry	Just past Hardscrabble Road on the right (1.3 miles)
Medical	Pine Strawberry Medical Center, 476-3258 (1.2 miles)
Post Office	Will hold general delivery for 30 days, 476-3274 (1.4 miles)
Showers	Pine Creek RV Park has showers for paying guests (see "Camping").

After 3 miles of the rocky power line road, the trail veers a bit south (right) of the power-line corridor. In another 0.5 mile, avoid a dirt road that forks right (south-southwest) and continue straight (southeast) for 50 yards to pass through a gate. Climb into a pleasant oak, juniper, and ponderosa forest (6,260'; N34°20'43", W111°29'50").

Watch carefully where the road forks when you reach another power line. Follow carsonite posts onto the right (southeast) fork and continue on Trail #251. The road descends to the south and southeast for the next mile.

Swing left (northeast) to pass East Tank (5,890'; N34°20'03", W111°29'10"). As you continue from this tank, look east-northeast for views of the flat top of the Mogollon Rim.

The road passes back under the power line (5,760') and then dips into the drainage of Tank Gulch, where water may be found (N34°20'24", W111°28'52"). The road climbs steeply up a rocky roadbed to the southeast for 0.1 mile (5,870'), then descends another 0.1 mile to N34°20'24", W111°28'41". At this point, look on the left side of the road for cairns that mark a very faint singletrack trail descending to the northeast. Signs indicate Trail #251. Turn onto this trail and follow cairns through rocky terrain.

The faint trail descends, occasionally steeply, with cairns marking most of the way, until you reach a sign for Oak Spring (5,180'; N34°21'04", W111°28'21"). The spring is a short distance behind the sign to the southeast—not on the canyon floor.

The trail leaves Oak Spring to the north. Soon there's a sign that indicates you're on Oak Spring Trail (#16). Turn right (northeast), continue into Oak Spring Canyon, and reach the bottom of the canyon in 0.1 mile. Follow a steep climb, through many switchbacks, out of the canyon and into a pleasant forest of tall ponderosa pines. Reach the top at mile 9.9 (5,650').

Pass by Bradshaw Tank and cross through the drainage below the tank, following cairns where the tread is obscure. Then pick up a clear singletrack continuing to the northeast.

When the trail meets Pine Creek, turn right and walk downstream 100 yards, then cross the creek to the east. Turn left (northeast) and follow a clear single-track trail away from the creek. The trail soon curves to the right (east) and follows the south edge of a tributary of Pine Creek. Now more of a road, the trail bends to the right (south). In 0.1 mile, carsonite posts mark a left (east) turn off the road onto a singletrack.

Within earshot of AZ 87, pass through a gate, walk 70 yards, and cross the highway with care to pick up a clear trail on the other side. This trail descends from the highway and bends right (northeast). Within 100 yards, the trail turns back to the north to cross a stream at some cairns. Shortly after that, there is a fork; take the left fork (west-northwest) and continue to the Pine Trailhead parking area and the end of Passage 26 (5,375'; N34°22'28", W111°26'35").

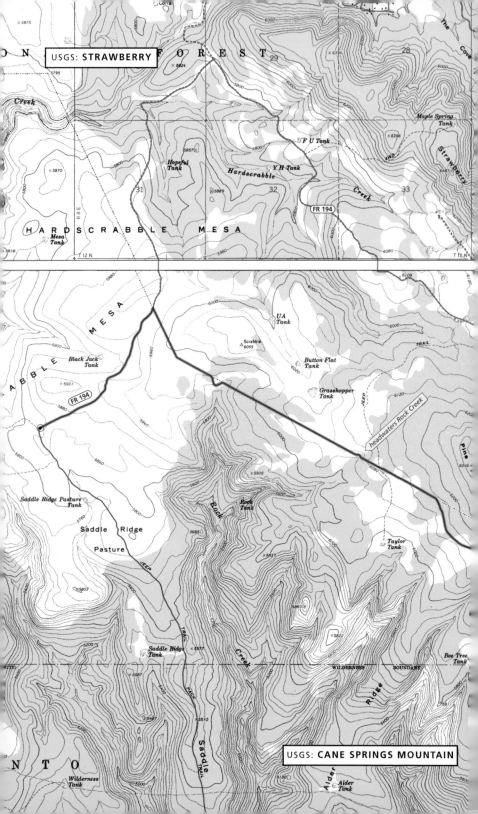

FOREST

Creek

Maple Spring
Tank

F U Tank

Hopeful
Tank

Hardscrabble

Y H Tank

Creek

FR 194

HARDSCRABBLE MESA

Mesa
Tank

MESA

UA
Tank

Scrabble
6055

Button Flat
Tank

Black Jack
Tank

FR 194

Grasshopper
Tank

TRAIL

JEEP

headwaters Rock Creek

Pine

Saddle Ridge Pasture
Tank

Saddle Ridge
Pasture

Rock
Tank

Rock

JEEP

Creek

Taylor
Tank

Ridge

Saddle Ridge
Tank

TRAIL

PACK

Saddle

Creek

WILDERNESS   BOUNDARY

Bee Tree
Tank

NTO

Wilderness
Tank

Alder

Alder
Tank

USGS: **PINE**

USGS: **BUCKHEAD MESA**

Passage 26
1:24,000 MAPS:
CANE SPRINGS MOUNTAIN, and
BUCKHEAD MESA

1/4   1/4

SCALE: 45/64 INCH = 1/2 MILE

Arizona Trail
(current segment)

Arizona Trail
(previous and next segments)

Access route

River or stream

Lake or pond

Marsh or swamp

Primary highway

Secondary highway

Light duty road

Unimproved road

Trail

Quarry or open mine pit

Pine

Strawberry Mountain

Strawberry Mtn

Bradshaw Tank

Oak Spring

Oak Spring Canyon

Ridge Tank

PINE

RIDGE

Water Tank

East Tank

Point Tank

Tank Gulch Tank

Tonto Natural Bridge

Spring

TONTO NATION

Passage 27
Highline: Pine Trailhead to FR 300

Fence along the Mogollon Rim near Kehl Spring

TOTAL DISTANCE	19.0 miles
QUALITY HIKING DISTANCE	19.0 miles
DIFFICULTY	Strenuous
TOTAL ELEVATION GAIN	4,667 feet
TOTAL DESCENT	2,779 feet
FROM MEXICO	447.2 miles
TO UTAH	324.7 miles
LAND MANAGERS	Tonto National Forest (Payson Ranger District)
RECOMMENDED MONTHS	March through November, depending on snow levels

INTRODUCTION   This passage is named for the trail it follows east of Pine toward the steep climb onto the magnificent Mogollon Rim. The Highline Trail dates to the nineteenth century, when ranchers traveled this route to neighboring homesteads. After an initial climb out of the Pine area, the trail rambles about 6.0 miles through mostly dry forests and the occasional stand of nice ponderosa pines. After mile 8.3 at the Geronimo Trailhead, cooler stands of pine and majestic fir trees are more common, and good campsites can be found.

After passing the Washington Park Trailhead, you gain more than 1,000 feet and there is little opportunity for camping. However, there are some great places to camp near General Springs Cabin at the very end of the passage.

This passage crosses at least a dozen drainages and several springs as it traverses across the steep sandstone slopes of the rim. Many of these are fairly reliable, but they do occasionally dry up. Check with the Forest Service before relying solely on these water sources.

Thanks to evenly spaced trailheads, it's easy to break this passage into shorter day hikes. (See "Alternate Access Point.") Where the trail occasionally fades, silver diamonds tacked to the trees show the way.

MOUNTAIN BIKE NOTES

Sections of this trail are fun on a bike, but many more are prohibitively difficult. If you attempt this passage, you'll be pushing the bike a lot.

WATER

Red Rock Spring: This source seems reliable (N34°22'18", W111°24'06").

Pine Spring: You should find a stronger flow here than at Red Rock Spring. A sign for the spring is by the trail.

Bear Spring: N34°24'46", W111°20'55"

Bray Creek

North Sycamore Creek

MAPS
USGS Quadrangles: Buckhead Mesa, Pine, Kehl Ridge, Dane Canyon
USFS: Tonto National Forest (North Half)
Other: Arizona Public Lands Information Center, AZT Passage Topo Map 27—Highline

BEGINNING ACCESS POINT

Smooth road to Trailhead

Pine Trailhead: Drive south of Pine on AZ 87 for 0.6 mile and turn left (east) to reach a large parking area and the trailhead (N34°22'28", W111°26 35").

Geronimo Trailhead: Drive south of Pine on AZ 87 for 2.2 miles and turn left (east) at a sign that says "Control Road" (FR 64). Drive 5.8 miles, and then turn left onto FR 440 at a sign for Camp Geronimo. Follow that road 2.0 miles to reach the small parking area for the Geronimo Trailhead on the right side of the road. The AZT passes this trailhead.

 Washington Park Trailhead: Drive south of Pine on AZ 87 for 2.2 miles and turn left (east) at a sign that says "Control Road" (FR 64). Drive 9.3 miles and turn left on FR 32. Continue 3.3 miles, and then turn right at a sign for Washington Park Trailhead. (Note that the mileage given on the signs here is wrong.) Make an immediate left turn and drive 1.0 mile to the large parking area at the trailhead (N34°25'51", W111°15'39"). Follow the trail from the north side of the parking lot. In about 100 yards, you'll reach the AZT at the intersection of the Highline Trail (#31) and the Colonel Devin Trail (#290).

 FR 300: See "Beginning Access Point" for Passage 28.

TRAIL DESCRIPTION Start on the trail at the northeast end of the parking lot (5,375'). Pass through a gate, continue 100 yards to a "T" intersection with the Highline Trail (#31), and turn right (southeast). You will stay on Trail #31 for the next 17.0 or so miles until you reach the Washington Park area. Where this trail is occasionally obscure, cairns and silver diamonds tacked to the trees show the way.

At a "T" intersection (5,640'; N34°22'36", W111°25'56"), turn right (east) toward Red Rock Spring.

Avoid the Donahue Trail (#27) by continuing straight (southeast) on the AZT. When the trail reaches a high vantage point on a ridge, distant landmarks of the AZT come into view to the south, including the Mazatzal Mountains and the craggy Four Peaks farther in the distance. There are a few flat campsites up here, but no water.

The trail rolls across steep, overgrown terrain to reach Red Rock Spring (6,080'; N34°22'18", W111°24'06"). You'll find a place to camp a short distance to the left (northeast). About 70 yards beyond the spring, continue straight (east) on the Highline Trail as the Red Rock Trail (#294) cuts right to descend to Control Road in the valley floor.

You'll pass Pine Spring. From here the AZT passes in and out of a number of drainages, trending mostly to the east. Descend to an intersection with the old roadbed of the Geronimo Trail (5,520'; N34°23'56", W111°22'05").

Turn right (east) and continue descending on the roadbed, which soon parallels a large stream. In 0.2 mile, follow the stream across an intersecting roadbed, make a turn

Opposite: The author at Pine Trailhead
Photo by Tom Jones

PINE TRAILHEAD

THE HIGHLINE TRAIL

TONTO NATIONAL FOREST

to the right (east), and descend through a beautiful forest of very large ponderosa pine trees. Silver diamonds on trees mark the AZT's path.

The trail makes a switchback to the left (northeast) and descends 50 yards to a couple of signs and a junction with a faint trail. Turn left (north) and follow the faint trail 85 yards to the two channels of Webber Creek. Cross carefully and continue on the other side to reach a dirt road (FR 440) and the Geronimo Trailhead.

You'll find many more campsites over the next 10 miles or so of this passage than in the first 9 miles. Follow the Highline Trail (#31) northwest out of the parking area. About 0.5 mile along this trail, you'll see a roadbed paralleling the trail on the left. Ignore this and continue on the singletrack. If you find the frequent trail forks here confusing, just follow the silver diamonds on the trees. Where the trail touches the edge of that parallel road atop a small ridge (6,040'; N34°24'45", W111°21'06"), follow the single-track trail (#31) to the northeast.

You'll reach a trough of water from Bear Spring and a "T" intersection with what looks like a road (6,030'; N34°24'46", W111°20'55"). Turn right (south). Where the road bends left, stay on a singletrack trail to the east. The AZT occasionally approaches the steep, rocky walls of the rim, passing through thick patches of crimson-stemmed manzanita, alligator juniper, oak, and ponderosa pines.

Pick your way across two broad sections of red slick-rock, and then cross Bray Creek. Cross another small stream in a lush oasis in 1.0 mile, and continue to a crossing of North Sycamore Creek. The trail is faint on the other side of the creek; walk down-stream about 20 yards and look for a faint tread heading east.

The trail rambles through cool pine forests and across several more streams. The stands of fir trees here are sublime.

Begin a steady descent through a series of switchbacks, terminating at a road. Turn right,

The Arizona Trail along the Mogollon Rim
Photo courtesy of The Arizona Trail Association

and then immediately take a left fork. Cross a creek, walk 40 yards, and turn onto a singletrack trail on the left that is marked by a hiking sign. Climb gradually out of the valley. Over the next 0.5 mile, the trail swings around the south side of a ridge before turning back to the north (left).

The trail soon becomes a bit confusing. The AZT reaches a road under a power line. Continue straight across the road to the north-northeast and follow the singletrack as it descends and crosses a small stream. Then make two quick switchbacks to end up pointing north. You'll reach the Colonel Devin Trail (#290) on an old road that heads north. To reach the Washington Park Trailhead, turn right (southeast) and descend 100 yards to the parking area (N34°25'51"; W111°15'39").

The AZT is now following the headwaters of the East Verde River, although the drainage may be dry here.

A singletrack trail (6,790'; N34°26'55", W111°15'05") on the right (east) leaves the road you've been climbing. A sign indicating the Tunnel Trail (#390) and the Colonel Devin Trail marks this intersection. Turn onto the singletrack, which immediately crosses the stream and then curves left (north-northeast). Shortly after the trail begins to climb steeply, you'll see a trail on the right that leads 0.25 mile to an uncompleted railroad tunnel, which was intended to carry ore from southern Arizona mining towns through the Mogollon Rim to Flagstaff. To continue on the AZT, follow a switchback to the left (northwest).

The trail crosses back to the left side of the East Verde River. Welcome to the top of the Mogollon Rim and the southern edge of the Colorado Plateau (7,200'; N34°27'09", W111°14'59"). Continue north less than 0.1 mile to cross FR 300, near the historical marker for the Battle of Big Dry Wash, and then walk another 0.4 mile to the parking area at General Springs Cabin and the end of Passage 27 (mile 19.0; 7,200'; N34°27'32", W111°15'00").

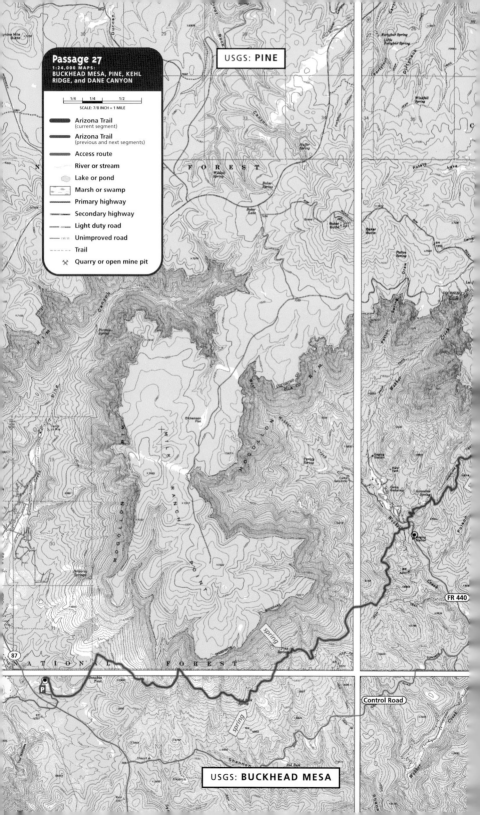

Passage 27

1:24,000 MAPS:
BUCKHEAD MESA, PINE, KEHL
RIDGE, and DANE CANYON

SCALE: 7/8 INCH = 1 MILE

| 1/4 | 1/4 | 1/2 |

━━━ Arizona Trail
(current segment)

━━━ Arizona Trail
(previous and next segments)

━━━ Access route

River or stream

Lake or pond

Marsh or swamp

Primary highway

Secondary highway

Light duty road

Unimproved road

Trail

✕ Quarry or open mine pit

USGS: **PINE**

USGS: **BUCKHEAD MESA**

Control Road

FR 440

87

Passage 28
Blue Ridge: FR 300 to AZ 87

General Springs Cabin

TOTAL DISTANCE	15.8 miles
QUALITY HIKING DISTANCE	13.8 miles
DIFFICULTY	Moderate
TOTAL ELEVATION GAIN	1,133 feet
TOTAL DESCENT	1,575 feet
FROM MEXICO	466.2 miles
TO UTAH	305.7 miles
LAND MANAGERS	Coconino National Forest (Mogollon Rim Ranger District)
RECOMMENDED MONTHS	April through November, depending on snow level

INTRODUCTION This passage is mostly flat, with two notable exceptions. The first is the 500-foot-deep gorge carved by East Clear Creek, which flows into Blue Ridge Reservoir. The second is the steep drop from Blue Ridge to AZ 87. Neither is particularly difficult, and this passage as a whole is relatively easy.

You'll cross pockets of pristine natural beauty, including the quiet sanctuary of General Springs Canyon, early in the passage. If only it lasted longer before the AZT climbs back out of the canyon. The drop into East Clear Creek is equally inspirational, passing thick stands of ponderosa pine and fir trees. Although much of the passage is crisscrossed with roads, these are not heavily traveled, and their presence does not spoil this quiet corner of the Mogollon Plateau.

MOUNTAIN BIKE NOTES

Parts of this passage are ridable, but the dip into East Clear Creek is not. From mile 9.5 to the end, the riding is very difficult because of extremely rocky terrain. Only the most hardcore, masochistic riders will enjoy this.

WATER

Unnamed stock tank: The water here is surprisingly clear for a stock tank (N34°32'31", W111°14'03").

East Clear Creek: This intermittent flow feeds Blue Ridge Reservoir (N34°33'04", W111°14'06").

Rock Crossing Campground: Available during summer months only, there is a water spigot at the restrooms, just off the AZT (N34°33'42", W111°13'07").

Blue Ridge Campground: At the south end of the campground (N34°35'29", W111°12'00"), a water spigot is available only during the summer.

MAPS

USGS Quadrangles: Kehl Ridge, Dane Canyon, Blue Ridge Reservoir
USFS: Coconino National Forest (South Half)
Other: Arizona Public Lands Information Center, AZT Passage Topo Map 28—
   Blue Ridge

BEGINNING ACCESS POINT

FR 300: From the intersection of AZ 87 and AZ 260 north of Pine, drive east 2.6 miles on AZ 87 then turn right (south) toward FR 300. Go 0.1 mile and turn left onto FR 300. Avoid the frequent side roads and drive 12.0 miles on FR 300 to a turnoff on the left (north) at a historical marker for the Battle of Big Dry Wash. This is where the AZT crosses FR 300. Turn left and follow a power line 0.3 mile to General Springs Cabin. The road curves right to a small parking area and the trailhead (N34°27'32", W111°15'00").

ENDING ACCESS POINT

 AZ 87: See "Beginning Access Point" for Passage 29.

TRAIL DESCRIPTION   The trail exits the parking area to the left (west) of an elk exclosure fence. This elk exclosure is designed to enhance stream habitat conditions for the endangered Little Colorado spinedace fish. Rock cairns and brown carsonite posts bearing the AZT symbol guide you through the forest along General Springs Canyon. At mile 0.3, the trail has been rerouted around a badly eroded section that needs rehabilitation. The deeper you follow the winding trail into the canyon, the more beautiful it becomes.

At a trail fork, turn left (north) to climb out of the drainage. After a series of steep switchbacks, the AZT reaches level ground and turns sharply right (north) to join an old road. In 0.5 mile, the road bends left (west-northwest) and reaches a second dirt road at a "T" intersection. Go straight across this road onto a singletrack trail, as a carsonite post indicates. The trail immediately curves back to the right and crosses under power lines in 0.1 mile.

The AZT zigzags along, following cairns by the power line. It crosses the dirt road FR 123 (N34°30'17", 111°13'59") and continues on the other side to the northwest.

For about the next 2.0 miles, the trail parallels FR 123. Follow the cairns and carsonite posts until you reach FR 123A, an old two-track road. Turn left (northwest) and continue to a fork, where you should bear right (north-northeast).

 There is a stock tank with clear water right next to the road (N34°32'31", W111°14' 03").

At 7,000' (N34°32'57", W111°14'01"), the road veers left (west). Leave the road and continue straight ahead (north) on a singletrack that crosses a fence and immediately begins a steep descent into the canyon of East Clear Creek. This is as far as mountain bikes can go comfortably. A dense forest in the canyon offers respite from the heat of the plateau.

Cross the flat, gravelly bottom of the canyon (N34°33'04", W111°14'06"). You may find water here, near the upper reaches of Blue Ridge Reservoir. Cross the canyon diagonally to your left (due west) and pick up a clear trail ascending the bank.

After climbing out of East Clear Creek Canyon, the trail levels abruptly on the plateau above the canyon, known as Blue Ridge. The trail heads almost due east, offering another nice view into East Clear Creek Canyon.

At about 0.3 mile before Rock Crossing Campground, you will come to a trail junction, with the AZT heading to the northeast (left). This trail lets the AZT traveler bypass the campground, which is closed most of the year. You will see signage indicating that the trail continuing east will take you to Rock Crossing Campground.

During summer when the campground is open, water and restrooms are available, and hikers and mountain bikers can stay in the campground for a fee. Horses are not permitted.

The Arizona Trail route around the campground goes northeast for about 0.5 mile, where it crosses FR 751. This is the location of a future trailhead. The trail heads east again, and in about 0.7 mile you come to a two-track road where this new route rejoins the old route north of the campground. This new route is well marked with carsonite posts and rock cairns.

As you enjoy views of the vast expanse of flat pine forest stretching to the north, the trail bends right to head a little south of east. It curves back to the north (N34°34'58", W111°11'59") to begin a rocky descent down the lush, pine- and oak-covered slopes of Blue Ridge.

Before you reach Blue Ridge Campground, you will come to a trail route bypassing the campground, for the same reasons as at the previous Rock Crossing Campground bypass. Follow the signs on an old two-track road that heads left (north) to FR 138, then turn right (south) on FR 138. In about 100 yards, you will see the entrance to the campground on the right and the Arizona Trail continuing north on the left.

During summer when it's open, this campground has water.

Head north on a clear singletrack. The trail passes through enchanting stands of aspen before reaching a road crossing.

After the road crossing, there is a stock pond. The trail bends to the right to pass the pond and then continues north. Avoid a side trail on the left that heads west-northwest.

Trend northeast on a clear singletrack, and then intersect a faint trail by a large cairn and a sign (N34°36'15", W111°11'44"). Turn left (west) and follow cairns and carsonite posts to mile 15.8 (6,838'; N34°36'25", W111°12'01"), where you'll find a parking area, an informal trailhead, and the end of Passage 28.

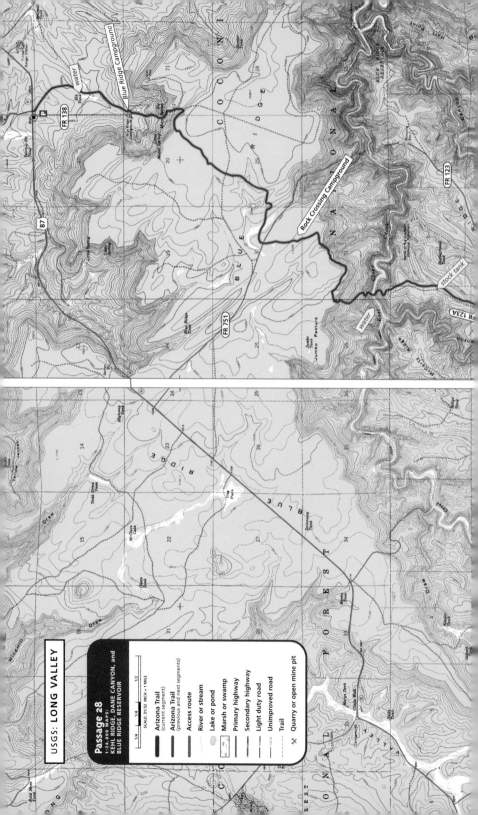

USGS: LONG VALLEY

Passage 28
1:24,000 MAPS:
KEHL RIDGE, DANE CANYON, and
BLUE RIDGE RESERVOIR

SCALE 31/32 INCH = 1 MILE

1/4   1/4   1/2

— Arizona Trail
  (current segment)

— Arizona Trail
  (previous and next segments)

  Access route

  River or stream

  Lake or pond

  Marsh or swamp

— Primary highway

— Secondary highway

— Light duty road

—— Unimproved road

—— Trail

✕ Quarry or open mine pit

Blue Ridge Campground

Rock Crossing Campground

water

water

stock tank

FR 138

FR 123

FR 751

87

COCONINO NATIONAL FOREST

BLUE RIDGE

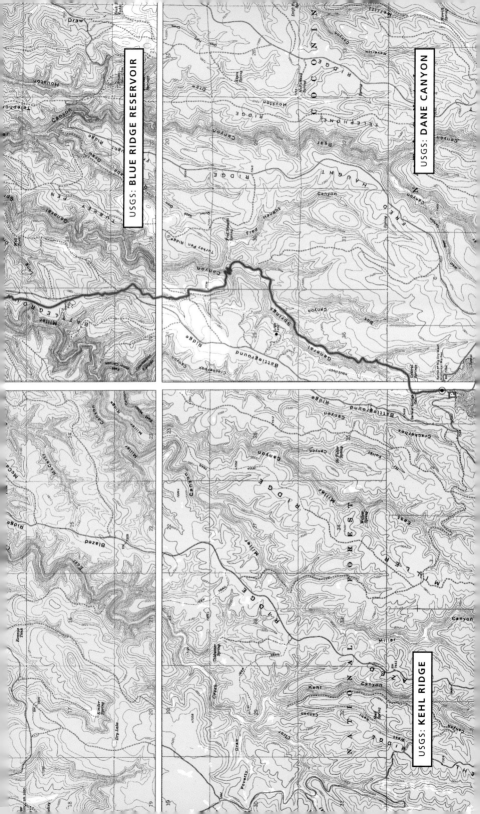

USGS: BLUE RIDGE RESERVOIR

USGS: DANE CANYON

USGS: KEHL RIDGE

Passage 29
Happy Jack: AZ 87 to Allan Lake

The Arizona Trail north of Blue Ridge Ranger Station

TOTAL DISTANCE	31.5 miles
QUALITY HIKING DISTANCE	15.0 miles
DIFFICULTY	Easy
TOTAL ELEVATION GAIN	2,484 feet
TOTAL DESCENT	1,849 feet
FROM MEXICO	482.0 miles
TO UTAH	289.9 miles
LAND MANAGERS	Coconino National Forest (Mogollon Rim Ranger District)
RECOMMENDED MONTHS	April through June, September through November. Summers are hot; snow is likely in winter. Monsoons in July and August can create muddy conditions.

INTRODUCTION This passage traverses some attractive terrain, but much of it (about two-thirds) follows roads that are open to motorized vehicles. In the absence of natural barriers on the Mogollon Plateau, vehicles have crisscrossed the area, and roads are more prevalent than trails. There are exceptions—for example, the first 5.1 miles of the south end of this passage are mostly singletrack trails in scenic forest canyons, although the route crosses and briefly follows roads at several points. Fortunately, the Forest Service and the Arizona Trail Association are working to add more singletrack that will bypass two-track roads. For that reason, parts of the passage may differ from the descriptions here.

There are no guaranteed water sources, but stock tanks are plentiful, and Pine Spring is fairly reliable. You'll see good campsites all along this passage.

MOUNTAIN BIKE NOTES

 The road to hell is paved with good intentions, but for mountain bikers on this passage it is paved with millions of pieces of lava rock of varying sizes. Forget the padded shorts and try a pillow. That's an overstatement, but there are stretches on this relatively flat passage where it seems to be the case. The worst part is the road from mile 5.7 to mile 8.6.

WATER

 Wochner Tank: On the 1970 Turkey Mountain USGS map, labeled Waldroup Tank.

 Unnamed pond: This water was good when I was here in June (N34°39'48", W111°16'21").

 Gonzales Tank: N34°42'49", W111°17'53"

 Pine Spring: Located 0.3 mile off the AZT, this is one of the best sources on this passage; call the Forest Service to verify flow (N34°46'27", W111°21'05").

 Bargaman Park, Shuff's, and Maxie Tanks

MAPS

USGS Quadrangles: Blue Ridge Reservoir, Hay Lake, Turkey Mountain, Jaycox Mountain, Hutch Mountain
USFS: Coconino National Forest (South Half)
Other: Arizona Public Lands Information Center, AZT Passage Topo Maps 29A and 29B—Happy Jack

BEGINNING ACCESS POINT

 AZ 87: From the intersection of AZ 87 and AZ 260 north of Pine, drive northeast 19.5 miles on AZ 87 then turn right (south) on FR 138. (This is about 0.8 mile west of the Blue Ridge Ranger Station on AZ 87.) Signs on the highway point to Moqui Campground. The trailhead is about 100 yards south on FR 138, on the left (east) side of the road (N34°36'25", W111°12'01").

ENDING ACCESS POINT

 Allan Lake: See "Beginning Access Point" for Passage 30.

TRAIL DESCRIPTION From the trailhead (6,838'), walk 100 yards north on the dirt road to AZ 87, turn right (east) on the highway, walk about 40 yards, and turn left (north) onto FR 138. Pass through a gate and continue along the road 0.1 mile to a sign indicating a singletrack trail on the right (northeast).

Cairns and brown carsonite posts show the way when the trail is faint. The AZT reaches a road and bends left to parallel it for 0.2 mile before crossing it to the northeast (6,700'; N34°37'26", W111°12'28"). The trail joins another road that forks immediately. Take the right fork and follow the road about 100 yards until it bends to the right. Leave the road on a singletrack trail continuing straight ahead (northeast).

The trail bends left (northwest) to descend into Jacks Canyon. In 0.2 mile (6,585'), join a very faint old road in the bottom of the scenic canyon and follow it west. The canyon bends sharply right (north). In 0.1 mile (6,595'; N34°38'45", W111°13'21"), the trail follows a very faint roadbed across the drainage and out of it to the west, immediately bends right (north), recrosses the canyon, and swings left again to follow the canyon to the west.

 The following description requires a bit of bushwhacking, so pay attention! Cross a small side drainage (N34°38'49", W111°13'33") coming from the right and turn sharply in that direction to pick up a faint singletrack that parallels the side drainage, heading north. Continue 0.1 mile to where a second, even smaller side drainage comes in from the left (west). Turn left and go up that drainage.

In about 0.5 mile, this streambed forks. Stay to the right (north-northwest); you'll reach a high-quality dirt road (6,740'; N34°39'11", W111°13'57"). Cross the road and continue northwest 0.6 mile to reach Route 9727H. Turn left (west) and follow this road, which is covered with chunks of lava rock, through pretty ponderosa forests.

 Pass Wochner Tank. This is shown as Waldroup Tank on the 1970 Turkey Mountain USGS map.

 The water was clearer at this unnamed pond than at Wochner Tank (6,900'; N34°39'48", W111°16'21").

You'll reach a "T" intersection with FR 93 (7,020'; N34°39'50", W111°16'59"). Turn right (north). Bear right (northeast) at a triangular intersection to stay on FR 93. Walk a little more than 0.1 mile to turn left (northwest) onto Route 93K.

In about 2.0 miles, the trail veers right (east) and continues another 1.0 mile to rejoin FR 93. Turn left (north-northwest), continue 0.4 mile, and then turn right (northeast) on FR 9364J.

Gonzales Tank is about 0.25 mile northwest of the intersection of FR 93 and FR 9364J (N34°42'49", W111°17'53"). Please be careful in this environmentally sensitive area.

After 0.7 mile of climbing on FR 9364J, the road curves left (north), and then, in another 0.3 mile, curves back to the right (east). At this point, at the signed turn just past the gate, veer off to the left (northwest) and follow the singletrack trail about 0.74 mile over a flat ridge before descending to FR 93A.

Turn right (northeast) and walk a short distance to FR 9356P. Turn left (northwest) onto this road and begin a steady climb. After topping out around 7,300', this road descends to Wild Horse Tank. Join FR 9361E at the tank, follow it north for 1.6 miles to FR 135, and bear left (west).

Continue to a signed singletrack to the left just before reaching a "T" road intersection. If you want to get water at Pine Spring, turn right at the "T" intersection and walk on this road for less than 0.1 mile to a second fork. Turn right and continue 0.2 mile to the spring (N34°46'27", W111°21'05"). Pine Spring flows into a stock pond that provides the easiest access to the water. There are some nice places to camp here.

If you do not want to go to Pine Spring, follow the trail as it passes through the trees west of the road just before the "T" intersection for about 0.14 mile, until it crosses FR 294 and the east end of Bargaman Park. The trail then follows a two-track north a short way, then heads west again on a two-track as it crosses Bargaman Park. In less than 0.1 mile, the trail leaves the two-track road headed west to become singletrack heading north.

Pass Bargaman Park Tank and then continue north to FR 135D. Turn right (northwest) and continue 1.9 miles on FR 135D to Shuff's Tank. Turn right (north), following signs and rock cairns to Maxie Tank.

Then continue cross-country, following the signs and heading north-northeast for 0.6 mile to FR 135 (mile 29.0; 7,600'). Cross this road and follow Route 135C for 0.2 mile to FR 92A, which will curve north-northwest around a low peak on the left.

You will reach FR 92, which is a busy, graded dirt road. There is a carsonite AZT sign at this road intersection, and plans are in the works to build a trailhead at this location. Continue north on a singletrack trail across the meadow to the edge of the woods, turn left (northwest), and you will reach paved Forest Highway 3 (Lake Mary Road to Flagstaff) in about 0.3 mile. This is the end of Passage 29.

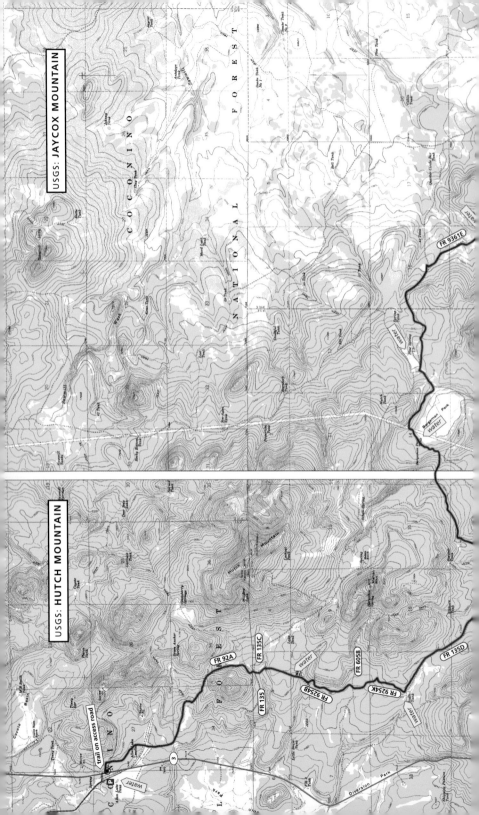

USGS: JAYCOX MOUNTAIN

USGS: HUTCH MOUNTAIN

USGS: HAPPY JACK

USGS: TURKEY MOUNTAIN

CONTINUED ON P. 232

FR 935P

FR 93A

(FR 934)

FR 93A

FR 93

water

COCONINO

NATIONAL FOREST

Bargaman

Draw

Sheep

Tank

Draw

Passage 29
1:24,000 MAPS:
BLUE RIDGE RESERVOIR, HAY
LAKE, TURKEY MOUNTAIN, JAYCOX
MOUNTAIN, and HUTCH MOUNTAIN

SCALE 7/8 INCH = 1 MILE

1/4   1/4   1/2

Arizona Trail
(current segment)

Arizona Trail
(previous and next segments)

Access route

River or stream

Lake or pond

Marsh or swamp

Primary highway

Secondary highway

Light duty road

Unimproved road

Trail

Quarry or open mine pit

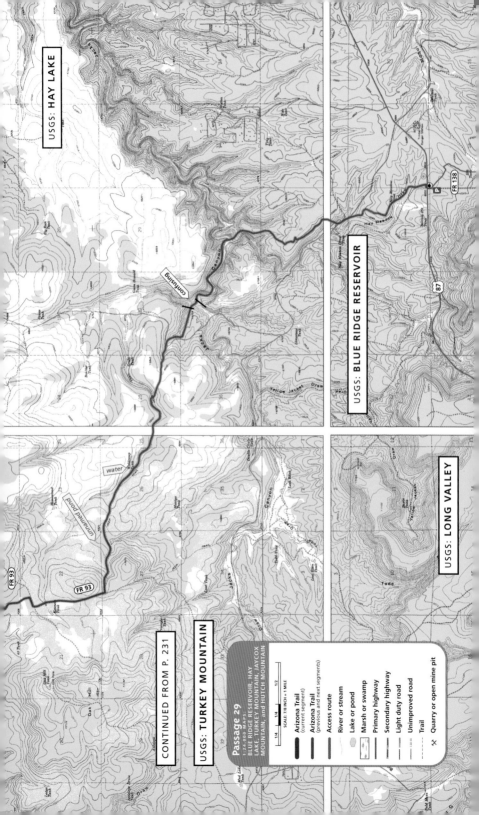

USGS: HAY LAKE

USGS: BLUE RIDGE RESERVOIR

USGS: LONG VALLEY

USGS: TURKEY MOUNTAIN

CONTINUED FROM P. 231

continuing

water

unnamed pond

FR 93

FR 93

FR 138

87

Passage 29
1:24,000 MAPS:
BLUE RIDGE RESERVOIR, HAY
LAKE, TURKEY MOUNTAIN, JAYCOX
MOUNTAIN, and HUTCH MOUNTAIN

SCALE 7/8 INCH = 1 MILE

1/4   1/4   1/2

Arizona Trail
(current segment)

Arizona Trail
(previous and next segments)

Access route

River or stream

Lake or pond

Marsh or swamp

Primary highway

Secondary highway

Light duty road

Unimproved road

Trail

✕ Quarry or open mine pit

Passage 30
Mormon Lake: Allan Lake to Marshall Lake

Arizona Trail near Mormon Lake

INTRODUCTION Environmental evaluations for this unfinished section of the AZT have been conducted, and the Forest Service has approved a final route. Construction of this passage around Mormon Lake is under way and is scheduled for completion by September 2005. This easy, 28-mile section crosses beautiful open meadows beside aspen and pine forests, with fine views of the San Francisco Peaks. Given the presence of Mormon Lake Lodge and of the small mountain community of Mormon Lake right in the middle, this passage is likely to become one of the most popular sections of the entire 770-mile Arizona Trail among all trail users: hikers, mountain bikers, and horseback riders. For current trail information, contact the Peaks Ranger District of the Coconino National Forest or the Arizona Trail Association (602-242-4794 or ata@aztrail.org).

TOTAL DISTANCE	Approximately 28.0 miles
QUALITY HIKING DISTANCE	Approximately 28.0 miles
DIFFICULTY	Easy
TOTAL ELEVATION GAIN	NA
TOTAL DESCENT	NA
FROM MEXICO	513.5 miles
TO UTAH	258.4 miles
LAND MANAGERS	Coconino National Forest (Peaks and Mormon Lake Ranger Districts)
RECOMMENDED MONTHS	April through October

MOUNTAIN BIKE NOTES

This section, when complete, will be almost entirely singletrack trail with excellent riding.

WATER

Water sources are yet to be identified in this passage but are likely to be Navajo Spring, Double Springs Campground, and Railroad Tank.

MAPS

USGS Quadrangles: Hutch Mountain, Mormon Lake, Ashurst Lake, Lower Lake Mary
USFS: Coconino National Forest (South and North)

BEGINNING ACCESS POINT

  Allan Lake: From the turnoff leading from Forest Highway 3 to Mormon Lake Village, continue south on Forest Highway 3 for 4.7 miles and then turn right onto a gated dirt road. There is no sign identifying this road, but there is a small sign on a tree for Game Management Unit 6A (N34°49'828", W111°26'281"). Drive about 100 yards and look for a place to park off the main road.

You can also reach this point from AZ 87 by driving north on Forest Highway 3.

ENDING ACCESS POINT

  Marshall Lake: See "Beginning Access Point" for Passage 31.

TRAIL DESCRIPTION

At the start, the trail generally winds northwest from near Fulton Canyon heading toward Railroad Spring, about 3.0 miles south of Mormon Lake. Rock cairns and brown carsonite posts with the AZT logo show the way. Occasionally, you will also see a wooden directional Forest Service sign. Singletrack trail is under construction here. The trail then continues northwest, paralleling FR 90 on the south and west side of the Mormon Lake basin. The trail route passes by Double Springs Campground on the west side of the lake basin and just northwest of Dairy Springs Campground.

Approximately 0.75 mile of the trail route coincides with the Lakeview Trail. Parking is provided at the existing Lakeview Trailhead, located near Double Springs Campground.

The trail crosses FR 240, heads northeast to the northwest side of Dairy Springs Campground, and then crosses FR 132 as it continues east toward the new Horse Mesa Trailhead. The trail route passes just south of the Pine Grove Campground when it crosses Forest Highway 3 (Lake Mary Road).

At Horse Mesa Trailhead, the trail veers north across Anderson Mesa toward Marshall Lake. The trail route is well marked by carsonite posts bearing the AZT logo. The trail skirts the Lowell Observatory and then crosses an open meadow before descending through a wooded hillside to reach a gravel road. Continue straight ahead (west) on the left fork of the road. You'll reach the end of Passage 30 at Marshall Lake Trailhead, on the left, at mile 28.0.

SUPPLIES, SERVICES, AND ACCOMMODATIONS

MORMON LAKE VILLAGE

This beautiful mountain community offers one of the best stops or staging areas anywhere along the entirety of the Arizona Trail's 770-mile route. In addition to privately owned cabins and RV spaces, Mormon Lake Lodge offers cabin rentals, camping, RV parking, showers, and laundry facilities. Visitors can also enjoy the amenities of a bar, restaurant, store, and post office. Mormon Lake Lodge, a Forever Resort, has been a major partner with the Arizona Trail Association in providing the necessary resources to complete the Arizona Trail around Mormon Lake. For more information, contact Mormon Lake Lodge, P.O. Box 3801, Mormon Lake, AZ 86038; (928) 354-2227; www.mormonlakelodge.com.

Distance from Trail 1.5 miles.

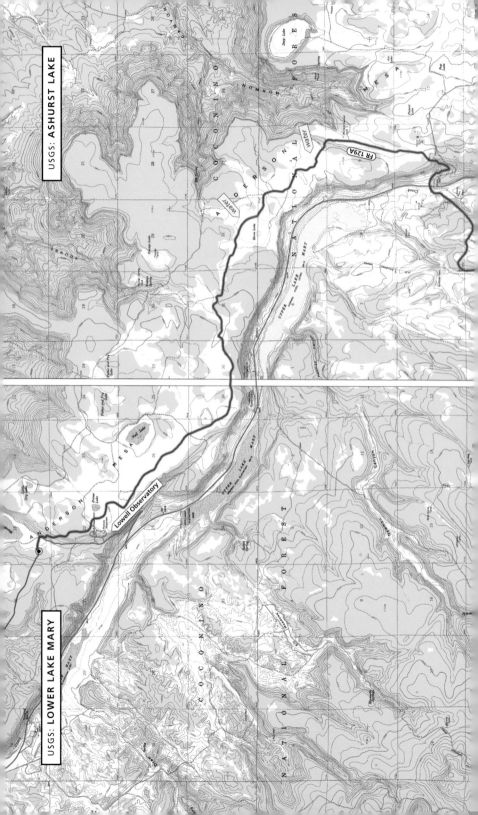

USGS: ASHURST LAKE

USGS: LOWER LAKE MARY

Lowell Observatory

FR 129A

water

water

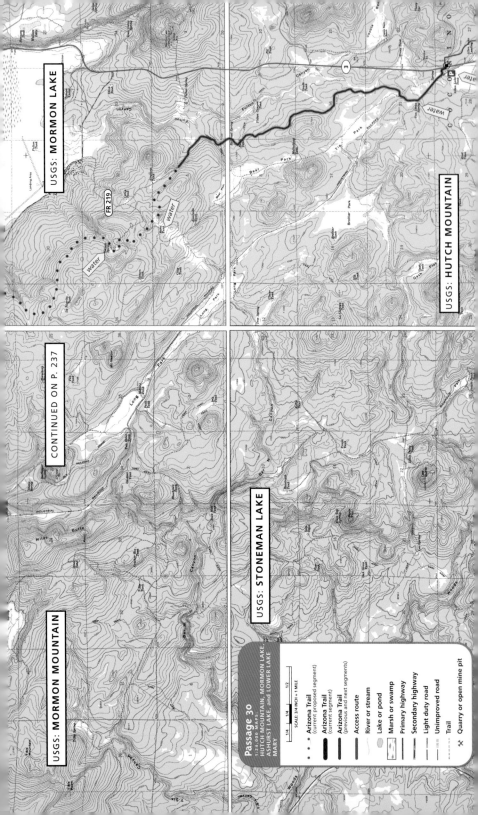

USGS: MORMON LAKE

USGS: HUTCH MOUNTAIN

USGS: MORMON MOUNTAIN

USGS: STONEMAN LAKE

CONTINUED ON P. 237

FR 219

Water

Water

water

Passage 30
1:24,000 MAPS:
HUTCH MOUNTAIN, MORMON LAKE,
ASHURST LAKE, and LOWER LAKE
MARY

SCALE 3/4 INCH = 1 MILE

1/4   1/4   1/2

• • • Arizona Trail
(current proposed segment)

▬▬ Arizona Trail
(current segment)

▬▬ Arizona Trail
(previous and next segments)

⋯⋯ Access route

  River or stream

  Lake or pond

  Marsh or swamp

  Primary highway

  Secondary highway

  Light duty road

  Unimproved road

  Trail

✕ Quarry or open mine pit

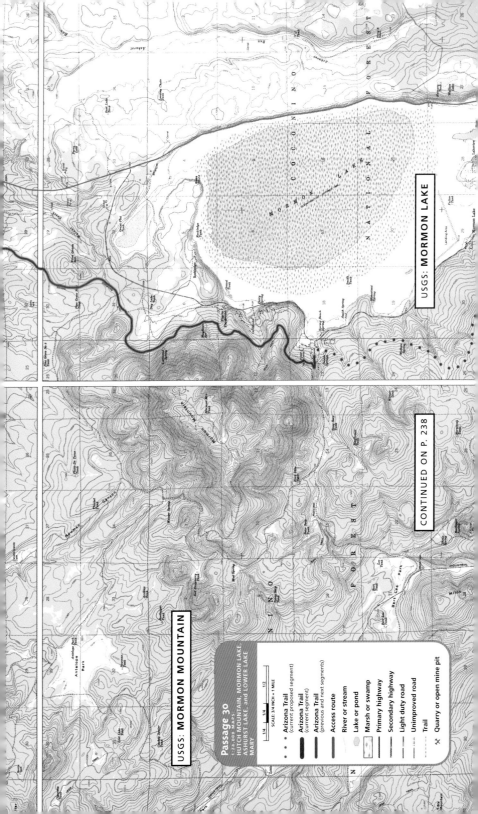

CONTINUED ON P. 238

USGS: MORMON LAKE

USGS: MORMON MOUNTAIN

Passage 30
1:24,000 Maps
HUTCH MOUNTAIN, MORMON LAKE,
ASHURST LAKE, and LOWER LAKE
MARY

SCALE 3/4 INCH = 1 MILE

1/4   1/4   1/2

N

• • • • **Arizona Trail** (current proposed segment)

━━━ **Arizona Trail** (current segment)

─── **Arizona Trail** (previous and next segments)

─── **Access route**

River or stream

Lake or pond

Marsh or swamp

Primary highway

Secondary highway

Light duty road

Unimproved road

Trail

✕ **Quarry or open mine pit**

Passage 31
Walnut Canyon: Marshall Lake to Cosnino (I-40)

Marshall Lake

TOTAL DISTANCE	18.2 miles
QUALITY HIKING DISTANCE	18.2 miles
DIFFICULTY	Easy
TOTAL ELEVATION GAIN	1,051 feet
TOTAL DESCENT	1,685 feet
FROM MEXICO	541.5 miles
TO UTAH	230.4 miles
LAND MANAGERS	Coconino National Forest (Peaks Ranger District)
RECOMMENDED MONTHS	April through October

INTRODUCTION This passage's peaceful traverse of Anderson Mesa from Marshall Lake and along Walnut Canyon belies its proximity to the city of Flagstaff. The Fisher Point area is a popular mountain-biking destination for local residents; however, because so many trails weave through the area, you will not see very many people on any stretch of trail.

At the Fisher Point area, you will come to a junction in the Arizona Trail. This passage heads east and traverses the edge of Walnut Canyon. The other option, a resupply route for thru-hikers, heads north into Flagstaff (see Passage 33).

MOUNTAIN BIKE NOTES

 Before you drop into Walnut Canyon, Anderson Mesa is rocky but level singletrack. There are several climbs into and out of canyons where you might need to walk your bike. The northern half of the passage is smooth singletrack through the forest.

WATER

There are no reliable water sources along this passage, but the city of Flagstaff is always nearby.

MAPS

USGS Quadrangles: Lower Lake Mary, Flagstaff East, Flagstaff West, Winona
USFS: Coconino National Forest (North Half)
Other: Arizona Public Lands Information Center, AZT Passage Topo
Map 31—Walnut Canyon

BEGINNING ACCESS POINT

 Marshall Lake: From Flagstaff, take the Lake Mary Road exit (339) off I-17 for 9.0 miles, then turn left (east) on FR 128 at the sign for Marshall Lake. Pass the observatory turnoff, then at 2.2 miles turn left before Marshall Lake (more of a marsh) and park at the AZT sign on the left. If you are coming from the south on Lake Mary Road, the Marshall Lake turnoff is 7.5 miles north of Pine Grove Campground.

ALTERNATE ACCESS POINT

 Walnut Canyon Trailhead: From Flagstaff, take the Country Club exit (201) from I-40 and head south. Turn left at the Old Walnut Canyon Road (FR 303); the road will turn to dirt. The trailhead is several miles past the pavement on the right. There is room for trailers.

ENDING ACCESS POINT

 Cosnino (I-40): See "Beginning Access Point" for Passage 32.

TRAIL DESCRIPTION   A wooden sign marks the singletrack's departure to the southwest of Marshall Lake (7,122'). The trail passes through a pleasant, flat woodland of ponderosa pine and oak. At mile 1.2, the trail begins a short descent into a canyon, then heads west and crosses a road to climb the other side of this small canyon. Cross another road at mile 3.5 before the trail descends steeply into lower Walnut Canyon. At the "T" intersection in the bottom of the canyon, turn right toward Fisher Point.

At mile 5.9, the trail forks. Take the right fork up and out of the canyon. The trail then skirts the edge of the canyon, with one steep climb into and out of a side canyon. A major trailhead is located on FR 303, the Old Walnut Canyon Road. At this point, the trail gradually transitions from a ponderosa pine forest into a piñon-juniper forest. The trail crosses the paved Walnut Canyon entry road and continues to head east before turning north to cross the interstate at Cosnino.

SUPPLIES, SERVICES, AND ACCOMMODATIONS

FLAGSTAFF

Most of these services are either near downtown, 1.0 mile west of Switzer Canyon Road on Route 66, or along East Route 66, closer to Switzer Canyon Road. The exceptions are Little America, east of passage mile 13.0 on Butler Avenue, and Woody Mountain Campground, 2.5 miles west of downtown on Route 66.

Distance from Trail	0.0 mile
Area Code	928
Zip Codes	86001 and 86004
ATM	Bank One, 100 W. Birch Ave., 779-7411
Bank	Bank of America, 125 E. Birch Ave., 779-3910
Bicycle Shop	Absolute Bikes, 18 N. San Francisco St., 779-5969
Camping	Woody Mountain Campground, 2727 W. Route 66, 774-7727
Dining	*Asian Gourmet,* 1580 E. Route 66, 773-7771; *Bellavia,* 18 S. Beaver St., 774-8301
Gear	Babbitt's Backcountry Outfitters, 12 E. Aspen Ave., 774-4775
Groceries	Albertson's, 1416 E. Route 66, 773-7955
Information	Chamber of Commerce, 101 W. Route 66, 774-4505
Laundry	Little America (see "Lodging"); White Flag Coin-Op Laundry, 16 S. Beaver St., 774-7614
Lodging	*Little America,* 2515 E. Butler Ave., 779-7900; *Western Hills Motel,* 1580 E. Route 66, 774-6633; *Best Western Kings House Motel,* 1560 E. Route 66, 774-7186
Medical	Flagstaff Medical Center, 1200 N. Beaver St., 779-3366
Post Office	104 N. Agassiz St. (86001), 527-2440
Showers	Little America (see "Lodging")

USGS: FLAGSTAFF EAST

Passage 31
LOWER LAKE MARY, FLAGSTAFF EAST, and WINONA

SCALE: 1.5/32 INCH = 1 MILE

1/4   1/4   1/2

Arizona Trail
(current segment)

Arizona Trail
(previous and next segments)

Access route

River or stream

Lake or pond

Marsh or swamp

Primary highway

Secondary highway

Light duty road

Unimproved road

Trail

Quarry or open mine pit

USGS: **WINONA**

USGS: **ASHURST LAKE**

USGS: **LOWER LAKE MARY**

Passage 32
Mount Elden: Cosnino (I-40) to Schultz Pass

Pond and grasses with the San Francisco Peaks in the distance

TOTAL DISTANCE	14.8 miles
QUALITY HIKING DISTANCE	14.8 miles
DIFFICULTY	Easy
TOTAL ELEVATION GAIN	1,897 feet
TOTAL DESCENT	363 feet
FROM MEXICO	559.7 miles
TO UTAH	212.2 miles
LAND MANAGERS	Coconino County, Coconino National Forest (Peaks Ranger District)
RECOMMENDED MONTHS	May through September

INTRODUCTION

The first half of this passage skirts the Turkey Hills and crosses the Rio de Flag toward Elden Pueblo. In this section, 2 miles of trail have yet to be constructed. The second half is part of the Mount Elden Trail System and skirts the base of Little Elden Mountain up to Schultz Pass.

MOUNTAIN BIKE NOTES

The trail west of the highway is part of the Dry Lake–Mount Elden Trail System, which is the most popular and challenging system of trails for mountain biking in the Flagstaff area. The northern 6.5 miles of the trail climb gradually up to the mountain pass.

WATER

The water in the Rio de Flag is contaminated with wastewater effluent from Flagstaff's water treatment facility. Instead, fill your bottles in town along US 89.

MAPS

USGS Quadrangles: Winona, Flagstaff East, Sunset Crater West, Humphreys Peak
USFS: Coconino National Forest (North Half)
Other: Arizona Public Lands Information Center, AZT Passage Topo Map 32—
Mt. Elden

BEGINNING ACCESS POINT

Cosnino (I-40): From the Cosnino exit (207) off of I-40, turn right and take your next right onto the frontage road. There is no official parking area; however, there is space to park along the frontage road.

ALTERNATE ACCESS POINT

Sandy Seep Trailhead: Take US 89 north from the Flagstaff Mall, then turn left to the trailhead just past the US 89 intersection with Townsend-Winona Road.

Little Elden Spring Horse Camp/Trailhead: Take US 89 north of Flagstaff past the Silver Saddle Road stoplight. Turn left onto Elden Spring Road (FR 556), a graded dirt road, to the trailhead or horse camp.

ENDING ACCESS POINT

Schultz Pass: Accessible from the east side of the mountains along Elden Spring Road (see second "Alternate Access Point"). Turn left on Schultz Pass Road (FR 420).

From the west side of town, take US 180 north and turn right (east) onto Elden Lookout Road. Immediately turn left (north) onto Schultz Pass Road (FR 420), which soon turns into a graded dirt road and arcs eastward to join FR 556 at the trailhead.

TRAIL DESCRIPTION   At the frontage road south of I-40, the trail will use an underpass under I-40 and another underpass under the railroad (this section was not completed at the time of publication). From there, the trail veers west, then parallels the railroad and currently ends at the Turkey Hills Road (FR 510B). The next 2.0 miles of trail will head northwest toward US 89 and cross the Rio de Flag. There is an underpass just south of the intersection of US 89 and Townsend-Winona Road. The trail leaves the underpass and heads north to meet up with the Sandy Seep Trail. Turn left onto the 1.4-mile Sandy Seep Trail. At the "T" intersection, turn right onto the Little Elden Trail and go 4.9 miles to Schultz Pass.

Opposite: Aspens with the San Francisco Peaks in the distance

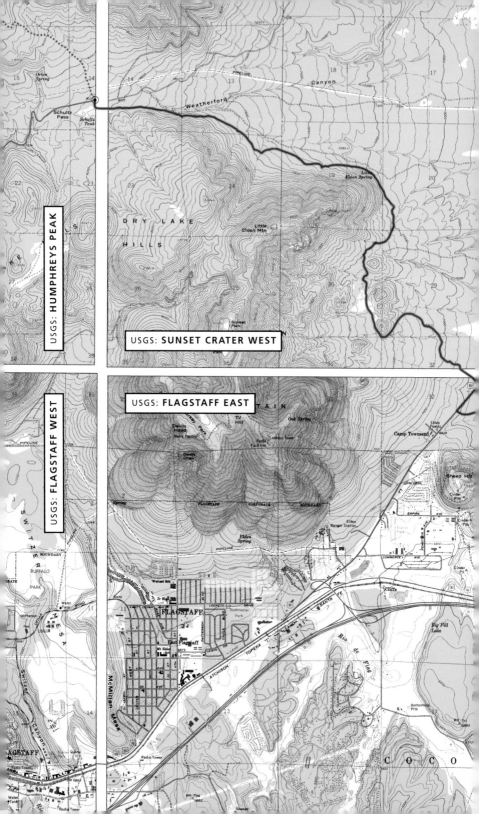

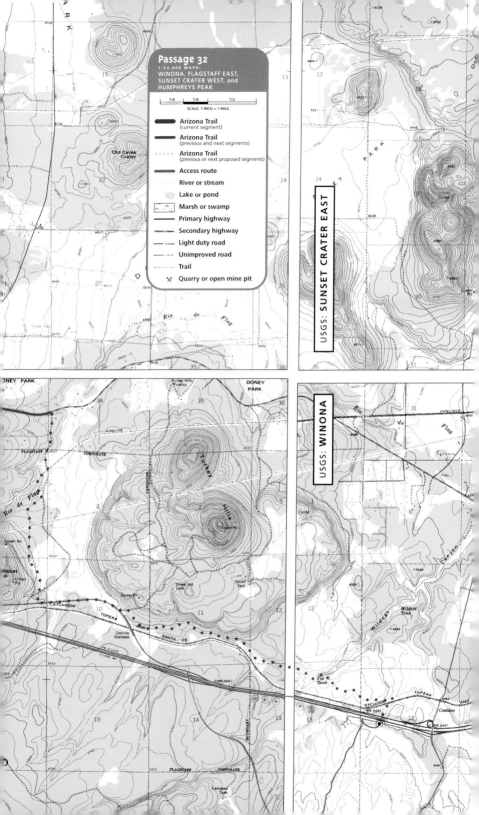

Passage 32

1:24,000 MAPS:
WINONA, FLAGSTAFF EAST,
SUNSET CRATER WEST, and
HUMPHREYS PEAK

1/4	1/4		1/2

SCALE: 1 INCH = 1 MILE

▬▬▬ **Arizona Trail**
(current segment)

▬▬▬ **Arizona Trail**
(previous and next segments)

•••• **Arizona Trail**
(previous or next proposed segments)

▬▬▬ **Access route**

River or stream

⬭ **Lake or pond**

Marsh or swamp

▬▬▬ **Primary highway**

▬▬▬ **Secondary highway**

▭▭▭ **Light duty road**

▬▬▬ **Unimproved road**

----- **Trail**

✕ **Quarry or open mine pit**

USGS: SUNSET CRATER EAST

USGS: WINONA

Passage 33
Flagstaff (Resupply Route): Fisher Point to Schultz Pass

Wildflowers near Buffalo Park with the San Francisco Peaks in the background

INTRODUCTION This urban route takes you across the center of the city of Flagstaff, with a diversity of experiences from beginning to end. This passage gives long-distance thru-hikers a chance to resupply in town and visit the city. The mileage of this route is not included in the total mileage of the Arizona Trail.

The passage starts along the Fisher Point area trail system, passes through an underpass at one of the city's busiest intersections at Enterprise Road, and then climbs

TOTAL DISTANCE	13.8 miles
QUALITY HIKING DISTANCE	10.2 miles
DIFFICULTY	Moderate
TOTAL ELEVATION GAIN	2,208 feet
TOTAL DESCENT	814 feet
FROM MEXICO	559.7 miles
TO UTAH	212.2 miles
LAND MANAGERS	Coconino National Forest (Peaks Ranger District), City of Flagstaff
RECOMMENDED MONTHS	April through October

to McMillan Mesa on an urban trail. Then the trail passes through beautiful Buffalo Park and into the Dry Lake Hills trail system.

MOUNTAIN BIKE NOTES

The portions of this trail route south and north of the city are some of the most popular mountain-biking trails in town. The hills make these challenging for some. Be aware that the Schultz Creek Trail is also open to motorcycles.

WATER
Resupply in town; the pond south of I-40 is effluent from the wastewater treatment facility.

MAPS
USGS Quadrangles: Flagstaff East, Flagstaff West, Sunset Crater West, Humphreys Peak
USFS: Coconino National Forest (North Half)
Other: Arizona Public Lands Information Center, AZT Passage Topo Map 33—
  Flagstaff

BEGINNING ACCESS POINT

Fisher Point: Fisher Point has no road access. The closest trail access is via Trail #106 from Canyon Vista Campground, 4 miles south of Flagstaff on FR 3.

ALTERNATE ACCESS POINT

Buffalo Park: From Route 66, take Switzer Canyon Road north and turn right on Turquoise Drive. Turn right at Forest/Cedar Avenue. At the top of the hill, turn left (north) to Buffalo Park (past the USGS complex).

ENDING ACCESS POINT

 Schultz Pass: See "Ending Access Point" for Passage 32.

TRAIL DESCRIPTION   At the junction of several drainages just west of Fisher Point, take the left fork up a tributary of Walnut Canyon. At Fisher Point, you will come to a junction in the AZT. Passage 31 heads east and traverses the edge of Walnut Canyon. The passage described here (Passage 33) is a resupply route for thru-hikers and heads north into Flagstaff.

At 1.0 mile up the hill, turn right at the fence walk-through and head north for 1.8 miles. Take the left fork at the next two major trail junctions. The trail drops down a steep hill and leads to a pond just below I-40.

From the bottom of the hill, follow the route around the east side of the pond, pass under I-40, and take the road to the right. You will end up at the intersection of Babbitt and Butler next to the Sam's Club. Turn right at Butler and take the underpass at Enterprise north to Route 66. Turn left at Route 66 to get to Switzer Canyon Road until the McMillan Mesa link is constructed. From Route 66, turn right onto Switzer Canyon Road. Turn right onto Turquoise Drive and head north to Forest/Cedar Avenue. Cross the intersection to the urban trail on the northeast corner, which leads you to Buffalo Park.

From the Buffalo Park entrance, take the trail to the north to the Forest Service boundary. This is the Oldham Trail, which links up with the Rocky Ridge Trail just north of Elden Lookout Road. Turn left on the Rocky Ridge Trail. At the Schultz Creek Trailhead, turn right onto the Schultz Creek Trail. Go northeast along the drainage, climbing toward Schultz Pass.

Opposite: Wildflowers and the I-40 bridge as seen from Rio de Flag Canyon

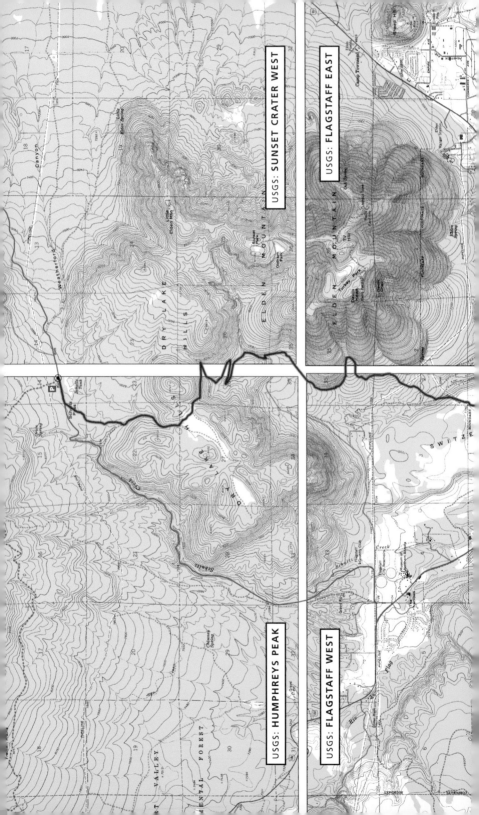

USGS: SUNSET CRATER WEST

USGS: FLAGSTAFF EAST

USGS: HUMPHREYS PEAK

USGS: FLAGSTAFF WEST

Passage 34
San Francisco Peaks: Schultz Pass to Cedar Ranch

The Arizona Trail through the San Francisco Peaks

TOTAL DISTANCE	26.4 miles
QUALITY HIKING DISTANCE	26.4 miles
DIFFICULTY	Strenuous
TOTAL ELEVATION GAIN	1,946 feet
TOTAL DESCENT	3,573 feet
FROM MEXICO	574.5 miles
TO UTAH	197.4 miles
LAND MANAGERS	Coconino National Forest (Peaks Ranger District)
RECOMMENDED MONTHS	May through October

INTRODUCTION   As of fall 2004, the Arizona Trail in this passage has not been constructed. The Peaks Ranger District of the Coconino National Forest has identified a route and completed a final environmental assessment for the route. There still remain some issues to resolve prior to trail construction, scheduled to begin in 2006. For more information, contact the Peaks Ranger District of the Coconino National Forest or the Arizona Trail Association (602-242-4794 or ata@aztrail.org).

This passage will skirt the west side of the San Francisco Peaks, whose high point, Humphreys Peak, is Arizona's tallest summit (12,633'). The AZT will also reach its highest point in this passage at 10,400'.

MOUNTAIN BIKE NOTES

The route of this passage, as planned, will be excellent for mountain bikers when the tread is complete. The entire passage will skirt but not enter the Kachina Peaks Wilderness.

WATER

Water sources have not as yet been identified along this passage. Based on the route plan, the main water sources appear to be at Schultz Pass, the very unreliable Kelly Tank, and East Cedar Tank. Thru-hikers should get current water-source information from the Peaks Ranger District or the Arizona Trail Association.

MAPS

USGS Quadrangles: Humphreys Peak, Sunset Crater West, White Horse Hills, S P Mountain, Chapel Mountain
USFS: Coconino National Forest (North Half)

BEGINNING ACCESS POINT

Smooth road to Trailhead   **Schultz Pass:** From downtown Flagstaff, drive north on US 180 (also North Fort Valley Road). After you pass the Sechrist School on your right, continue 1.2 miles and then turn right (north) where a sign indicates Schultz Pass Road (FR 420). Follow this paved road 0.7 mile through two right-angle turns. After the road turns to dirt, continue 4.5 miles to a parking area on the right (south) side of the road (N35°17'05", W111°37'48").

ENDING ACCESS POINT

Bumpy road to Trailhead   5.2 miles   **Cedar Ranch:** See "Beginning Access Point" for Passage 35.

TRAIL DESCRIPTION   The Forest Service's proposed route for the Arizona Trail from Schultz Pass to Cedar Ranch runs along the west side of the San Francisco Peaks just outside the Kachina Peaks Wilderness. The following trail route description is taken from an official Forest Service document that's part of the environmental assessment.

The advantages of the selected route are that it would provide safe and high-quality recreation opportunities. The trail is nonmotorized, in keeping with the vision of the

Arizona Trail statewide to provide for hiking, equestrian, and mountain bike opportunities. The trail route is scenic, with long-distance vistas, a variety of high-elevation plant communities (aspen, limber pine, and mountain meadows), and up-close views of Agassiz and Humphreys Peaks. The route represents a balance of providing this high-elevation experience while being sensitive to wildlife, cultural, and wilderness values.

The Humphreys Trailhead link will allow Arizona Trail hikers the choice of taking the Humphreys Trail to reach the highest point in Arizona. At the same time, the trail link and interpretive loop trail give a well-designed place to go for the thousands of people who visit the trailhead parking lot each year.

Along this route the Arizona Trail hiker or rider will experience long, contiguous, and unbroken stretches of singletrack trail, seldom crossing social trails or roads. After trail obliteration work is complete, the evidence of these trails will quickly become substantially unnoticeable to the passing AZT user. The AZT user will be able to enjoy a quality of experience with noticeable opportunities for feelings of solitude, remoteness, and a lack of human disturbance, for long periods of time.

There is no doubt this will be a popular trail used by many people. The design features and mitigation measures will ensure that environmental effects from increased levels of use are not significant. The managed trail corridor provides greater opportunity for maintaining the qualities of the area in a safe, environmentally sensitive way.

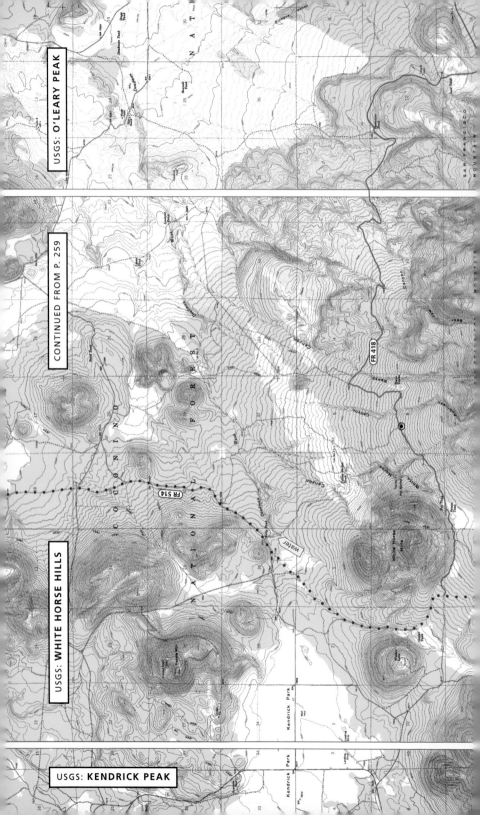

CONTINUED FROM P. 259

USGS: O'LEARY PEAK

USGS: WHITE HORSE HILLS

USGS: KENDRICK PEAK

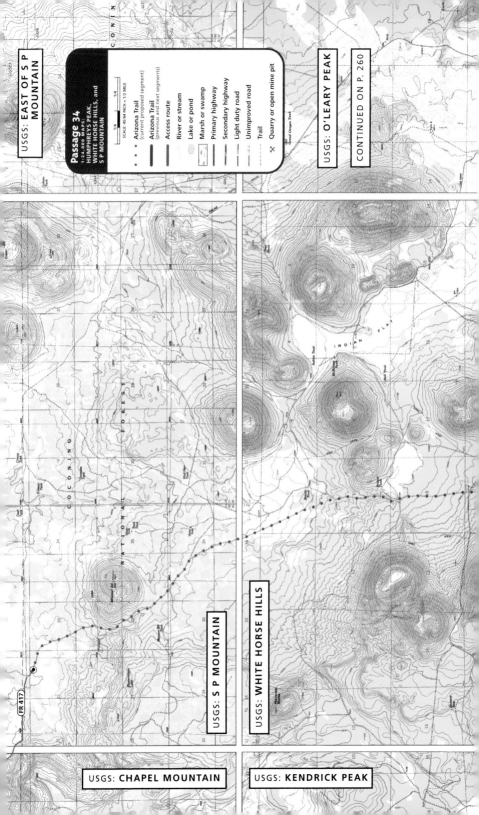

Passage 34
1:24 000 MAPS:
HUMPHREYS PEAK,
WHITE HORSE HILLS, and
S P MOUNTAIN

SCALE 45/64 INCH = 1/2 MILE

1/4   1/4

• • • Arizona Trail
        (current proposed segment)

        Arizona Trail
        (previous and next segments)

        Access route

        River or stream

        Lake or pond

        Marsh or swamp

        Primary highway

        Secondary highway

        Light duty road

        Unimproved road

        Trail

×   Quarry or open mine pit

CONTINUED ON P. 260

COCONINO   NATIONAL   FOREST

INDIAN   FLAT

FR 417

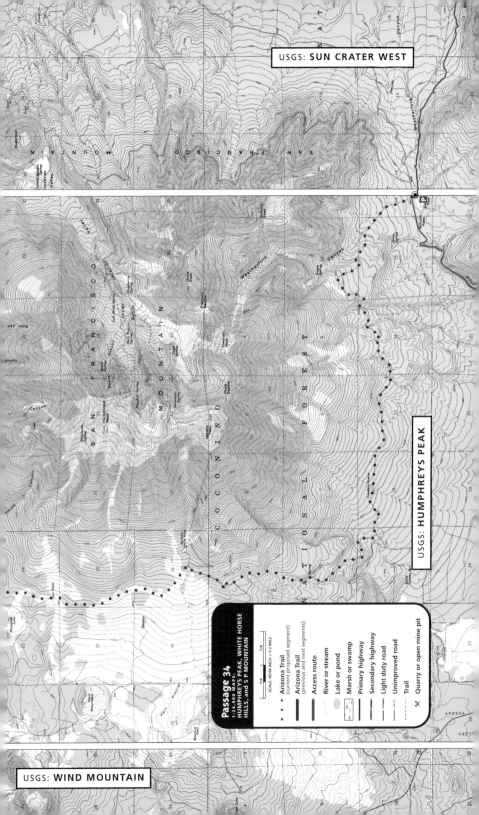

USGS: **SUN CRATER WEST**

USGS: **HUMPHREYS PEAK**

USGS: **WIND MOUNTAIN**

Passage 34
1:24,000 MAPS:
HUMPHREYS PEAK, WHITE HORSE
HILLS, and S P MOUNTAIN

SCALE 45/64 INCH = 1/2 MILE

1/4   1/4

•••• Arizona Trail
(current proposed segment)

■■■■ Arizona Trail
(previous and next segments)

—— Access route

River or stream

Lake or pond

Marsh or swamp

Primary highway

Secondary highway

——— Light duty road

----- Unimproved road

.... Trail

✕ Quarry or open mine pit

Passage 35
Babbitt Ranch: Cedar Ranch to Moqui Stage Station

Babbitt Ranch

TOTAL DISTANCE	28.7 miles
QUALITY HIKING DISTANCE	28.7 miles
DIFFICULTY	Easy
TOTAL ELEVATION GAIN	1,034 feet
TOTAL DESCENT	787 feet
FROM MEXICO	600.9 miles
TO UTAH	171.0 miles
LAND MANAGERS	Kaibab National Forest (Chalender Ranger District, Tusayan Ranger District), Arizona State Land Department
RECOMMENDED MONTHS	Spring and fall are best. Summer temperatures can be uncomfortable, and winter snow is a possibility.

The AZT on this passage is mainly on ranch roads. But traffic is infrequent and the unique terrain is an integral part of the rich variety of landscapes along the Arizona Trail. The views to the south toward the San Francisco Peaks are stunning. Try to imagine the scene 2 million years ago when lava was spewing over thousands of square miles.

The route is easy to follow because volunteers have done a good job marking the various road intersections with AZT-branded 4x4 posts. The final 5.0 miles follow a singletrack trail that is occasionally obscure but makes a nice diversion from the road.

Note that this passage crosses Arizona state lands, and a state lands permit is required for camping. To acquire a permit, write to Arizona State Land Department—Public Records, 1616 West Adams, Phoenix, AZ 85007. Phone: (602) 542-4631.

This passage also crosses land owned by Babbitt Ranches. Please respect private property. You can contact the ranch at P.O. Box 520, Flagstaff, AZ 86002. Phone: (928) 774-6199.

Note: As of late 2004, the management of Babbitt Ranches and Coconino County are working on plans to relocate the Arizona Trail off the ranch roads and build a new singletrack trail in the near future. The route has been identified and plotted using GPS, and the necessary state trust land easements have been acquired by Coconino County.

MOUNTAIN BIKE NOTES

This passage follows dirt ranch roads over its first 19.0 miles and then jumps onto a faint but ridable singletrack. The entire passage offers fun riding, with views of surreal landscapes rarely seen at most fat-tire destinations.

WATER

Dirt Tank: N35°38'20", W111°49'10"

Upper Lockwood Tank: N35°43'07", W111°49'17"

Lockwood Tank: N35°43'45", W111°47'48"

MAPS

USGS Quadrangles: S P Mountain, Chapel Mountain, Lockwood Canyon, Peterson Flat, Harbison Tank
USFS: Kaibab National Forest (Chalender and Tusayan Ranger Districts)
Other: Arizona Public Lands Information Center, AZT Passage Topo Maps 35A and 35B—Babbitt Ranch

BEGINNING ACCESS POINT

Bumpy road to Trailhead   5.2 miles

Cedar Ranch: From Flagstaff drive north on US 180 about 33.0 miles and turn right (east) onto FR 417 near mile marker 247. (If you reach the Kaibab National Forest, you've gone too far by 0.4 mile.) Continue 5.2 miles to a point a short distance north of Cedar Ranch Camp where a side road, FR 9008A, leaves FR 417 to the left (N35°32'51", W111°46'57"). The passage begins here and follows FR 9008A north-northeast.

ENDING ACCESS POINT

Moqui Stage Station: See "Beginning Access Point" for Passage 36.

TRAIL DESCRIPTION   Head north-northeast on FR 9008A, as indicated by 4x4 posts with the AZT brand (6,375'). Walk through a sparsely vegetated landscape of juniper trees and rabbitbrush to a fork at mile 3.6. Continue straight (north) on a lower-quality road; don't follow the main road, which breaks off to the right. Around mile 4.0, you'll pass a house that is part of Tub Ranch Camp. Continue up a hill to the north and pass through a gate (N35°36'10", W111°45'31"). Follow the road's left fork, which angles up a low ridge and deposits you on a beautiful high plateau with great views.

The road enters small hills dotted with trees. Cross a wash in 0.2 mile, bear left (southwest), and climb gradually. After some power lines come into view, you'll reach a fork. Bear right and continue 0.1 mile to another fork. Stay right again and continue straight ahead to the north.

You'll pass Dirt Tank, which is on the left about 100 yards away (N35°38'20", W111°49'10"). Cross under the buzzing power lines, follow a right fork to the north, up a hill, and begin a long traverse of another broad, featureless plateau.

After bearing north and finally northwest, you'll pass Upper Lockwood Tank (N35°43'07", W111°49'17"). Follow the old road as it curves to the right around the back of the tank and heads northeast along a tributary of Lockwood Canyon.

You'll reach Lockwood Tank (6,375'; N35°43'45", W111°47'48") at a fence with two gates. Go straight through the gate in front of you, bear left, and continue through another distinctive gate to FR 301 on the north side of the tank. Turn left and head northwest.

A cattle guard, a fence, and several signs mark your crossing into the Kaibab National Forest. (The road you're following becomes FR 301.) Cross the cattle guard and look to the left for a wooden sign that says "Kaibab National Forest." Behind this sign, head west on a very faint singletrack trail. Look for several large rock cairns that dot the trail ahead. Aim for a lone juniper tree in the flat and walk past it in 0.1 mile. Look for 4x4 posts with the AZT brand to help you navigate here.

The trail improves as it reaches the trees and bends briefly to the left (southwest) before curving back to the northwest. Cross an old dirt road at a right angle. The trail winds and rolls through a dry piñon-juniper forest as it parallels the main road, FR 301, to the northwest. The trail becomes less distinct as it crosses FR 301. Follow the singletrack to the northwest on the other side.

The trail breaks out of the trees into a clearing and all but disappears. If you can't see the faint trace heading across the clearing, take a compass bearing of 330° and head for the opposite side. There you'll reach a fork in the trail that marks the end of Passage 35 (mile 28.7; 6,640'; N35°47'14", W111°52'31"). The right fork is the continuation of the AZT into Passage 36. To reach the parking area at Moqui Stage Station, turn left (west) and continue 0.2 mile to a simple Forest Service sign marking the trailhead.

Arizona Trail horseback rider.
Photo courtesy of The Arizona Trail Association

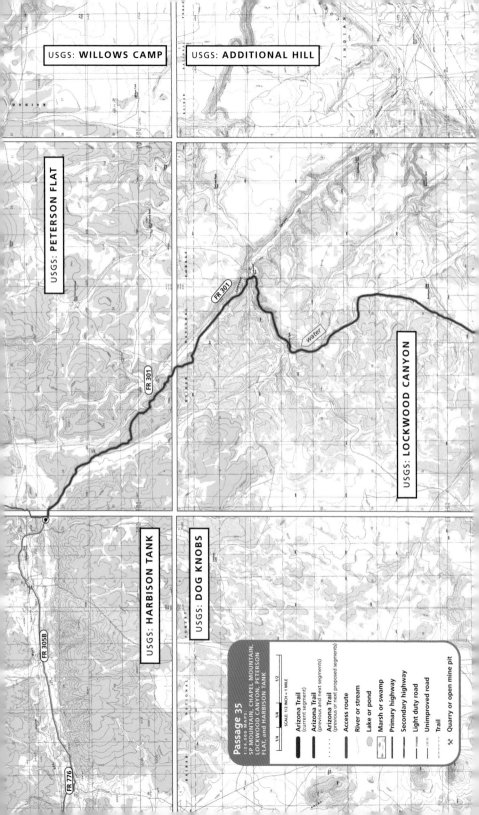

USGS: **WILLOWS CAMP**

USGS: **ADDITIONAL HILL**

USGS: **PETERSON FLAT**

USGS: **LOCKWOOD CANYON**

USGS: **HARBISON TANK**

USGS: **DOG KNOBS**

FR 301

FR 301

FR 305B

FR 776

water

Passage 35
SP MOUNTAIN, CHAPEL MOUNTAIN,
LOCKWOOD CANYON, PETERSON
FLAT, and HARBISON TANK

SCALE: 1/2 INCH = 1 MILE

1/4   1/4   1/2

Arizona Trail
(current segment)

Arizona Trail
(previous and next segments)

Arizona Trail
(previous or next proposed segments)

Access route

River or stream

Lake or pond

Marsh or swamp

Primary highway

Secondary highway

Light duty road

Unimproved road

Trail

Quarry or open mine pit

USGS: **S P MOUNTAIN**

USGS: **CHAPEL MOUNTAIN**

USGS: **EBERT MOUNTAIN**

FR 9008A

FR 417

Dirt Tank

Passage 36
Coconino Rim: Moqui Stage Station to Grandview Lookout Tower

Grandview Lookout Tower

Arizona Trail Association

INTRODUCTION This passage offers a classic northern Arizona hiking or mountain biking experience, with long stretches of beautiful ponderosa pine forest, prime elk habitat, and tantalizing views of the Grand Canyon. To break this passage into smaller sections, use the Russell Tank area as an intermediate trailhead. This is on FR 311 about 1.7 miles south of FR 310, the Coconino Rim Road.

This relatively flat stretch has abundant campsites. There is not much fresh water, but the frequent tanks and ponds may be promising. As you head northwest along

TOTAL DISTANCE	19.0 miles
QUALITY HIKING DISTANCE	19.0 miles
DIFFICULTY	Easy
TOTAL ELEVATION GAIN	1,790 feet
TOTAL DESCENT	905 feet
FROM MEXICO	629.6 miles
TO UTAH	142.3 miles
LAND MANAGERS	Kaibab National Forest (Tusayan Ranger District)
RECOMMENDED MONTHS	April through November

the Coconino Rim, some of the drainages dropping to the northeast may contain water. However, you will only find water in the upper reaches of these valleys if the ground is saturated from winter snowmelt or recent rainfall. The trail is frequently marked with 4x4 posts emblazoned with the AZT symbol.

MOUNTAIN BIKE NOTES

The entire length of this passage is open for riding, and for the most part it is easy going. One spot midway in the passage requires a short bike detour (signed) where the trail switchbacks down and up the steep walls of a drainage. Watch out for the surprisingly abundant prickly pear cactus.

WATER

Although there is a restroom at Grandview Lookout Tower, there is no water.

 Russell Tank: N35°52'18", W111°52 44"

MAPS

USGS Quadrangles: Harbison Tank, Peterson Flat, Grandview Point
USFS: Kaibab National Forest (Tusayan Ranger District)
Other: Arizona Public Lands Information Center, AZT Passage Topo Map 36—
   Coconino Rim

BEGINNING ACCESS POINT

Moqui Stage Station: 11.0 miles south of Tusayan and about 56.0 miles north of Flagstaff on US 180, turn east onto FR 320 at mile marker 224. Turn right (east) at an intersection in 3.8 miles, staying on FR 320. Continue 0.2 mile and turn right (south) on FR 305 (not marked). Follow this road south, east, and south again for 4.0 miles to FR 776. Turn left (east) onto FR 776 and continue another 4.0 miles. Turn left (east) on FR 305B and drive 5.0 miles to FR 301. Turn right (south) and continue 0.5 mile to Moqui Stage Station on the left, marked by a simple Forest Service sign.

Park here, walk up a road that curves to the right (northeast), pass an old stone well in 50 yards, and follow a singletrack trail east through the trees 0.1 mile to intersect the very clear AZT (N35°47'14", W111°52'31"). To follow the AZT northbound, turn left toward Russell Tank.

ENDING ACCESS POINT

Grandview Lookout Tower: See "Beginning Access Point" for Passage 37.

TRAIL DESCRIPTION The AZT descends to cross a dirt road 0.5 mile north of the intersection by Moqui Stage Station. Go straight across and continue north on a reclaimed two-track road that meanders through ponderosa pines. As the road fades, pass through a gate into a fenced area, and then continue on a faint two-track just west of north. Anderson Tank is just out of view on the right.

In 1.0 mile, after you pass through another gate at mile 3.4, the road virtually disappears. Turn left and parallel the fence line due north—don't be tricked by a decoy path that continues straight ahead to the northeast.

A faint two-track soon develops. When the fence ends, follow the two-track straight ahead. Cross FR 320. Soon, you'll pass a small, metal water tank at mile 4.0 (6,780'), after which the AZT follows Russell Wash through a deepening ponderosa forest (6,960'; N35°51'49", W111°52'34"). At this point, the trail veers left (west) out of the wash.

The clear tread soon veers back to the right (north) and, after another 0.7 mile, passes through a modern gate near the large Russell Tank (7,055'; N35°52'18", W111°52'44"). At Russell Tank, there is a modern outhouse about 100 yards off the trail to the west.

The AZT continues north and passes through another gate. Cross FR 310. After rambling through some oak-lined drainages, the trail trends to the west. Then the AZT breaks onto the edge of the Coconino Rim, offering far-ranging views to the north.

After a mile, a trail sign indicates a bike bypass taking the left (westernmost) route. Hikers should stay right. Where the trail fades in about 0.1 mile, continue to a fence, turn back to the right, and follow a faint tread that switchbacks down the slope. If you lose this elusive trail, make your way toward the bottom of the wash. The trail crosses the bottom 25 yards east of the fence and is much clearer as it climbs the north side for 0.2 mile to reach a road. Here, the bike bypass rejoins the main route, which continues north on a singletrack (7,290'; N35°54'13", W111°53'34"). Over the next 3 miles, cross through several gates and minor washes and get your first close-up views of the Grand Canyon to the north (right).

Toward the end of the passage, you'll begin to see interpretive signs explaining the effects of dwarf mistletoe on ponderosa pine populations. Northbound AZT hikers will encounter these signs in reverse order, so you won't find out what dwarf mistletoe actually is until you reach the beginning of the interpretive trail.

When you reach FR 307, turn left onto this road, cross a cattle guard, and turn right (due north) to rejoin the singletrack. A few steps farther, you will join the plush gravel tread of a developed loop trail and follow it west to Grandview Lookout Tower and the end of Passage 36 (7,530'; N35°57'29", W111°57'20"). You'll find a restroom, but no water, near the lookout tower.

Grandview Trailhead

Arizona Trail Association

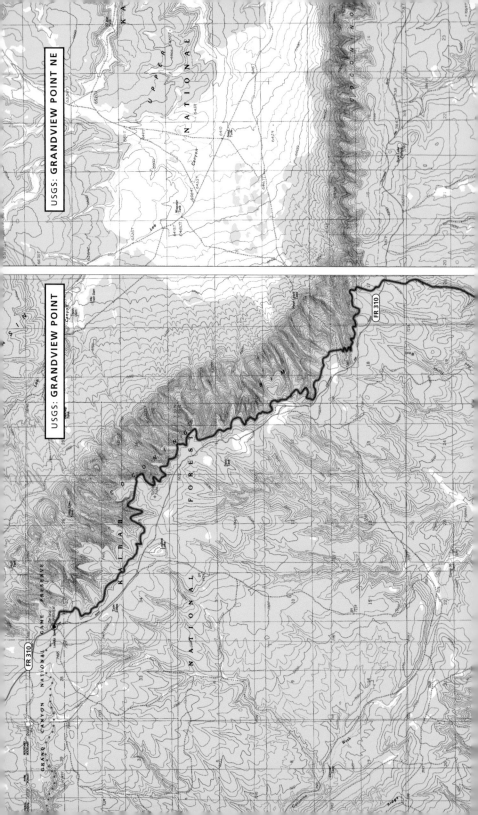

USGS: GRANDVIEW POINT NE

USGS: GRANDVIEW POINT

FR 310

FR 310

FR 310

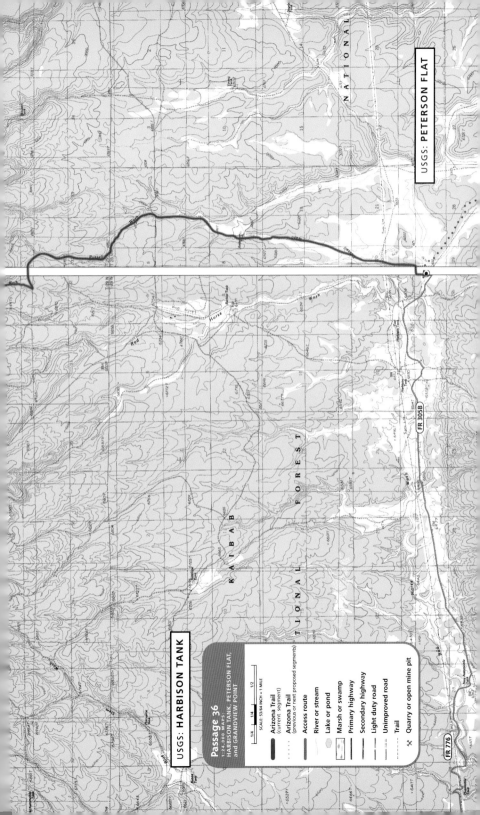

USGS: PETERSON FLAT

USGS: HARBISON TANK

Passage 36
1:24,000 MAPS
HARBISON TANK, PETERSON FLAT,
and GRANDVIEW POINT

SCALE 53/64 INCH = 1 MILE

1/4   1/4   1/2

Arizona Trail
(current segment)

Arizona Trail
(previous or next proposed segments)

Access route

River or stream

Lake or pond

Marsh or swamp

Primary highway

Secondary highway

Light duty road

Unimproved road

Trail

✕   Quarry or open mine pit

FR 776

FR 305B

NATIONAL

KAIBAB

NATIONAL FOREST

Passage 37
Grand Canyon—South Rim: Grandview Lookout Tower to Yaki Point/South Kaibab Trailhead

Near Grandview Point, South Rim of the Grand Canyon

TOTAL DISTANCE	23.3 miles
QUALITY HIKING DISTANCE	15.0 miles
DIFFICULTY	Easy
TOTAL ELEVATION GAIN	981 feet
TOTAL DESCENT	1,303 feet
FROM MEXICO	648.6 miles
TO UTAH	123.3 miles
LAND MANAGERS	Kaibab National Forest (Tusayan Ranger District), Grand Canyon National Park
RECOMMENDED MONTHS	April through November, depending on snow level

INTRODUCTION An official route for this passage is not yet finalized. The route described here is not official but is the likely general route. Starting at the Grandview Lookout Tower, it leads first to the north edge of Tusayan and then into Grand Canyon National Park alongside US 180 through the park entrance station. After entering the park, you're once again walking near the road to the Yaki Point/South Kaibab Trailhead. But until an Arizona Trail route is finalized, most hikers will hike north from the Grandview Lookout into the park, then either hike into the canyon via Grandview Point or make their way to Grand Canyon Village for amenities.

MOUNTAIN BIKE NOTES

 The route described in this passage, from the Grandview Lookout Tower into Tusayan, is via the Tusayan Bike Trail. Pretty nifty riding, too! But from Tusayan to the Grand Canyon rim, it's paved road to Yaki Point. Of course, you can't ride a bicycle below the rim into the canyon's inner gorge area. But see "Mountain Bike Notes" in Passage 38 for information on having your bike transported to the North Rim while you hike through the canyon.

WATER

 Mile 4.4, Watson Tank: This tank sometimes has water (N35°57'28", W112°01'21").

 Mile 14.3, Tusayan: Water is always available at a number of places in this town (N35°58'28", W112°07'32").

 South Kaibab Trailhead: There is water at the trailhead at the end of this passage (N36°03'12", W112°05'00").

MAPS

USGS Quadrangles: Grandview Point, Tusayan East, Phantom Ranch
USFS: Kaibab National Forest (Tusayan Ranger District)
Other: Tusayan Bike Trail, Grand Canyon Map (provided at the park entrance station)

BEGINNING ACCESS POINT

 Grandview Lookout Tower: Follow Grand Canyon National Park's Rim Drive (AZ 64) to its southernmost dip, about 11.0 miles east of Grand Canyon Village. From this junction, follow FR 310 (Coconino Rim Drive) 1.3 miles south to the trailhead (N35°57'29", W111°57'20").

ENDING ACCESS POINT

 Yaki Point/South Kaibab Trailhead: See "Beginning Access Point" for Passage 38.

TRAIL DESCRIPTION Across FR 310, west of the Grandview Lookout Tower, is a parking lot that has a trail sign noting a bike trail and a distance of 16 miles to Tusayan.

Until it is determined how the Arizona Trail will enter the Grand Canyon, this bike trail will serve as the route. The trail is decent and easy to follow, but as far as a route to enter one of the world's greatest natural wonders, it leaves a lot to be desired. The plus is that it's a lovely area, and you are not likely to run into any of the hordes of people that will be in the Grand Canyon area.

From the trailhead, the trail goes west through open forest. It crosses a road at mile 1.3 (7,380'; N35°57'22", W111°58'35") and continues west.

Eventually the trail drops into an unnamed canyon and comes to Watson Tank at mile 4.4 (N35°57'28", W112°01'21"). Depending on the time of the year, this tank might have water.

From here, the trail goes about 0.2 mile, turns right (north), and climbs up to FR 303. The route now follows this road for about 1.7 miles to a junction with FR 825 at mile 6.8 (6,920'; N35°57'40", W112°02'52"). Turn right (north) here and stay on this dirt road until it ends at mile 7.9 (6,950'; N35°58'17", W112°03'14").

The trail is now a singletrack again, but not for long. It heads southwest for about 0.5 mile and arrives at a gate and FR 818. Turn right (north) here and follow this road up to mile 9.3, which is a junction with FR 815. Take FR 815 for about 0.25 mile to FR 814 and turn left (southwest) on FR 814.

Follow FR 814 until it reaches FR 2709 at mile 10.9 (6,850'; N35°58'13", W112°04'48"). This road is also known as Bike Route #2 on the Tusayan Bike Trail map. Follow Bike Route #2 to Bike Route #1, which takes you very close to Tusayan and then heads north.

SUPPLIES, SERVICES, AND ACCOMMODATIONS

GRAND CANYON VILLAGE

Distance from Trail Approximately 2.5 miles
Area Code 928
Zip Code 86023
ATM See "Bank"
Bank Bank One (Market Plaza), 638-2437
Camping Mather Campground, (800) 365-CAMP
Dining Bright Angel Restaurant (Bright Angel Lodge); Marketplace Delicatessen (Market Plaza)
Gear See "Groceries"
Groceries Canyon Village Marketplace (Market Plaza), 638-2262
Information Canyon View Information Plaza, 638-7888; Backcountry Information Center, 638-7875
Laundry See "Camping"
Lodging Rooms in a variety of lodges on or near the canyon rim can be reserved through Amfac Parks & Resorts, (303) 297-2757.
Medical There is a clinic near the south end of the village; dial 911 for emergencies.
Post Office In Market Plaza, 638-2512
Showers See "Camping"

Winter morning at the Grand Canyon near Mather Point

The bike trail ends on AZ 64/US 180, 0.3 mile north of Tusayan, after crossing under the highway through a large concrete walkway. This point is 0.4 mile south of the Tusayan Ranger District office.

Once you reach AZ 64/US 180, walk north, following the road, about 1.0 mile to the park entrance station. Pay your $10 and enter Grand Canyon National Park. Continue on for 3.0 to 4.0 miles until you reach the junction where AZ 64 goes east. Follow AZ 64 east about 1.0 mile to the Yaki Point/South Kaibab Trailhead. It's well signed and easy to locate. You'll find portable bathrooms and water here, but overnight camping is prohibited.

If you wish to go to Grand Canyon Village, which is worth the trip, proceed past the junction to the visitor center near Mather Point. From the visitor center, shuttles will take you to Grand Canyon Village.

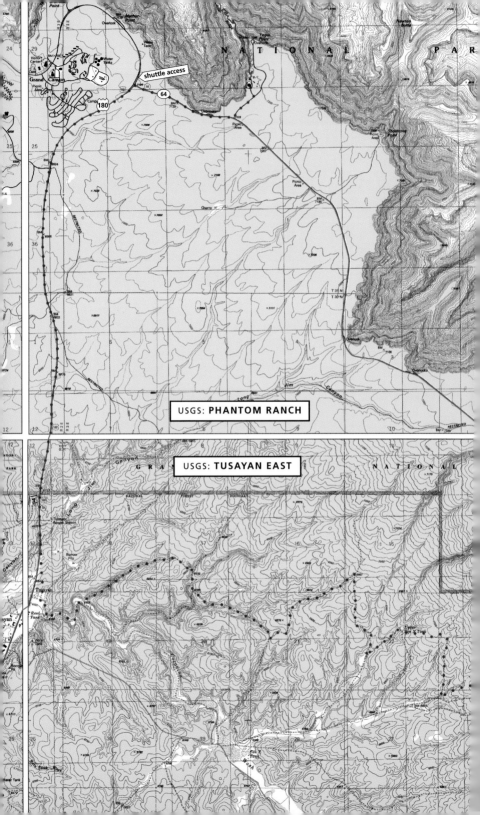

shuttle access

64

180

USGS: **PHANTOM RANCH**

USGS: **TUSAYAN EAST**

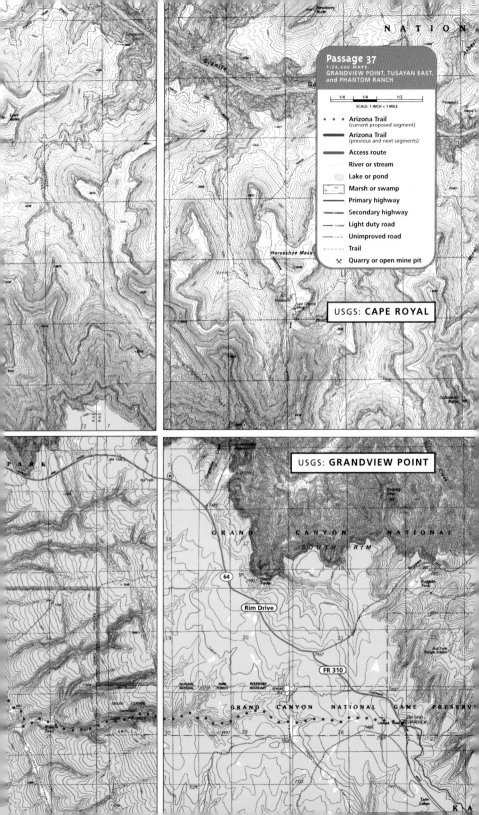

USGS: **CAPE ROYAL**

USGS: **GRANDVIEW POINT**

Passage 38
Grand Canyon—Inner Gorge: Yaki Point/South Kaibab Trailhead to North Kaibab Trailhead

Sunset colors the cliffs of the South Rim of the Grand Canyon

TOTAL DISTANCE	Approximately 21.4 miles
QUALITY HIKING DISTANCE	Approximately 21.4 miles
DIFFICULTY	Strenuous
TOTAL ELEVATION GAIN	5,760 feet
TOTAL DESCENT	4,723 feet
FROM MEXICO	671.9 miles
TO UTAH	100.0 miles
LAND MANAGERS	Grand Canyon National Park
RECOMMENDED MONTHS	May, June, September, and October. Temperatures exceed 100 degrees in summer. The North Rim is closed in winter and may not open until mid-May; check with the National Park Service for projected opening dates.

INTRODUCTION Through the high Kaibab Plateau in northern Arizona, the Colorado River has carved a canyon 277 miles long and averaging 10 miles from rim to rim. It took 6 million years to create this mile-deep canyon. In his comprehensive book *A Field Guide to the Grand Canyon*, Stephen R. Whitney notes, "Among the earth's great river gorges the Grand Canyon is unmatched in its overall vastness, topographic complexity, striking landforms, and range of colors."

Many hikers consider this passage the crown jewel of the AZT. Nowhere else in the country does a few hours' walk take you through 2 billion years of geologic history. Photographs and words cannot capture the massive scale of the Grand Canyon. The relatively few individuals who physically traverse the canyon, feeling each foot of elevation loss and gain in their knees and thighs, are the only ones who will have a real sense of the grandeur of this magical place.

Hiking into and back out of the Grand Canyon is a potentially life-threatening undertaking. Park Service literature and signs near trailheads are plastered with warnings about heat exhaustion and dehydration. A desert climate prevails partway into the canyon, and temperatures exceeding 100 degrees are not uncommon. It is particularly demanding and dangerous to attempt to hike into and out of the canyon in one day—invest a minimum of two days and one night for a safe, fun traverse of the canyon. To experience the canyon more fully, spend two nights at the bottom. You'll appreciate it on the hike out, which most people commence at 5 a.m.

To spend a night or two at the bottom of the Grand Canyon, you must plan well in advance. In the area of the AZT, you may stay only at Bright Angel Campground or Phantom Ranch, near mile 7.0 of this passage. (You also may consider Cottonwood Campground at mile 14.4, but that makes for a long first day of hiking.) At the campground, you will need all of your normal equipment, including the means to cook your own food. At Phantom Ranch, you can take a break from camping and enjoy a bed with sheets and blankets, a shower and towels, air conditioning, and even an outgoing telephone. Even if you're not staying there, you can sign up for the hearty meals at Phantom Ranch; reservations must be made well in advance.

Permit applications for backcountry campgrounds are accepted at the Grand Canyon National Park backcountry office up to four months in advance—submit an application as early as possible. Write to Backcountry Information Center, P.O. Box 129, Grand Canyon, AZ 86023. Phone inquiries are accepted Monday through Friday, 1 p.m. to 5 p.m., at (928) 638-7875.

Reservations for Phantom Ranch are taken up to 23 months in advance, and the rooms often fill very early. Call Xanterra Parks and Resorts at (303) 297-2757.

Due to its great popularity, camping in the Grand Canyon is tightly controlled by the Park Service. Rangers regularly patrol all areas of the canyon, and violations will result in fines and loss of future travel privileges inside the canyon.

Southbound Hikers: Be aware that park rangers do not recommend hiking up the established route of the AZT, the South Kaibab Trail, because it is steep, sun-exposed, and devoid of any water, natural or man-made. The alternative is to hike up the Bright Angel Trail, which will deposit you in Grand Canyon Village, about

3.5 miles west of the South Kaibab Trailhead on the South Rim. The Bright Angel Trail has several water sources.

MOUNTAIN BIKE NOTES

 Mountain bikes are not allowed beneath the rim of the Grand Canyon. To have your bike transported the 212 miles to the North Rim while you hike this passage, contact Trans Canyon Shuttle Service at (928) 638-2820. Advance reservations are required. The shuttle leaves the South Rim at 7 a.m. and arrives at the North Rim at noon. For southbound travelers, the shuttle leaves the North Rim at 1:30 p.m. and reaches the South Rim at 6:30 p.m. This service is available May 15 through October 15.

WATER

 Bright Angel Campground: You can find potable water here or at Phantom Ranch at mile 7.3.

 Rest house

 Rest area

MAPS

USGS Quadrangles: Phantom Ranch, Bright Angel Point
USFS: Kaibab National Forest (Tusayan Ranger District)
Other: Trails Illustrated #207 (Grand Canyon National Park)

BEGINNING ACCESS POINT

 Yaki Point/South Kaibab Trailhead: There is no parking at the trailhead (N36º03'12", W112º05'00"). You must take a shuttle from Grand Canyon Village, near the intersection of US 180 and AZ 64. Inquire at the visitor center.

ENDING ACCESS POINT

 North Kaibab Trailhead: See "Beginning Access Point" for Passage 39.

TRAIL DESCRIPTION   The South Kaibab Trail is well marked, and although it is less popular than its cousin to the west, the Bright Angel Trail, you're still likely to see quite a few people. If you encounter mule trains, stand aside and let them pass.

After leaving the trailhead (7,198'), drop immediately along numerous switchbacks. The trail straightens somewhat and trends north-northwest, and then the sharp drops resume along Cedar Ridge. After passing under the prominent pinnacle of O'Neill Butte, the trail levels briefly on a stunning high plateau before plunging through countless switchbacks toward the inner rim. On a final flat shelf above the Colorado River, you'll reach the intersection with the Tonto Trail. Continue straight to the

Arizona Trail in the Grand Canyon

WILDERNESS ALERT

Congress established **Grand Canyon National Park** in 1919 to preserve its 1.2 million acres of breathtaking vistas, high alpine forests, and 2-billion-year-old geologic record. The regulations governing visits here are more restrictive than those for designated wilderness areas. Please remember and practice these rules governing this American treasure:

- Camping is allowed in designated sites and by permit only.
- Campfires are prohibited; use a stove for cooking.
- Keep water sources clean by washing at least 200 feet from them. Strain dishwater and then scatter it.
- Bury human waste 6 inches deep and 200 feet from any water source. Used toilet paper must be packed out.
- Let nature's sounds prevail. Keep loud voices and noises to a minimum.
- Pets are not allowed, except for signal and guide dogs.
- No bicycles below the canyon rim.
- Pack out all trash, including cigarette butts and toilet paper; don't attempt to burn it.
- Stay on main trails and do not shortcut switchbacks.
- Leave what you find, including rocks, plants, and archaeological remains.
- Do not feed wild animals anywhere in the park.

north for the spectacular, winding descent into the inner gorge. On a geologic scale, you have now traveled 1.2 billion years back in time.

Just above the mighty Colorado River, you'll reach an intersection with the River Trail. Turn right (east) and continue through a tunnel and across the river on a suspension bridge. Follow the trail west (there are some ruins about 0.1 mile past the bridge), and then north along Bright Angel Creek. You will reach the left turn to Bright Angel Campground. After you pass the ranger station, bear right at a fork and soon reach the Phantom Ranch area. Continue to the canteen to check in or purchase a snack (2,560'; N36°06'20", W112°05'37").

Assuming you're well rested after a stay at Bright Angel Campground or the plush Phantom Ranch, set out to the north along Bright Angel Creek. You'll pass the turnoff to the Clear Creek Trail, which offers a nice day hike for those taking a rest day in the Phantom Ranch area. Continue along this relatively easy stretch of trail to reach Cottonwood Campground (4,040').

Pass through a gorgeous canyon of red rock in about 1.5 miles, and then cross to the left side of Bright Angel Creek on a sturdy bridge. In another 0.1 mile (4,580'), you'll find a rest house with fresh water. In a short distance, the trail begins climbing to the left (northwest) as it leaves Bright Angel Canyon. Follow Roaring Springs Canyon for the final climb to the North Rim. You'll see this side canyon's namesake falls, which do indeed roar. Pass a small, developed rest area with water and restrooms and then continue another 2.5 miles to reach the North Kaibab Trailhead, and the end of this passage (8,235'; N36°13'01", W112°03'21").

If you plan to walk to the lodge and other services at the North Rim, you can save about 0.6 mile by avoiding the main road and bearing left at a sign that says "Grand Lodge 1.1 miles." It's actually farther to the lodge, but in about 0.5 mile this path will take you to a general store, laundry facilities, and showers near a campground across the highway.

SUPPLIES, SERVICES, AND ACCOMMODATIONS

GRAND CANYON NORTH RIM

The main development of the North Rim centers around the Grand Canyon Lodge at the far southern end of AZ 67, which is 2.3 miles south of the North Kaibab Trailhead (or about 1.7 miles by the shortcut trail). Here you can find lodging, dining, postal service, phones, and a limited store. For lodging reservations, which should be made as early as possible due to limited availability, call (303) 297-2757. For other information, call the lodge directly at (928) 638-2611.

A campground 1.3 miles north of Grand Canyon Lodge on AZ 67 has a general store, laundry, and showers. This general store is the best place in the area to find camping supplies.

Along the North Kaibab Trail, Grand Canyon

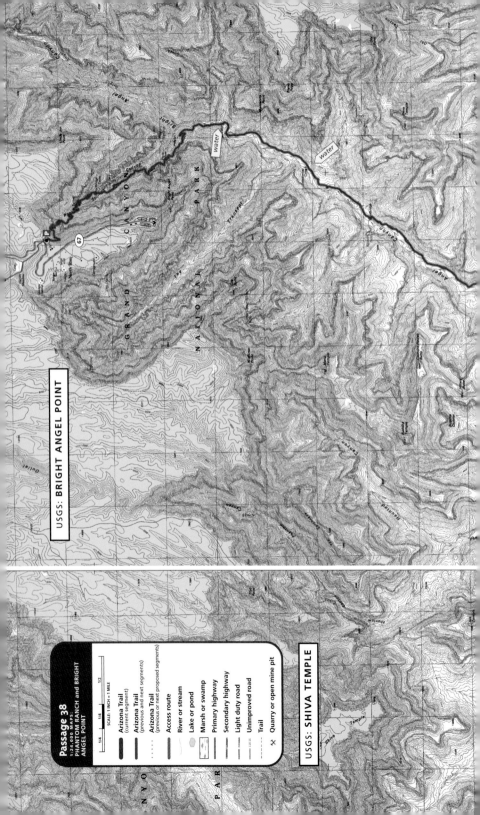

USGS: BRIGHT ANGEL POINT

USGS: SHIVA TEMPLE

Passage 38
1:24,000 MAPS:
PHANTOM RANCH and BRIGHT
ANGEL POINT

SCALE: 1 INCH = 1 MILE

1/4   1/4   1/2

Arizona Trail
(current segment)

Arizona Trail
(previous and next segments)

Arizona Trail
(previous or next proposed segments)

Access route

River or stream

Lake or pond

Marsh or swamp

Primary highway

Secondary highway

Light duty road

Unimproved road

Trail

✕ Quarry or open mine pit

USGS: PHANTOM RANCH

USGS: GRAND CANYON

Passage 39
Grand Canyon—North Rim: North Kaibab Trailhead to National Park—National Forest Boundary

Forest north of the Grand Canyon's North Rim

TOTAL DISTANCE	11.8 miles
QUALITY HIKING DISTANCE	11.8 miles
DIFFICULTY	Moderate
TOTAL ELEVATION GAIN	1,511 feet
TOTAL DESCENT	628 feet
FROM MEXICO	693.3 miles
TO UTAH	78.6 miles
LAND MANAGERS	Grand Canyon National Park
RECOMMENDED MONTHS	May through October

INTRODUCTION This passage traverses the relatively little-used northern side of Grand Canyon National Park to the Kaibab National Forest, through rolling, forested hills. You are unlikely to see many other people on this passage. The trail follows graded dirt roads for a total of 2.0 miles, but the bulk of the passage follows a primitive, remote utility corridor.

For those with horses, the park has a place for you to camp just north of the North Rim parking lot. Follow the road at the end of the parking lot and head north, up a hill, and bear left as you travel up the road. At press time there was no sign. Call the park to check availability.

As it is for humans, conditioning is a big issue for horses traveling on the North Rim. At 8,800 feet in elevation, they, too, feel the effects of the high altitude. De-hydration is also a concern, so make sure you and your livestock consume enough water and electrolytes.

MOUNTAIN BIKE NOTES

 This passage is open to bikes, with mostly intermediate riding. There are some steep hills. The trail may be obscure or nonexistent, requiring some walking.

WATER

There is no reliable water on this passage.

MAPS

USGS Quadrangles: Bright Angel Point, Little Park Lake
USFS: Kaibab National Forest (North Kaibab Ranger District)
Other: Trails Illustrated #207 (Grand Canyon National Park); Arizona Public Lands
    Information Center, AZT Passage Topo Map 39—Grand Canyon North Rim

BEGINNING ACCESS POINT

 North Kaibab Trailhead: The parking area is on the east side of AZ 67, 41.0 miles south of Jacob Lake and 2.3 miles north of Grand Canyon Lodge. The trailhead is at the south end of the parking lot (N36°13'01", W112°03'21").

ENDING ACCESS POINT

 National Park–National Forest Boundary: See "Beginning Access Point" for Passage 40.

TRAIL DESCRIPTION From the parking lot (8,235'), carefully cross the highway due west, pass an AZT marker, and follow a well-defined trail down a drainage to a high-quality dirt road. Turn left (west) and follow the road past the parking lot for the Widforss Trail to a road junction. Bear left and follow the road 0.1 mile to a singletrack trail that departs on the right side. The trail soon joins a utility corridor. Stay on this corridor as it crosses several dirt roads. Many deer and turkeys that show little fear of humans inhabit this grassy area.

The trail reaches AZ 67 (8,795'). Cross the highway carefully and follow a dirt road east for 60 yards. Then turn left (north) onto a primitive road and continue along the utility corridor you had been following. The utility corridor reaches a steep-sided drainage. Just down the south slope, turn right (east) onto a singletrack trail through the trees. The trail heads down, crosses a drainage, and switchbacks up the north slope, crossing the utility corridor several times.

Rejoin the utility corridor and reach this passage's second-highest point. A steep descent begins. A flat stretch then takes you to where the trail leaves the utility corridor through the trees to the left, a few hundred yards southeast of the national park's north entrance station. (If you stay on the utility corridor, you'll pass through the grounds of a small residence used by the NPS.) Follow the trail to the parking lot just east of the entrance station, and then pick up a road going east around the back of the NPS residence (N36°20'10", W112°06'56"). Be sure to stop at the park entrance station and tell the rangers that you are using the AZT. Many rangers are unaware of the trail, so your stopping helps to spread the word.

Pass through a gate and follow the road along a gradual climb. In another 0.2 mile, look for a trail departing on the left (northeast) (N36°19'53", W112°06'09"). In 0.7 mile, cross a fence at the National Park Service–National Forest boundary and reach a long meadow. If you can't see a trail, walk north-northeast 0.1 mile through the meadow to a gate and climb a short, steep slope to reach the trailhead on FR 610 (mile 11.8; 8,995'; N36°20'26", W112°05'22"). This is the end of Passage 39.

Opposite: Old-growth aspen trees along the Arizona Trail, Kaibab National Forest

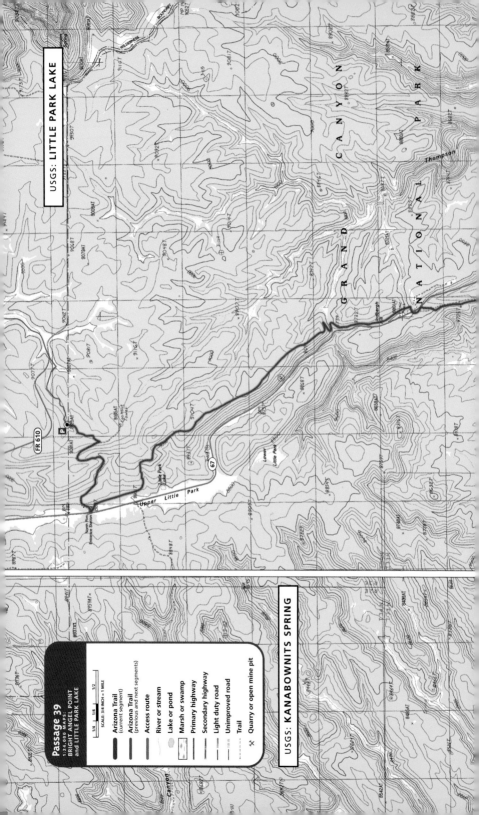

USGS: LITTLE PARK LAKE

USGS: KANABOWNITS SPRING

Passage 39

1:24,000 MAPS:
BRIGHT ANGEL POINT
and LITTLE PARK LAKE

SCALE 3/4 INCH = 1 MILE

1/4   1/4   1/2

Arizona Trail
(current segment)

Arizona Trail
(previous and next segments)

Access route

River or stream

Lake or pond

Marsh or swamp

Primary highway

Secondary highway

Light duty road

Unimproved road

Trail

× Quarry or open mine pit

GRAND CANYON

NATIONAL PARK

FR 610

P

67

Upper Little Park

Lower Little Park

North Rim
Entrance Station

Thompson

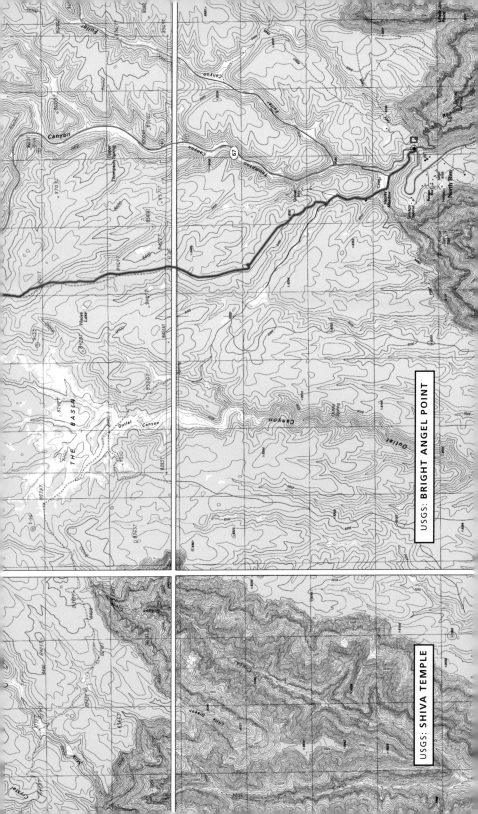

USGS: BRIGHT ANGEL POINT

USGS: SHIVA TEMPLE

Passage 40
Kaibab Plateau South: National Park–National Forest Boundary to Telephone Hill

The Arizona Trail as it works its way toward the East Rim Viewpoint

TOTAL DISTANCE	22.0 miles
QUALITY HIKING DISTANCE	22.0 miles
DIFFICULTY	Easy
TOTAL ELEVATION GAIN	1,808 feet
TOTAL DESCENT	2,078 feet
FROM MEXICO	705.1 miles
TO UTAH	66.8 miles
LAND MANAGERS	Kaibab National Forest (North Kaibab Ranger District)
RECOMMENDED MONTHS	May through October

INTRODUCTION This section of the AZT, which follows the Kaibab Plateau Trail (#101), might just offer the trail's easiest and most pleasant walking. It crosses a much-overlooked and delightful area of northern Arizona, passing through an idyllic forest of spruce, pine, and aspen. For about a mile, the trail dodges in and out of stately trees along the East Rim of the Grand Canyon, offering breathtaking views of Marble Canyon to the east and the Vermilion Cliffs to the north, the final Arizona landmark before the canyon country of Utah.

Water is plentiful except under drought conditions. You can camp almost anywhere, as long as you're out of sight of the trail and roads.

MOUNTAIN BIKE NOTES

 With singletrack almost the entire way, this passage offers one of the best moderate rides in the country, passing through evergreen forests and peaceful meadows, with far-reaching views from the East Rim.

WATER

 Pond: This appears to be a reliable source (N36°21'55", W112°05'07").

 Crystal Spring: There is a pond near the spring (N36°23'26", W112°05'42").

 Dog Lake: The water's a little murky, but it seems to be permanent (N36°25'23", W112°05'22").

 Another murky pond: N36°28'28", W112°06'47"

 Large pond: N36°30'38", W112°07'53"

 Crane Lake: N36°31'47", W112°08'50"

MAPS

USGS Quadrangles: Little Park Lake, Dog Point, Cane, Telephone Hill
USFS: Kaibab National Forest (North Kaibab Ranger District)
Other: Arizona Public Lands Information Center, AZT Passage Topo Maps 40A and 40B—Kaibab South

BEGINNING ACCESS POINT

 National Park–National Forest Boundary: From Jacob Lake, drive south on AZ 67 for 26.0 miles and turn left (east) onto FR 611. (This is 4.5 miles north of the Grand Canyon National Park entrance station and about 1.0 mile south of Kaibab Lodge.) Drive 1.1 miles and turn right (east) onto FR 610. Wind south and then east 5.1 miles to a pullout on the north side of the road, near a brown AZT post (N36°20'26", W112°05'22").

ENDING ACCESS POINT

Telephone Hill: See "Beginning Access Point" for Passage 41.

TRAIL DESCRIPTION   Follow a faint tread northeast into the valley behind the AZT sign (8,995'). The trail soon becomes much clearer and is marked by carsonite posts bearing AZT stickers. After a mile, the trail follows an old road left (west-northwest) into an adjacent valley. In 0.1 mile, it joins another valley and turns back to the right (north) to meander through beautiful forests punctuated by meadows.

 At a sign indicating the Kaibab Plateau Trail (#101), leave the road and turn right (north) onto a faint singletrack. In 200 feet, you'll pass a pond (N36°21'55", W112°05'07").

After 2.3 miles, the trail leaves the valley by climbing a side drainage to the left (southwest). In 0.1 mile, the trail curves back to the right (north) to climb more steeply into a thick spruce-fir forest. Within the next mile, cross diagonally over two old roads and stay on the singletrack.

When you reach a jeep road, as indicated by carsonite posts, turn right (north). The road forks in 0.7 mile; take the right fork.

 You'll reach a pond at Crystal Spring (8,780'; N36°23'26", W112°05'42"). The two-track road ends here. Follow the singletrack to the north.

A gradual descent ends (8,718'). Avoid side trails and climb to the northeast through giant, old-growth ponderosa pines. The trail levels along the East Rim, with awesome views east into the Saddle Mountain Wilderness. Soon you can see Marble Canyon, upstream from the Grand Canyon. Far to the north lie the colorful Vermilion Cliffs.

The trail winds along the rim and reaches the vehicle-accessible East Rim Viewpoint (8,822'). With restroom facilities and good picture-taking and napping possibilities, East Rim Viewpoint makes a fine rest stop; however, camping is not allowed in the vicinity. Join a dirt road for a brief distance, staying near the rim. Then follow a singletrack that goes around the right (east) side of a camping area. Avoid trail #7, which descends off the rim, and stay on the very clear singletrack as it ambles along the rim to the north.

As you leave the East Rim Viewpoint, where the trail widens into a road, pick up a singletrack taking off to the left by a carsonite post. Go about 40 yards, cross another road at a right angle, and continue on a two-track road to the west-northwest.

You'll pass a murky yet scenic pond called Dog Lake (N36°25'23", W112°05'22").

A half mile past Dog Lake, follow a faint two-track northwest through a long meadow for 0.6 mile. When you reenter the trees, the AZT leaves the road to the left on a singletrack. The trail crosses two old roads and then begins a major descent through a series of switchbacks. Reach the peaceful valley called Upper Tater Canyon (8,540').

Turn right (north) onto an old two-track road and walk along the narrow, flat meadow. Watch for a carsonite AZT sign and be careful to avoid a fainter, two-track road that climbs out of the valley to the left. Near the north end of the valley, the road you're following curves to the left. Look for carsonite posts marking a singletrack trail breaking off to the right. Follow this 0.1 mile, then turn right onto a two-track that climbs northwest away from the meadow. Cross a fence and an adjacent road at a right angle, and then follow a singletrack on the other side.

 The trail winds through the forest, passing another murky pond (8,680'; N36°28'28", W112°06'47").

Cross a well-graded dirt road, FR 221. Continue on a singletrack, cross another road in 0.2 mile, and pick up a fainter two-track trending just east of north. In 0.5 mile, follow a singletrack that leaves the right side of the road and curves northwest through a pleasant grove of aspen trees. You'll soon see AZ 67 in sprawling Pleasant Valley to the west.

In less than a mile, the two-track fades to a singletrack that is occasionally a bit obscure. This descends to a broad, grassy extension of Pleasant Valley (8,500'; N36°29'39", W112°07'01") and then climbs an old jeep road to the northwest. As the trail regains the trees, follow a left fork less than 100 yards to a singletrack that continues straight ahead to the northwest. Brown carsonite posts clearly mark the route.

 Roll through the forest and meadows, entering a very large meadow 15 miles from the start of the passage. As the trail fades, follow a faint two-track to the left (west) along the north edge of the meadow, passing a pond. Descend to another meadow and follow a singletrack to the right (north) past a large pond (N36°30'38", W112°07'53").

The AZT climbs (8,620') and then descends to parallel AZ 67.

 The trail reaches Crane Lake, in the middle of another large meadow (8,540'; N36°31'47", W112°08'50").

As the trail fades, go straight across the meadow to the northwest, following brown carsonite posts. You'll enter yet another meadow. The trail heads north-northwest along the east side, and then climbs steeply into the trees (8,550'). This 0.5 mile ascent takes you to the top of Telephone Hil (8,845'). Follow the trail to the west and north until you reach FR 241 and the end of Passage 40 (8,860'; N36°33'06", W112°10'30").

USGS: CANE

USGS: DOG POINT

USGS: TELEPHONE HILL

FR 221

FR 241

67

water

water

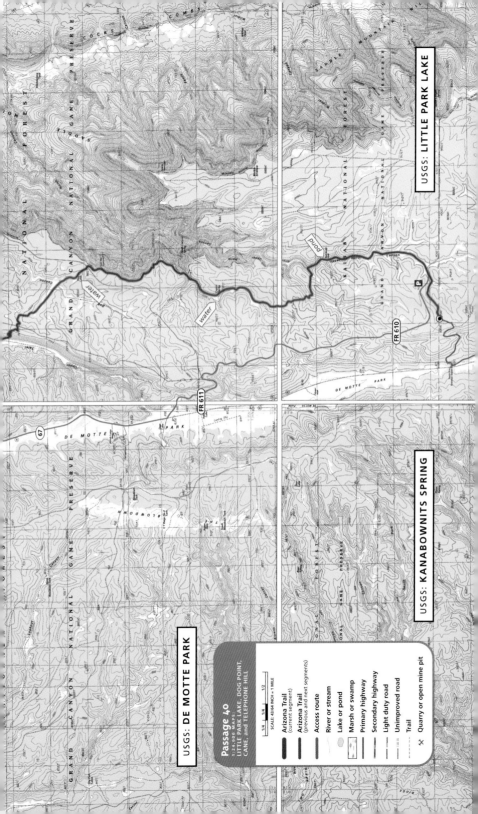

USGS: LITTLE PARK LAKE

USGS: DE MOTTE PARK

USGS: KANABOWNITS SPRING

pond

water

water

FR 611

FR 610

P

67

Passage 40
1:24,800 MAPS:
LITTLE PARK LAKE, DOG POINT,
CANE, and TELEPHONE HILL

SCALE 43/64 INCH = 1 MILE

1/4   1/4   1/2   1 MILE

— Arizona Trail
(current segment)

— Arizona Trail
(previous and next segments)

— Access route

River or stream

Lake or pond

Marsh or swamp

Primary highway

Secondary highway

Light duty road

Unimproved road

Trail

✕ Quarry or open mine pit

Passage 41
Kaibab Plateau Central: Telephone Hill to US 89A

Kaibab Plateau

TOTAL DISTANCE	17.0 miles
QUALITY HIKING DISTANCE	17.0 miles
DIFFICULTY	Easy
TOTAL ELEVATION GAIN	571 feet
TOTAL DESCENT	1,897 feet
FROM MEXICO	727.1 miles
TO UTAH	44.8 miles
LAND MANAGERS	Kaibab National Forest (North Kaibab Ranger District)
RECOMMENDED MONTHS	April through October

INTRODUCTION This passage continues the pleasant hiking and mountain biking experience of the Kaibab Plateau Trail (#101). As the trail gradually descends, the spruce trees of the previous passage give way to stands of ponderosa pine and the land is noticeably drier. You're unlikely to see any free-flowing water.

The trail crosses many dirt roads in this passage, but they are not busy. Hunting is popular here in the fall; consult the Forest Service at (928) 643-7395 for information on hunting seasons.

MOUNTAIN BIKE NOTES

The cycling is mostly easy on this passage, with a clear trail and just a few steep climbs and descents.

WATER

 Stock pond: N36°40'25", W112°09'27"

 Big Ridge Tank: N36°42'54", W112°11'15"

MAPS
USGS Quadrangles: Telephone Hill, Jacob Lake
USFS: Kaibab National Forest (North Kaibab Ranger District)
Other: Arizona Public Lands Information Center, AZT Passage Topo Maps 41A and 41B—Kaibab Central

BEGINNING ACCESS POINT

Bumpy road to Trailhead 0.1 mile

Telephone Hill: About 13.5 miles south of Jacob Lake on AZ 67, look for a sign pointing to FR 429 on the right-hand side. Do not turn right onto FR 429, but instead turn left (east) onto FR 241. In 0.1 mile, the AZT crosses the road, but there is no parking here (N36°33'06", W112°10'30"). Continue another 0.1 mile to a little campsite on the left, where you may be able to park.

ENDING ACCESS POINT

Smooth road to Trailhead

US 89A: See "Beginning Access Point" for Passage 42.

TRAIL DESCRIPTION From a brown AZT post by the road (8,860'), follow a singletrack trail east and then north. An old jeep road soon branches to the left (west). Avoid the road and stay on the singletrack. The AZT develops into an old roadbed as it descends steadily to where it reaches a low point (8,605') near AZ 67.

The trail then climbs and turns left (northeast) onto a faint singletrack. Cross over a well-traveled road and continue north 0.1 mile to join a faint road trending north-northwest. A singletrack takes over, bearing north-northwest. In 0.4 mile, a steep switchbacking descent leads to the bottom of a beautiful forest canyon.

The trail bends left (northwest) to climb out of the canyon. After a high point, cross a jeep road and make a rolling descent on an old road to the northwest. The AZT crosses FR 205 (near a parking area and a restroom) and continues to the north.

Following carsonite posts, the AZT soon crosses two obscure roads, then rolls over flat terrain to meet a dirt road. Turn left (west-northwest) and walk 100 yards along the road to a faint singletrack taking off to the right (north). Over the next mile, the trail joins an old road for a short distance and then leaves it to the north a couple of times.

Next you'll reach a stock pond (8,358'; N36°40'25", W112°09'27"). From the pond, the trail turns 90 degrees to the left and descends to an old jeep road. In 3 miles, pass by a gravel pit and continue on a very wide, old roadbed to the northwest.

The next water source is the dirty water of Big Ridge Tank (7,732'; N36°42'54", W112°11'15"). At the far side of the tank, follow a singletrack trail to the right (north-northwest).

After crossing a dirt road, the trail turns into a clear two-track road. At an intersection, turn left (north) and continue 0.2 mile to a sign that marks a singletrack trail climbing away from the road to the right (north). Follow this trail 0.5 mile to reach the parking lot and trailhead at this passage's end (7,518'; N36°44'07", W112°11'17").

SUPPLIES, SERVICES, AND ACCOMMODATIONS
JACOB LAKE INN
Jacob Lake is not a town but a small resort at the intersection of US 89A and AZ 67. From the trailhead at the end of passage 41, hike 50 yards north to US 89A, turn left (west), and carefully walk a little over 2 miles beside the road to Jacob Lake. The inn offers lodging, dining, laundry, showers ($3), and a small store. Phone: (928) 643-7232. The Kaibab Plateau Visitor Center is next to the inn. Phone: (928) 643-7298.
Distance from Trail 2.2 miles

Opposite: Kaibab National Forest
Photo courtesy of The Arizona Trail Association

USGS: HOUSE ROCK

USGS: JACOB LAKE

Passage 41
1:24,000 MAPS
TELEPHONE HILL, and
JACOB LAKE

SCALE: 1/2 INCH = 1 MILE

1/4   1/4   1/2

Arizona Trail
(current segment)

Arizona Trail
(previous and next segments)

Access route

River or stream

Lake or pond

Marsh or swamp

Primary highway

Secondary highway

Light duty road

Unimproved road

Trail

✕   Quarry or open mine pit

USGS: CANE

USGS: TELEPHONE HILL

Passage 42
Kaibab Plateau North: US 89A to Winter Road

Carsonite post along the trail

TOTAL DISTANCE	17.0 miles
QUALITY HIKING DISTANCE	17.0 miles
DIFFICULTY	Moderate
TOTAL ELEVATION GAIN	188 feet
TOTAL DESCENT	1,177 feet
FROM MEXICO	744.1 miles
TO UTAH	27.8 miles
LAND MANAGERS	Kaibab National Forest (North Kaibab Ranger District)
RECOMMENDED MONTHS	April through October

INTRODUCTION This passage contains the AZT's final major ecosystem change. The trail begins in a uniform forest of ponderosa pines and descends into high desert dotted with sagebrush, stands of juniper trees, and creeping prickly pear. The trail is frequently faint, but cairns and signs for "Trail #101" mark the route.

MOUNTAIN BIKE NOTES

The riding on this passage is mostly easy. Downed timber and soft ground present the toughest obstacles.

WATER

Joes Reservoir: This stock pond might provide the only water on the passage. You can drive to it on forest roads if you want to check the water supply in advance (N36°51'11", W112°09'17").

MAPS

USGS Quadrangles: Jacob Lake, Cooper Ridge, Buck Pasture Canyon, Coyote Buttes
USFS: Kaibab National Forest (North Kaibab Ranger District)
Other: Arizona Public Lands Information Center, AZT Passage Topo Maps 42A and 42B—Kaibab North

BEGINNING ACCESS POINT

US 89A: From Jacob Lake, head east on US 89A for 2.2 miles, then turn right (south) on FR 205. The trailhead is 50 yards ahead on the left (N36°44'07", W112°11'17").

ENDING ACCESS POINT

Winter Road: See "Beginning Access Point" for Passage 43.

TRAIL DESCRIPTION From the parking area (7,518'), follow the dirt road north 50 yards to the paved highway. Bear diagonally right and carefully cross the highway to a dirt road on the other side. Look for a sign on the right that says "Kaibab Plateau Trail #101." Follow a faint singletrack into the trees behind the sign, trending slightly east of north. After 0.2 mile, reach a barbed-wire fence. Turn right and follow the fence line for 20 yards, and then curve left to follow a bend in the fence. In the next 0.5 miles the AZT winds its way along or near the fence. The trail is easy to follow as it makes its way to a ravine (N36°44'22", W112°10'41").

The trail trends north, crossing a road at a right angle. Follow signs for Trail #101. Continue northward, staying above Orderville Canyon on your left and keeping the dirt FR 257 on your right. The trail veers right (northeast) to cross at a right angle.

After you cross another road at mile 4.0, the trail becomes invisible but cairns show the way. The route parallels Orderville Canyon, which remains on the left. Stay away from frequent two-track roads that will try to pull you away to the right. Look for cairns to assist you. Notice the transition from ponderosa pine forest to a drier ecosystem.

Cross FR 249 about 5.5 miles from the start of this passage and continue due north through a burn area, following cairns. The AZT continues to trend between northeast and northwest, crossing the occasional road. The trail descends into a shallow ravine, which it follows through ponderosa pines. The ravine ends abruptly at a gigantic clearing covered with sagebrush.

The route is obvious, as a clear swath has been cut through the sage, heading north along the far right (east) side of this open area. Where the sagebrush ends, it becomes harder to follow the trail. Just keep the trees—piñon and juniper—close on your right and follow denuded ground that indicates a trail.

 You'll come to an intersection with the Navajo Trail (N36°51'06", W112°09'03"), which leads 0.25 mile west to Joes Reservoir (N36°51'11", W112°09'17").

The trail winds through a pleasant high-desert forest of juniper and small pines for the next mile, then enters another large field of sage and promptly disappears. Look for an obscure swath through the sagebrush about 10° west of north. Then cross a faint road at a right angle and reenter the trees. In a mile, the forest gives way to an eerie landscape of dead trees and the trail disappears again (N36°52'57", W112°08'33"). Continue in the same direction. Reach the other side of this strange, silent veldt (N36°53'06", W112°08'27").

In 0.5 mile, you'll cross another large field of sage, but there is an obvious trail corridor through this one. The AZT crosses a two-track road and a sturdy barbed-wire fence. In 0.2 mile, after another road-and-fence combination, a trail lined with logs and debris winds to the northeast. You'll reach Winter Road, or BLM Road #1025 (6,538'; N36°55'05", W112°06'25"). A decent campsite exists about 250 yards west of Winter Road.

Aspens along Trail #101 near Little Round Valley

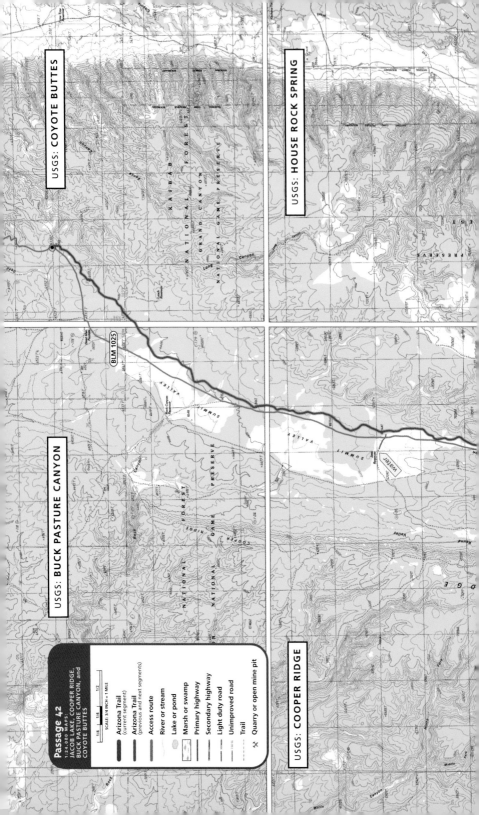

USGS: COYOTE BUTTES

USGS: HOUSE ROCK SPRING

USGS: BUCK PASTURE CANYON

USGS: COOPER RIDGE

BLM 1025

Passage 42
1:24,000 MAPS:
JACOB LAKE, COOPER RIDGE,
BUCK PASTURE CANYON, and
COYOTE BUTTES

SCALE 3/4 INCH = 1 MILE

1/4   1/4   1/2

Arizona Trail
(current segment)

Arizona Trail
(previous and next segments)

Access route

River or stream

Lake or pond

Marsh or swamp

Primary highway

Secondary highway

Light duty road

Unimproved road

Trail

✕   Quarry or open mine pit

Passage 43
Buckskin Mountain: Winter Road to Utah Border

Coyote Valley, at the northern terminus of the Arizona Trail

INTRODUCTION The AZT ends in the north much like it began in the south—out in the middle of nowhere. This is entirely appropriate, of course, because getting to the middle of nowhere is what hiking the AZT is all about.

This spectacularly beautiful final passage marks a return to the high-desert ecosystem of small cacti, colorful shrubs, and hardy piñon and juniper trees. You'll enjoy sweeping views of Utah to the north and the brightly colored Vermilion Cliffs to the east. The AZT is clear and easy to follow over most of this passage.

TOTAL DISTANCE	10.8 miles
QUALITY HIKING DISTANCE	10.8 miles
DIFFICULTY	Easy
TOTAL ELEVATION GAIN	582 feet
TOTAL DESCENT	2,121 feet
FROM MEXICO	761.1 miles
TO UTAH	10.8 miles
LAND MANAGERS	BLM (Arizona Strip District)
RECOMMENDED MONTHS	March through November

MOUNTAIN BIKE NOTES

The excellent mountain biking of the Kaibab Plateau continues here, with mostly intermediate riding and the occasional technical section. A northbound ride is decidedly easier than heading south, because of the elevation loss.

WATER

There is no reliable water on this passage.

MAPS

USGS Quadrangles: Coyote Buttes, Pine Hollow Canyon, UT
USFS: Kaibab National Forest (North Kaibab Ranger District)
Other: Arizona Public Lands Information Center, AZT Passage Topo Map 43—
Buckskin Mountain.

BEGINNING ACCESS POINT

Bumpy road to Trailhead 19.0 miles

Winter Road: From US 89A, 6.0 miles south of Fredonia (or about 23.0 miles north of Jacob Lake), turn east-northeast 0.3 mile south of mile marker 603 and enter a dirt road that looks like a parking lot (N36°54'44", W112°25'08"). There is no sign on the highway, but 100 yards down the road a sign says "Buckskin Mountain 10; Paria Plateau 29." This is the Winter Road (BLM Road #1025).

Continue about 19.0 miles, avoiding side roads and sticking to the best surface at forks, to reach an obscure spot where brown carsonite posts mark the AZT's crossing (N36°55'05", W112°06'25"). Park on the side of the road. The northbound trail departs to the left as you're driving in.

ENDING ACCESS POINT

Bumpy road to Trailhead 10.0 miles

Utah Border Trailhead: It may help to set your odometer to zero in Page, Arizona. From Page, head west on AZ 98 for 2.5 miles to US 89 and turn right (north). At mile 6.4, you'll pass Wahweap Marina, which offers camping. Cross the state line at mile 13.0. At mile 38.0 from Page, just after mile marker 25, you'll pass through a roadcut and the highway will begin a big, sweeping curve to the right. At the end of the guardrail on the left, turn left (south) onto a dirt road. This is 0.2 mile south of mile marker 26. (From Kanab, this turnoff is about 36.0 miles "south" according to signs—actually geographically east—on US 89.)

Follow the dirt road 10.0 miles, and then turn right (west) onto a well-graded dirt road. Continue 0.2 mile to a parking area, restrooms, and several campsites (N37°00'04", W112°02'03"). The trailhead is on the left as you drive in. Park in designated spots only.

TRAIL DESCRIPTION From Winter Road (6,538'), follow a clear singletrack northwest through a pleasant juniper and piñon forest, rolling in and out of washes and crossing the occasional dusty road. One of these is at N36°56'52", W112°06'17". Then begin a gradual descent to a shallow valley. The trail is sometimes obscure here, but occasional cairns mark the way. The trail becomes clearer after crossing a faint road (N36°57'25", W112°06'03").

After crossing a primitive road (N36°58'29", W112°05'53"), the trail bends right to trend east-northeast. After a high point (6,460'), the AZT begins a long descent toward Utah by joining the drainage of North Larkum Canyon. The trail dances in and out of this canyon until it exits on the left (north) and climbs gradually to the adjoining ridge (6,220' feet; N36°59'16", W112°03'53"). Straight ahead, you'll see the colorful Vermilion Cliffs.

After 8.5 miles from your starting point, the trail descends via switchbacks to the northeast and Coyote Valley comes into view. You'll reach the bottom of the switchbacks after 10 miles. Continue northeast across the sagebrush-covered valley to a low, rocky ridge. The trail descends the other side of this ridge to a parking lot marked by ramadas, picnic tables, restrooms (no water), and an informational kiosk at the trailhead (4,995'; N37°00'04", W112°02'03"). This is the northern end of the AZT.

Entering Utah at the end of the Arizona Trail

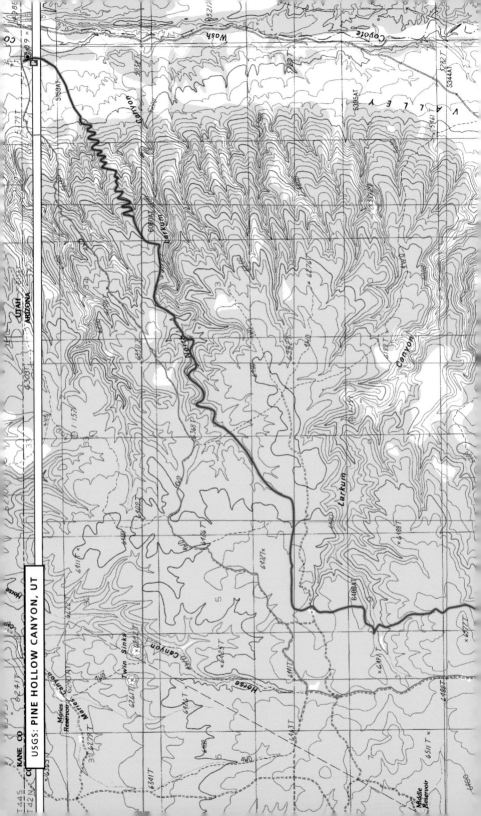

USGS: PINE HOLLOW CANYON, UT

Passage 43
1:24,000 MAPS
COYOTE BUTTES and
PINE HOLLOW CANYON, UTAH

SCALE 53/64 INCH = 1/2 MILE

Arizona Trail
(current segment)

Arizona Trail
(previous and next segments)

Access route

River or stream

Lake or pond

Marsh or swamp

Primary highway

Secondary highway

Light duty road

Unimproved road

Trail

× Quarry or open mine pit

USGS: COYOTE BUTTES

Appendix A: Land Management Offices

ARIZONA TRAIL ASSOCIATION
P.O. Box 36736
Phoenix, AZ 85067-6736
(602) 252-4794
www.aztrail.org

U.S. FOREST SERVICE (USFS)
Coronado National Forest
300 W. Congress St.
Tucson, AZ 85701
(520) 670-4552

Sierra Vista Ranger District
5990 S. Hwy. 92
Hereford, AZ 85615
(520) 378-0311

Nogales Ranger District
303 Old Tucson Rd.
Nogales, AZ 85621
(520) 281-2296

Santa Catalina Ranger District
5700 N. Sabino Canyon Rd.
Tucson, AZ 85750
(520) 749-8700

Tonto National Forest
2324 E. McDowell Rd.
Phoenix, AZ 85006
(602) 225-5200

Mesa Ranger District
P.O. Box 5800
Mesa, AZ 85211
(480) 610-3300

Globe Ranger District
7680 S. Six Shooter
Canyon Rd.
Globe, AZ 85501
(928) 402-6200

Tonto Basin Ranger District
HC 02, Box 4800
Roosevelt, AZ 85545
(928) 467-3200

Payson Ranger District
1009 E. Highway 260
Payson, AZ 85541
(928) 474-7900

Coconino National Forest
2323 E. Greenlaw Lane
Flagstaff, AZ 86004
(928) 527-3600

Mogollon Rim Ranger District
HC 31, Box 300
Happy Jack, AZ 86024
(928) 477-2255

Mormon Lake Ranger District
4773 S. Lake Mary Rd.
Flagstaff, AZ 86001
(928) 774-1147

Peaks Ranger District
5075 N. Hwy. 89
Flagstaff, AZ 86004
(928) 526-0866

Kaibab National Forest
800 S. 6th St.
Williams, AZ 86046
(928) 635-8200

Tusayan Ranger District
P.O. Box 3088
Grand Canyon, AZ 86023
(928) 638-2443

North Kaibab Ranger District
430 S. Main
Fredonia, AZ 86022
(928) 643-7395

NATIONAL PARK SERVICE (NPS)
Coronado National Memorial
4101 E. Montezuma
Canyon Rd.
Hereford, AZ 85615
(520) 366-5515

Saguaro National Park
3693 S. Old Spanish Trail
Tucson, AZ 85730
(520) 733-5153

Grand Canyon National Park
P.O. Box 129
Grand Canyon, AZ 86023
(928) 638-7888

BUREAU OF LAND MANAGEMENT (BLM)
State Office
(See PLIC in Appendix C.)

Phoenix District Office
21605 N. 7th Ave.
Phoenix, AZ 85027
(623) 580-5500

Tucson Field Office
12661 E. Broadway
Tucson, AZ 85748
(520) 258-7200

Arizona Strip Field Office
345 E. Riverside Dr.
St. George, UT 84770
(435) 688-3246

OTHER JURISDICTIONS
Pima County Natural
Resources, Parks and
Recreation Department
3500 W. River Rd.
Tucson, AZ 85741
(520) 877-6000

Pinal County
P.O. Box 727
Florence, AZ 85232
(520) 866-6411

City of Flagstaff–
Urban Trails System
211 W. Aspen Ave.
Flagstaff, AZ 86001
(928) 779-7632

Arizona State Land
Department–Public Records
1616 West Adams
Phoenix, AZ 85007
(602) 542-4631

Coconino County Parks
HC 39, Box 3A
Flagstaff, AZ 86001
(928) 744-5139

Appendix B: Equipment Checklist

Always Carry These Ten Essentials

Matches and lighter
Knife
Emergency shelter (tarp or ground cloth)
Food and plenty of water
Mirror or whistle for signaling
Extra clothing
Headlamp or flashlight with extra batteries
Compass and maps
First-aid kit
Sunglasses and sunscreen

Consider Adding These Items for Day Hikes

Daypack
Moleskin
Insect repellent
Cord or rope
Trowel for digging catholes
Lightweight hat and gloves
Extra socks
Long-sleeved shirt and long pants
Insulating layer—top and bottom
(fleece, wool, etc.)
Rain gear
Camera and film

Consider Adding These Items for Overnight or Thru-Hikes

Sleeping bag
Insulating ground pad (noninflatable
because of cacti)
Pillow
Tent or other shelter
Ground cloth
Stove, fuel, and eating/cooking utensils
Extra bags for garbage
Food bags (for hanging)
Extra clothing
Long underwear
Light camp shoes
Water filter or iodine tablets
Toiletries and personal hygiene kit
Sewing kit
Repair kits for tent, stove, water filter, etc.
Pack cover

Optional Items

Water bag
Chair
Snakebite kit
Journal or reading material
Watch
Fishing gear
Binoculars
Candle lantern
Walking stick
Radio
GPS receiver

Appendix C: Map Sources

Arizona Public Lands Information Center (PLIC)
1 N. Central
Phoenix, AZ 85004
(602) 417-9300
(800) 986-1151
az_plic@blm.gov

Wide World of Maps
2626 W. Indian School Rd.
Phoenix, AZ 85017
(602) 279-2323
(800) 279-7654

Appendix D: Maps Required by Thru-Hikers

Arizona Public Lands Information Center (PLIC)
AZT Passage Topographic Maps
These 1:24,000-scale maps can be used instead of the USGS quadrangles. They show land-ownership color and are available from the PLIC for $10 each (plus shipping). At the time of this printing, maps were available for 33 of the 43 AZT passages. Some passages require two maps, so there are a total of 40 maps available. See a current list at www.aztrail.org.

1—Huachuca
2—Canelo East
3—Canelo West
4—Temporal Gulch
5—Santa Rita Mountains
9—Rincon Mountains
10—Redington Pass
11—Santa Catalina Mountains
12—Oracle Ridge
13—Oracle
14A and 14B—Black Hills
17—Alamo Canyon
18—Reavis Canyon
19A and 19B—Superstition
   Wilderness
20—Four Peaks
21—Pine Mountain/Boulder
   Creek
22—Saddle Mountain
23—Mazatzal Divide
24—Red Hills
26—Hardscrabble Mesa
27—Highline
28—Blue Ridge
29A and 29B—Happy Jack
31—Walnut Canyon
32—Mt. Elden
33—Flagstaff

35A and 35B—Babbitt Ranch
36—Coconino Rim
39—Grand Canyon North Rim
40A and 40B—Kaibab South
41A and 41B—Kaibab Central
42A and 42B—Kaibab North
43—Buckskin Mountain

U.S. Forest Service (USFS) Maps
Coronado National Forest
   (Nogales/Sierra Vista Ranger
   Districts)
Coronado National Forest
   (Safford/Santa Catalina
   Ranger Districts)
Tonto National Forest
Coconino National Forest
Kaibab National Forest
   (Tusayan Ranger District)
Kaibab National Forest (North
   Kaibab Ranger District)

U.S. Geological Survey (USGS)
7.5-Minute Quadrangles
Agua Caliente Hill
Ashurst Lake
Black Mountain
Blue Ridge Reservoir
Boulder Mountain
Bright Angel Point
Buck Pasture Canyon
Buckhead Mesa
Campo Bonito
Cane
Cane Springs Mountain
Canelo Pass
Chapel Mountain
Cooper Ridge
Coyote Buttes
Croizer Peak
Cypress Butte
Dane Canyon
Dog Point

Empire Ranch
Flagstaff East
Flagstaff West
Four Peaks
Grandview Point
Grayback
Harbison Tank
Hay Lake
Helvetia
Huachuca Peak
Humphreys Peak
Hutch Mountain
Iron Mountain
Jacob Lake
Jaycox Mountain
Kearny
Kehl Ridge
Lion Mountain
Little Park Lake
Lockwood Canyon
Lower Lake Mary
Mammoth
Mazatzal Peak
Mica Mountain
Miller Peak
Mine Mountain
Mineral Mountain
Montezuma Pass
Mormon Lake
Mount Bigelow
Mount Fagan
Mount Hughes
Mount Lemmon
Mount Wrightson
North of Oracle
North Peak
O'Donnell Canyon
Oracle
Patagonia
Peterson Flat
Phantom Ranch
Picketpost Mountain
Piety Hill

Pine
Pine Hollow Canyon, UT
Pinyon Mountain
Putnam Wash
Reno Pass
Rincon Peak
S P Mountain
Sabino Canyon
Sonoita
Sunset Crater West

Tanque Verde Peak
Teapot Mountain
Telephone Hill
Theodore Roosevelt Dam
Turkey Mountain
Tusayan East
Two Bar Mountain
Vail
White Horse Hills
Winona

Other Maps
Hiker's Map of the Huachuca
  Mountains, Leonard Taylor
Trails Illustrated #237 (Saguaro
  National Park)
Tusayan Bike Trail, Grand
  Canyon Map
Trails Illustrated #207 (Grand
  Canyon National Park)

Appendix E: Bibliography and Suggested Reading

Bennett, Sarah. *Mountain Biking Arizona.* Helena, Mont.: Falcon Press, 1995.

Dell, John, and Steve Anderson. *Southern Arizona Trails Resource Guide.* Tucson, Ariz.: Pima Trails Association, 1998.

Dollar, Tom. *Guide to Arizona's Wilderness Areas.* Englewood, Colo.: Westcliffe Publishers, 1998.

Geronimo. *Geronimo: His Own Story.* New York: The Penguin Group, 1996.

Lankford, Andrea. *Biking the Arizona Trail.* Englewood, Colo.: Westcliffe Publishers, 2002.

Ray, Cosmic. *Fat Tire Tales and Trails.* Flagstaff, Ariz.: Self-published, 1998.

Sheridan, Thomas E. *Arizona: A History.* Tucson, Ariz.: The University of Arizona Press, 1996.

Sieve, Jerry, and M. John Fayhee. *Along the Arizona Trail.* Englewood, Colo.: Westcliffe Publishers, 1998.

Snyder, Ernest E. *Arizona Outdoor Guide.* Phoenix: Golden West Publishers, 1994.

Southwest Parks and Monuments Association. *Poisonous Dwellers of the Desert.* Tucson, Ariz.: Southwest Parks and Monuments Association, 1995.

Tighe, Kelly, and Susan Moran. *On the Arizona Trail: A Guide for Hikers, Cyclists, and Equestrians.* Boulder, Colo.: Pruett Publishing, 1998.

Tilton, Buck. *America's Wilderness: The Complete Guide to More Than 600 National Wilderness Areas.* San Francisco: Foghorn Press, 1996.

Townsend, Chris. *Crossing Arizona.* Woodstock, Vt.: The Countryman Press, 2002.

Trimble, Marshall. *Arizona: A Cavalcade of History.* Tucson, Ariz.: Treasure Chest Publications, 1990.

Whitney, Stephen R. *A Field Guide to the Grand Canyon.* Seattle: The Mountaineers, 1996.

Zwinger, Ann Haymond. *Downcanyon: A Naturalist Explores the Colorado River through the Grand Canyon.* Tucson, Ariz.: The University of Arizona Press, 1995.

The Arizona Trail Association

In sharing the nearly 800 miles of the Arizona Trail, hikers, backpackers, equestrians, mountain bikers, cross-country skiers, nature photographers, and wildlife enthusiasts also share responsibility for its establishment, maintenance, and eventual completion. The best way to make a difference for this spectacular long-distance trail is by supporting and joining in the efforts of the Arizona Trail Association (ATA).

The ATA accomplishes its work in partnership with more than 20 agency partners and many community and business supporters. Yet the most important tasks are often achieved by individual volunteers—people from all walks of life who love the outdoors and want to help preserve the scenic landscapes and rich ecosystems of one of the country's fastest-growing states. By assisting in trail construction, maintenance, and stewardship, as well as publicity, fund-raising, education, and research, these dedicated individuals not only enjoy the Arizona Trail themselves, they ensure the quality of the trail experience for future generations.

The ATA invites anyone interested in becoming part of the legacy of the Arizona Trail to join the organization and begin to personally share in the success of this project. Individuals who become involved in the ATA have an immediate opportunity to help bring the construction of the trail to completion. A 501(c)(3) nonprofit organization, the ATA welcomes contributions, whether in the form of membership dues or donations designated expressly for trail development; all contributions are tax deductible.

For a membership application, a list of member benefits, and further information, please contact:

Arizona Trail Association
P.O. Box 36736
Phoenix, AZ 85067-6736
(602) 252-4794
www.aztrail.org

Index

NOTE: Citations followed by the letter "p" indicate photos; citations followed by the letter "m" indicate maps.

About the Author

TOM JONES is an avid hiker, mountain biker, rock climber, and telemark skier. He hiked the Colorado section of the Continental Divide National Scenic Trail and wrote *Colorado's Continental Divide Trail: The Official Guide,* published by Westcliffe Publishers. He lives in Evergreen, Colorado.

About the Photographer

JERRY SIEVE has been photographing the American landscape since 1977. His many trips across the United States, Canada, and Mexico have resulted in exceptional photography published in books, calendars, and magazines nationwide. He is widely known for his work with *Arizona Highways* magazine. Originally from Cincinnati, Sieve has lived in Arizona since 1976 and is an avid outdoor enthusiast. For more insight into Jerry's work, please see sieveimages.com or visit Galeria del Valle Escondido in Cave Creek, Arizona.